14.50

BF
311
.B89
2002

D0770912

Journey Into the Realm of Consciousness

How the Brain Produces the Mind

By

Eugene M. Brooks, M.D.

Colorado Christian University
Library
180 S. Garrison
Lakewood, Colorado 80226

© 2002 Eugene M. Brooks M.D. All rights reserved.

No part of this book may be reproduced, stored in a retrieval system, or transmitted by any means, electronic, mechanical, photocopying, recording, or otherwise, without written permission from the author.

ISBN: 1-4033-2886-2 (e-book)
ISBN: 1-4033-2887-0 (Paperback)
ISBN: 1-4033-2888-9 (Hardcover)

Library of Congress Control Number: 2002105675

This book is printed on acid free paper.

Printed in the United States of America
Bloomington, IN

1stBooks — rev. 11/18/02

TABLE OF CONTENTS

About the Author.. ix
Foreword... x
Introduction 1
Chapter One: Philosophical Background 4
   Three Basic Approaches.. 4
   Realism.. 4
   Representationalism 6
   Idealism 9
   Animism.. 10
   Panpsychism.. 11
   Epipohenomenalism... 11
   Summary 12
Chapter Two: More Recent Theories 13
   Linguistics... 13
   Artificial Intelligence 13
   40 Hertz Rythm of Neurons 13
   Quantum Mechanics... 14
   Identity Theory.. 15
   Other Theories... 15
   The Unconscious (Subconscious) 17
   Summary 19
Chapter Three: Consciousness Cores 20
   The Consciousness (or Qualitative) Cores 20
   Distinctions Between Qualia and Consciousness Cores 27
   Bridging the Gap Between Mind and Body 29
   Location of the Consciousness Cores............................... 30
   Nervous System, Brain, Nerve Cells, and Impulses.......... 31
   Summary 31
Chapter Four: Equivalence of Terms................................... 32
   Sensory and Sensation.. 35
   Preperceptual Processes 36
   Perception in Representationalsim 37
   Summary 39
Chapter Five: Creations of the Brain................................... 40
   Ultimate Reality is Unknowable 42
   Summary 44
Chapter Six: Directionality 45
   Primary and Secondary Qualities 45
   Explanation of Directionality 50

Distance 50
Size 51
Shape 52
Motion 52
Solidity...53
Size and Shape Constancy 56
Interworking of Primary and Secondary Qualities.........................57
Secondary Qualities and Consciousness Cores..............................58
Summary 60
Chapter Seven: Multiplicity and Dynamicity of Consciousness 61
Multiplicity of Consciousness...61
Time Relationships of Consciousness..64
Multiplicity and Evolution 66
Further Arguments Favoring Multiplicity of Consciousness...........67
Dynamicity of Consciousness..68
Summary 69
Chapter Eight: First and Third Person Perspectives 71
Appreciate Consciousness Only from the Inside 72
Summary 74
Chapter Nine: The Self. Preliminary Considerations 75
Summary 77
Chapter Ten: Underlying Philosophical Problems 79
Activity Versus Passivity of Perception...79
Illusions as Indicators of Activity 81
Directness Versus Indirectness in Perception 84
Summary 85
Chapter Eleven: Location of Consciousness 86
Background 86
Consciousness Elements Originate All Over the Body....................87
Location of Consciousness...89
Mind-body Problem 90
Further Matters of Conventional Language and Concepts...............90
Robots 92
Summary 92
Chapter Twelve: Synecdoche 93
Synecdoche in General..93
Synecdoche and Representationalism 98
Summary 99
Chapter Thirteen: Extracting the Consistently Associated.........................100
Shorthand 100
Extracting and Retaining the Consistently Associated 102
Extracting and Motor Skills 103

Difference Between Extracting the Consistently Associated and
Synedoche 104
Extracting and Memory.. 105
Summary 105
Chapter Fourteen: Contributions From Physiology............................. 106
Neuroanatomy 106
Intercellular Transmitters... 107
Emotion 109
Modules.. 109
Plasticity 111
Association... 112
Carbon Monoxide Poisoning.. 114
Experiments with Light.. 114
Modules Distinguished from Conscious Cores 114
Summary 115
Chapter Fifteen: Preconscious Processes and Monitoring................... 116
Preconscious Processes 116
Monitoring.. 117
Interests and Anxieties 118
Selectivity in Perception.. 119
Dreams 120
Hallucinations 122
Summary 123
Chapter Sixteen: Identitiy Theory 124
New Concept of Consciousness Needed 124
Consciousness is Experiencing 125
Identitiy Theory-Nerve Cell Activity Experienced as Consciousness .. 126
Abstract Concepts Test Identity Theory (The Mental Develops from the
Physical)... 132
Abstractions Based on Contacts with Reality--Additional Illustrations 134
Summary 135
Chapter Seventeen: The Self 136
Self as a Concept.. 136
Self as Perceiver of Consciousness Contents 138
The Self and Memory... 139
Revision of Terminology 140
Summary 141
Chapter Eighteen: Hierarchies.. 142
Random Access 144
Emotion and Hierarchical Development 145
Summary 145

Chapter Nineteen: Memory 146
  Consciousness and Memory...146
  Perceptual Patterns and Memory 149
  Searching of Memory..150
  Boolean Search Strategy 151
  Sensory Impulses and Memory 151
  Motor Memory...153
  Perceptions from Within 154
  Summary 155
Chapter Twenty: Higher Centers...156
  Linking of Consciousness Cores...157
  Relationship of Association to Logic and Experience 159
  Summary 160
Chapter Twenty-one: Representations 161
  Partial Resolution of the question of Representations 161
  Perception is Largely Recognition..161
  Relation of Representations to Synecdoche and Qualia...................163
  Representations--Recursive Comparisons 163
  Summary 165
Chapter Twenty-two: Additional Aspects of Consciousness 166
  Consciousness is in the Present...166
Consciousness Components May Already Be Before Us 166
  Redefinition of Sensory 170
  Nerve Cells, Impulses, and Identity 170
  Summary 172
Chapter Twenty-three: Attention and Automaticity............................173
  Attention 173
  Automaticity 177
  Freedom of Will 178
  Volition 178
  Curiosity...179
  Summary 180
Chapter Twenty-four: Becoming Consciousness 181
  The Crux of Becoming Consciousness 181
  The *Reductio* in Relation to an Observer 185
  Origin of the Self...186
  The Real Self..187
  Memory and Consciousness May Be in the Same Neurons.............187
  Consciousness as the Surface of Memory...188
  Introspection 190
  Higher Centers and Memory...192
  Other Theories of the Arrival of Consciousness 193

Meditation 194
Summary 195
Chapter Twenty-five: Consciousness and Meaning 197
Meaning.. 197
Meanings Are Hierarchical 197
Objects as Meanings 198
Consideration of Multiplicity... 199
Further Considerations of Equivalence 199
Unconscious Meanings 200
Meaning, Consciousness, and Synecdoche................................. 201
Semantic Considerations.. 202
Experiencing the Latest Hierarchy Level as Meaning 205
Computer Intelligence.. 207
Context 208
Summary 208
Chapter Twenty-six: Elaboration and Completion 210
Identity and Reality 210
Rocks and Reality 213
Hierarchical Development of Objects and the Binding Problem 214
Objects as Concepts 215
Objects and Emotions 215
Time and Space 216
Synecdoche as Reality.. 217
Nerve Cells are Consciousness 218
Difficulties with Accepting Identity Theory 219
Revisiting the Initial Premise 222
General Summary 224
Bibliography 227
Index... 235

Illustrations

1) Distance...51
2) Size..52
3) Motion..53
4) Solidity..53
5) Size and Shape Constancy 57
6) Synecdoche in Stick Drawings.........................97
7) Nerve Cell..106
8) Cellular Junctions...107
9) Summation 158

ABOUT THE AUTHOR

Dr. Brooks is a physician having been graduated from the Vanderbilt University with a degree in medicine and an undergraduate degree in chemistry. As a practicing psychiatrist, psychoanalyst, and neurologist, he has had extensive first hand experience in the observation of consciousness and the human mind. His background includes clinical professorships in the medical schools of Wayne State University and Michigan State University. He is uniquely qualified for his in depth analysis and clear exposition of the process by which consciousness occurs as well as the mechanisms for attention, context, curiosity, the understanding of meaning, the appreciation of reality, and the pivotal functions of emotion and memory.

FOREWORD

We present an entirely plausible theory of the mechanisms by which our brains make us aware of ourselves and of the world around us. The enigma of consciousness has been considered to be impossible to fathom by many serious scholars and the problem has defied explanation throughout history. Our explanation of consciousness extends beyond the simple difference between being conscious and being unconscious. We take a thoroughly scientific approach while holding the language to a non-technical level with the exception of a few terms which we fully explain.

By "consciousness" we simply mean awareness in the ordinary sense of the word. At this point to extend the description of consciousness much beyond "awareness" is to endeavor to preempt the book. Even though the term sounds simple enough, philosophers frequently disagree as to the definition. An expanded definition or description depends upon the theory of consciousness that one adopts. The description has a number of facets which shall become clear as the details unfold.

Beginning with an overview of previous theories of consciousness, we carry the reader along with us as we construct our own theory, which extends well beyond prior thinking. The concepts unfold from our designated building blocks or bedrock "cores" of consciousness, through several of the brain's devices and arrive at the operational surface of full blown consciousness. The book lays much groundwork for the theoretical underpinnings leading to the development of humanoids with synthetic minds. In the overall consideration humanoids seem inevitable even though they may be for the betterment or detriment of mankind.

William James in 1890 (publication 1950, a) stated "That brains should give rise to a knowing consciousness at all, this is the one mystery which returns no matter what sort the consciousness and of what sort the knowledge may be." Freud, in 1925 (publication 1950, a), referred to consciousness as "inexplicable." Nagel (1974), Popper and Eccles (1977), McGinn (1995), Velmans (1995, a) and others believe it to be virtually impossible for the brain, which after all is a physical organ, to produce the mind which is generally regarded as non-material. But consciousness is a real phenomenon and it is obvious that there must be a mechanism by means of which it occurs. We shall clarify progress that has been made and offer deep inroads toward credible resolutions of the remaining problems. In addition to "consciousness cores" our theory is based on the identity of nerve cell activity with consciousness, the hierarchical structure of memory, and the equating of memory with the pre-conscious.

The theory develops through several stages, all of which are needed for a full understanding of consciousness. Some of the stages are counterintuitive, a characteristic which we believe is responsible for the fact that consciousness has hitherto been so perplexing. We arrive at a complete and scientifically sound theory. Since consciousness is a central feature of the human mind, a number of its connections with other aspects of the mind become apparent. These include the relationship of consciousness with meaning, with the self, with free will, with reality in general. Light is also cat upon other concepts typically associated with the field of psychology. The latter concepts incorporate among others memory, attention, curiosity, and abstractions. Our theory of consciousness is actually no less than a theory of the basic psychological and neurological mechanisms of the mind.

Several entirely new concepts are introduced which thoroughly alter the conventional thinking and which render the usual terminology in relation to consciousness no longer sufficiently accurate. However, we continue to use the conventional concepts and the usual terminology until we expressly and clearly revise them.

The manuscript for this book was first copyrighted in February 1994 and included most of the theory contained herein. An additional copyright was obtained in September 1994, and others in 1998, 1999, June 2000, November 2000,2001, and March 2002, as new ideas or revisions were incorporated.

INTRODUCTION

Years ago I attended a fascinating lecture given by Warren S. McCullough (1947). He was a leading neuroscientist who was very instrumental in the science of cybernetics and in the development of computers. Computers were in their infancy and still used vacuum tubes. He commented that a computer could duplicate the human brain but that it would take the power of Niagara Falls to run it and the water of Niagara Falls to cool it. After the lecture I posed a question to him: "Is it known how the brain produces consciousness?" He responded by asking, "What is consciousness?" I replied that it was awareness, to which he added that it was *"awareness of awareness."*

His statement impressed me as containing something profound yet puzzling. At times I thought it explained consciousness. Later, I learned that Freud had said something similar to an extent, that consciousness was a *"superordinate sense organ"* and *"...a sense-organ for the perception of psychic qualities"* (1938a, p.544). After having organized a theory explaining consciousness, I now feel that I understand the statements by McCullough and Freud. I am much indebted to the former for having initiated my thinking about consciousness, however, I now realize that his answer covered only one aspect of this fascinating subject.

I once presented a lecture on consciousness to the Detroit Philosophical Society. In brief, I described it as analogous to a miner wearing a head lamp in an otherwise totally dark mine. In whatever direction he turned his head, the beam of light illuminated the area within his visual field. This gave him the illusion that the mine was fully lighted. The explanation was much oversimplified but in essence, it illustrated that the features of consciousness are based on reality but are partly illusion. The wonders of consciousness or of the mind result from the functioning of a machine. The machine is a biological one. It is a soft machine, made of nerve cells instead of metal parts. But it is a machine nevertheless. Somehow this machine, using nerve impulses which are electrochemical processes, creates the "mental" phenomenon we know as consciousness.

I firmly believe that the nervous system or brain produces the mind and that the nervous system therefore has to perform seemingly "magic tricks." Consider consciousness to be a miracle if you wish. Or regard it as an illusion in part. It is certainly a marvel. But in this book we raise the questions, "How does it work? How is it possible for a nervous system, a package of nerve cells similar in a way to the silicon chips of computers, to produce this result? How can a machine, something which is physical,

1

produce something which is non-physical?" The latter question reflects the ancient "mind-body problem."

This book actually arrives at a clear answer to the enigma. The answer, in brief, is that nerve cell impulses *are* consciousness. But this is far too short an answer. It is comparable to saying we build a house by taking materials and putting them together and that the materials *are* the house. While both statements are correct they are by no means a full or satisfying explanation. We need to explain the steps of the process which take place between the visual sighting of an object, such as a rock or a tree, and the consciousness of the object.

Psychologists have discovered the mechanisms for some of the performances of perception but the final step, sentience, has been thoroughly puzzling. These mechanisms constitute the remainder of the answer for which this book presents some very credible and understandable physiological and psychological processes. It then develops and combines these processes until a coherent answer to the riddle of consciousness is reached.

As recently as 1994, Francis Crick (pp. 15 and 228) made the criticism of the intellectual environment that consciousness has no real home outside the sphere of philosophy. This was also observed by Daniel Dennett in 1991 (p. 25). Crick pointed out that Benjamin Libet, whose experimental work in psychology is widely mentioned, "wisely did not embark on his experiments on consciousness in alert people until he had obtained the security of academic tenure." One much used textbook of medicine, in its extensive index, does not even mention the word, consciousness. The same is true of a popular textbook of psychology. It is believed that, together with certain prejudicial attitudes, the subject was considered to be too little understood to waste time and effort pursuing it. The situation has changed greatly in the past few years thanks in no small measure to Crick's having declared it to be a legitimate subject for scientific investigation (Horgan, 1994). Also, President George H. W. Bush declared the 1990's to be "the Decade of the Brain" and his action stimulated great activity aimed at explanation of the issues. Nevertheless, some of the concepts mentioned in this book incorporate views which still meet considerable emotional resistance.

Since most of our concepts about perception and consciousness derive from philosophy and since empirical science has made relatively little progress with the basic concepts, we will begin in this exposition from the foundation which philosophy has provided. Philosophy is briefly reviewed in the book in order to glean from it what is substantively useful and to be used as background. More detailed works have been written a number of times (Dennett, 1991; Kelly, 1986; Joad, 1975; Holt, 1922). While our intent is neither to support nor refute any particular philosophical thinking, it will become apparent that theories or facts to be presented will have a bearing on particular philosophical approaches. Toward the end of the book surprising concepts of meaning, reality, and several psychological functions are developed in relation to consciousness.

In the writing of this book my wife, Annabelle, deserves my utmost appreciation for her willingness to listen for coherence and to challenge the ideas as they unfolded, thereby forcing their clarification. I also want to thank my sons, Mark, C.P.A., for his suggestions and James, M.D., for his suggestions and for proof reading the manuscript. Further I wish to thank some of my friends, particularly Jerome Elbert, Ph.D., Henry Green, M.D., George Ritter, M.D., and Lawrence Cowan, Ph.D. for their comments and to express my gratitude to my numerous teachers, particularly the psychoanalysts. Without an extensive grounding in the psychoanalytic understanding of the unconscious and the dynamic nature of mental processes, the writing of this book would hardly have been possible.

Chapter One

Philosophical Background

Three Basic Approaches

The effort by philosophers to solve the enigmatic problems associated with explaining the nature and origins of consciousness began with the ancient Greeks. Historically there have been three main philosophical approaches: realism, representationalism, and idealism (Holt 1922; Kelly 1986, pp. 2-11). There are also many individual variations and combinations of these approaches but the general themes will be described in a very brief and simplified form which is adequate for the general reader as well as coherent and understandable. It should be pointed out that all three approaches have deep-seated problems and are quite controversial. Of the many philosophers, almost all of them having their own divergent views, it would be virtually impossible to give a brief summary which would correctly apply to each. For philosophers the following summary will be an oversimplification but it is suitable for our purpose of understanding consciousness

Realism

Perception, which we will regard as fairly synonymous with consciousness, involves an object which is perceived and a brain which does the perceiving. We prefer to conceptualize the historically established theories about perception in terms of what is external and what is internal. Objects which are perceived are considered to be external and the mind to be internal. This scheme seems to provide a simple way to categorize the three theories.

For a mind to become conscious of objects which are perceived as being external to itself, requires either that objects have to be brought into the mind in order for perception to occur, or that objects do not exist external to the brain but are present only in the mind (some form of idealism). Realism strongly opposes idealism and maintains that objects definitely exist external to the mind. Realism also opposes representationalism which holds that objects exist outside the mind but some type of image of the objects is formed in the mind and the mind then becomes conscious of the image. (Holt, 1922; Hebb, 1980; Hirst, 1959; Kelly, 1986.)

The realist approach is the closest to common sense and the most easily understood of the three approaches. In regard to the brain's relation to the outside world, realism is the most externally oriented of the three theories.

4

It is at the opposite pole from idealism which tends to place the world entirely within the mind. We will consider the middle ground to be occupied by representationalism.

Widespread philosophical recognition was accorded the realist approach in 1903 following the publication of an article by professor G. E. Moore entitled "The Refutation of Idealism." Idealism had dominated the previous century. In 1911 a group of realists cooperatively wrote a philosophical exposition entitled "The New Realism." Hence, they came to be known as Neorealists or Modern Realists. While their views differed considerably, they agreed that they should take a scientific turn and that any theory should be based upon empirical evidence. They also agreed in expressing a rejection of the various non-realist theories. The rejection applied particularly to any form of idealism. Holt's summary statement (1922) mentioned that "Realism is committed to a rejection of all mystical philosophies."

In this regard Hebb (1949) observed:

> Modern psychology takes completely for granted that behavior and neural function are perfectly correlated, that one is completely caused by the other. There is no separate soul or life-force to stick a finger into the brain now and then and make neural cells do what they would not otherwise. Actually this is a working assumption only... It is quite conceivable that some day the assumption will have to be rejected...the working assumption is a necessary one, and there is no real evidence opposed to it. Our failure to solve a problem so far does not make it insoluble. One cannot logically be a determinist in physics and chemistry and biology, and a mystic in psychology.

The Modern Realists took positions which were considerably more in the middle ground between the "external" position of the Common Sense Realists and the "internal" position of the idealists. But the realists in general disagreed with the basic concept of representationalism. Holt (1922) stated, "[Realism] conceives of objects as directly presented to consciousness and being precisely what they appear to be...Objects are not represented in consciousness by ideas; they are themselves directly presented." One point receiving emphasis therefore, is the view that perception of objects takes place without the formation of a mental image of which consciousness subsequently becomes aware. On this point Kelly (1986, p. 3) stated:

> As a realist, of course, I reject the classical representationalist view that we ... perceive not physical objects themselves but certain mental entities (images, ideas, sense-data) which represent them. This is the point on which I expect I will have many allies.

Kelly very strongly supported realism while following the "Objectivist" philosophy of Ayn Rand, the highly recognized author of *Atlas Shrugged* and *The Fountainhead*. At the present time realism has lost popularity due empirical considerations.

According to realism, an object such as a tree is located in the outside environment exactly where we see it and the way we see it. While the realists do not deny the role of the sense receptors or the brain, the theory provides no explanation of how these are used to accomplish perception. E. B. Holt (1992) made the following statement summarizing his article: "[When the] environment is known, it is brought into direct relations with some variety of agency or process which is the knower." Such statements are very non-specific as to the mechanisms which might be involved but represent the considered judgment of their authors in expressing approximately all that they can say with any feeling of certainty. Realists often acknowledge, implicitly if not overtly, that no explanation is offered as to the neurological mechanisms by which perception is accomplished. They argue that objects are perceived with little or no process involving interpretation or judgment on the part of the mind. This characterization applies mainly to the philosophy known as "common sense realism." Kelly (1986) states:

> I argue that in perception we are directly aware of physical objects and their properties, and that perceptual judgments about those objects and properties can be based directly on perception, without the need for any inference.

Representationalism

The representationalist idea was first propounded by the early Greeks. It was then given great emphasis by Rene Descartes (1596-1650) over three hundred years ago. John Locke (1632-1704) is also credited with its promulgation. As mentioned above, the approach can be looked upon philosophically and even in spatial orientation as a middle ground theory between realism and idealism.

At least since the time that the idea was expressed by Descartes and Locke, it has *seemed* fairly obvious and inescapable that the perception of objects must result from some sort of representation of them in the mind. If we are looking at a piano, the piano must be represented internally, must somehow be brought into our brain. Even though the perception cannot literally consist of a little piano inside our skull, something has to be there. We do see a piano. We also remember seeing it; we "picture" it in our minds. Perhaps it would help in conceptualizing the matter if we consider the representation to be what has been called an image, or some type of symbolization, or what Locke called an "idea." According to representationalist theory, the object results in a representation being present in the mind and the mind or consciousness then "sees" the representation rather than the object itself. This conceptualization stands in contrast to the realist theories which hold that we see objects "directly."

The bare idea of a representation seems like a necessary and minimal assumption. It does not have to indicate how a representation would be formed or of what it would consist. Bertrand Russell (1929) and A. J. Ayer (1940) proposed that representations are somehow derived from or caused largely by the object. Others consider them to be produced to a greater or lesser degree by the nervous system (Broad, 1923; Hirst 1959; Price 1973).

Representationalism sounds very reasonable and has great appeal until one examines it closely. Until very recently at least, most philosophers adopted some version of this theory. It now seems to have been replaced to a considerable extent by the "identity theory" but still with little or no in-depth explanation. There are different ways of conceiving of a representation as being in the mind yet no one, prior to the theory presented herein, has had, in our opinion, an even plausible explanation of how a representation would be formed.

As obvious as the idea of a representation seems to be, we have learned that what seems obvious is not necessarily true. We have learned that the earth is not flat and that the sun does not move around the earth. Philosophers, using reason alone, have found a serious problem with the idea of a representation. No matter how one conceives of the representation, a basic criticism of the theory has been that it always leads in the end to a *reductio ad absurdum,* a reduction to the absurd. A representation is formed in the mind. Consciousness is then a sort of inner eye which is required to see the representation. If one continues using the same principle a second representation is needed in order to represent the first and then a second inner eye, and on and on. Critics derisively speak of a Cartesian theater (the term being taken after Descartes) where the representation is presented, and of a homunculus, a little man in the brain, who perceives the representation (Ryle, p. 8). We will often use the term "central observer" instead of the homunculus, for the inner eye, as it is somewhat more respectable. Bruner, in 1973 (p. 10), firmly stated that theories involving actual likenesses of objects have been "long since given up." Yet no one has offered a reasonable theoretical substitute for a likeness even though we are definitely capable of "picturing" objects.

Frances Crick, Nobel co-laureate for the discovery of the composition of the DNA molecule, stated,

> Most neuroscientists believe there is no homunculus in the brain. Unfortunately it is easier to state the fallacy than to avoid slipping into it. The reason is that we certainly have an illusion of the homunculus: the self. There is probably some good reason for the strength and persistence of this illusion. It may reflect some aspect of the overall control of the brain, but what the nature of this control is we have not yet discovered.

In suggesting that the homunculus "reflects some aspect of the overall control of the brain", Crick brings out a relationship of the homunculus beside that of a perceiver of representations. Our theory of consciousness will propose a mechanism for the overall control of the brain in a later chapter in the form of what we call "memory hierarchies."

Different authors have introduced different terms to be used for the representation ("sense-data" and "phenomenal qualities", often shortened to "qualia") depending on technical differences in theory. The term "sense-data" (singular, sense datum), the first of such terms, and qualia are the ones most generally used. In this writing we will not discard the idea of a representation, but we will alter the concept from the way it has been conceived previously to such an extent that it would hardly be considered to be the same concept. A considerable portion of the remainder of this book, with a number of facets, will be applicable to that topic. The matter of representations is one of the central problems in the explanation of consciousness.

The almost unavoidable attractiveness of the idea of a representation is credited mainly to Descartes. He is regarded as having so deeply influenced the entire conceptualization of the mind that he even shaped the language on the subject ever since. It is quite difficult to discuss or write about the mind or consciousness without either overtly or implicitly relying on his concepts. Descartes systematically developed the idea of consciousness as a central observer of representations which are somehow internalized. He also separated the concept of the mind from that of the brain. He regarded the brain as part of the body but the mind consisted of some unknown substance separate from the brain (Kelly p.10; Ryle p.8). This concept seems to have begun in Western philosophy about 450 B.C. with Anaxagoras. It was given further emphasis by Plato (in the Phaedo), by Aristotle, St. Augustine and others. Such a separation still persists in the well known "mind-body problem."

The blame, which has been heaped upon Descartes as having so heavily and lastingly influenced our language and our thinking about the role of a representation in consciousness, may not be entirely deserved. Even though he promulgated such ideas very effectively, the ideas seem to be a natural outgrowth of the situation which existed from his time to the present. In the absence of any better understanding of the mechanism for the perception of objects, what is more natural than to apply one's common experience to one's theory? It indeed seems most natural to believe that objects we see are internalized and that they have some representation in our minds. The idea has yet to be fully replaced despite the fact that it usually leads to a "reduction to the absurd." Philosophers as well as scientists have made many attempts to avoid the *reductio.* In fact most of the theories today seem to be largely motivated by that goal. Many authors merely avoid mentioning it or at least avoid coming face to face with it. In this book we will face it directly and suggest a very plausible way to overcome it.

Ryle (1949) considered the views of Descartes on the nature of the mind to be one of Descartes' "main philosophical legacies" but nevertheless to be a "myth." He clearly and at times almost poetically exploded Descartes' "myth." According to Ryle (p.11), Descartes even believed that a person's "body and his mind are ordinarily harnessed together, but after the death of the body his mind may continue to exist and to function." Descartes lived at a time when science was breaking away from scholasticism and his writing was still heavily influenced by religion. The "mind", as he saw it, is certainly suggestive of the soul. However, there are many who believe that Descartes only professed to be so strongly dominated by religion in order to avoid punishment by the church as had happened to Galileo. Consciousness is still considered to be the soul by a number of authors. (For example, see Panksepp, 1998, and Popper and Eccles, 1997)

Idealism

Idealism tends to place the world entirely within the mind and therefore can be regarded as the most internal of the three overall approaches to an understanding of consciousness. Traditionally the existence or non-existence of God was of paramount importance to philosophy but the mind and its relation to reality took a prominent position in the various theories.

[W]hen the word ["idealism"] came into general philosophical use about the middle of the 18th century, idealism was taken as the view that there was no material world but only ideas existing in immaterial minds (Acton, 1965).

9

George Berkeley (1685-1753) and David Hume (1711-1776), two of the "English philosophers", were major contributors to the world's thinking about idealism. For temporal comparison recall that Descartes died in 1650. The idealist views of Immanuel Kant (1724-1804), are often singled out for special attention and it is his perspective (see Kant, 1965) that will be summarized briefly.

Unlike more extreme forms of idealism, Kant's version does not rely on the mind for perception to the extent of excluding the role of objects. It holds that we see the object but not as it really exists; objects as they actually exist are "unknowable." Kant is translated as saying, "What objects may be in themselves...remains completely unknown to us." This is because the nervous system perceives through its own apparatus, that is, through its sense organs and brain mechanisms, and imposes its own qualities upon an object. We normally assume the "real" appearance of an object to be just as we see it, yet common experience tells us that in an important sense this is not so. For example, under an ordinary microscope the appearance of an object can be radically different from what it is to the naked eye. With the advent of the electron microscope, the change in the "reality" becomes even more radical and the atomic and subatomic levels are almost beyond the consideration of appearance. Idealists regard the ultimate perception of objects either "directly", as theorized by realists, or by means of perfect representations, to be impossible.

The major criticism of idealism is that it is considered to lose touch with reality, there being no real contact with the outside world. Idealism, not only that of Kant, is accused of implying solipsism, that we live in a dream world, that each of us can be sure only that he or she is real. Idealism may appear to be extreme and unbelievable but the Kantian version with its thesis that we cannot know things as they are intrinsically or "in-themselves", is considerably short of solipsism and becomes altogether credible in view of scientific information.

Animism

There are also theories of the mind which regard the mind or consciousness, if they distinguish between the two, as something mystical, similar to the concept of soul or spirit. Such beliefs or theories range from the ancient animism to panpsychism.

Animism is the belief, still present today in primitive cultures, that entities such as the wind, mountains, forests, and volcanoes, have spirits and in some way are alive and conscious and can be pleased or displeased, etc. With a few twists, animism is still current in scientific circles (Horgan, 1994). The earliest Greek philosophers, somewhat like the view later adopted by Descartes, regarded the psyche or mind as a very special kind of matter. Their particular animist views changed "with the moral or ethical theory of the soul developed by Democritus, Socrates, and Plato." Plato (in Timaeus) called the universe "a living body endowed with a soul" (Popper, 1977, p. 67) but there is some question whether or not this should be taken literally.

Panpsychism

Panpsychism is usually regarded as a more modern, more intellectual version of animism. It still contains the suggestion of mysticism and holds that all animals, plants, inanimate objects, and even the smallest particles of matter are imbued with some sort of rudimentary sensation or "soul." Spinoza (1632-1677), who was a contemporary of Locke, arrived in his theorizing at a position of panpsychism. He stated that substances have an infinite number of attributes but man was able to know only those two attributes which made up his own being, namely thought and extension in space. Since thought was said to be an attribute of substances, then "all things are alive" or animate to some extent. This was applied to "all things" large and small and meant even grains of sand should be regarded as possessing consciousness. Present day quantum theories of consciousness, according to some authors (Hameroff, 1996; Zohar, 1990), present a more sophisticated basis for panpsychism but we will elaborate upon them in the next chapter.

Leibniz (1646-1716), also a contemporary of Locke, disagreed with him and taught a form of panpsychism. The mind to Leibniz was a collection of "monads." These were mere points in space. As points, they had no three dimensional extension. And since they had no physical extension they were regarded as being non-material, as souls or spirits. The monads were ultimate units or elementary microcosms of a "high level." They had relatively clear perceptions. A group of lesser monads, having more obscure perceptions, formed the body. Bodies as we see them were the *outside appearances* of collections of souls or spirits. Ideas sprang from the monads. The ideas were innate and merely waiting to be developed. There were also empirical ideas. These were ideas which were brought out by experience. Leibniz regarded his theory of monads with their pre-established harmony as providing a solution of the mind-body problem.

Epiphenomenalism

Epiphenomenalism (*epi*: on, Greek) is a theory which is not flagrantly mystical but is nevertheless regarded as non-scientific. It is the theory that the relationship of the mind to the body is that of an epiphenomenon. An epiphenomenon would be similar to the whistle of a train as it passes by—a phenomenon which results from another phenomenon but which has no effect upon the first one. As applied to the mind, this means that the mind or consciousness simply accompanies brain activity as an epiphenomenon and has no power to result in activity. Consciousness particularly is simply a by-product of brain function. This relegates the mind to an insignificant, useless position since it is the brain and not the mind which controls action. Computers would be somewhat analogous in that they can control activity but without consciousness. Epiphenomenalism implies that the mind and body, more specifically the mind and the brain, are separate. Such a philosophical position is known as dualism in contrast to monism, the belief that the mind and brain are one. Dualism, in one form or another, is still often singled out and given prominence.

Summary

Historically, the three most widely known theories which attempt to explain consciousness are representationalism, realism, and idealism. Realism holds that there is an external reality and the mind simply becomes conscious of it directly, without the employment of representations intermediate between objects and consciousness. Representationalism states that objects are somehow taken into the mind, that by some means there is a representation formed and the mind then becomes aware of the representation. A problem with this view is the implication that the act of seeing the representation must be accomplished by a central observer. But in turn, the manner in which the activity is accomplished by the central observer requires a second representation and begins a "reduction to the absurd." The third theory, idealism, maintains that either in large or small measure, we do not become aware of reality, that the mind is instrumental in producing what we take to be reality.

Many theorists still find themselves forced reluctantly and rather tenuously to resort to epiphenomenalism or panpsychism. The sound made by a train whistle is epiphenomenal and is believed by epiphenomenalists to be analogous to the production of consciousness by the brain: consciousness exists but it has no effect, the brain is responsible for all behavior without a role for consciousness. Panpsychism, the idea that all matter, even atoms, have some degree of consciousness, is a philosophical notion which is the unavoidable logical extension of reasoning which some theorists, even current theorists, have adopted.

Chapter Two

More Recent Theories

Linguistics

Two twentieth century philosophers, Ludwig Wittgenstein (1969) and Wilfred Sellars (1963) held that words stand for objects and therefore represent reality. We have learned to use particular words in describing objects and, as long as the meaning of these words is consistent in our minds and in the minds of others, then the words describe reality as we know it. Linguists tend to believe that we think in words and that consciousness is based on the utilization of words. In this view, perception seems to have no firm grounding in reality and the view is therefore considered to be a type of idealism. According to the theory, words are based on concepts, and concepts are based on other concepts. This conveys the impression that perception lifts itself by its own bootstraps unless the concepts originate in something more elementary—something physical and in closer contact with external reality. The theory does not postulate such. The words, no matter how accurate or how well understood, are mere descriptions. They are neither objects nor sensations. While thinking often seems to be in words, particularly conscious thoughts, most students of the mind would agree that much thinking is at a sub-verbal level.

Artificial Intelligence

Since the advent of computers, particularly in the past two decades, computer experts have comprised an increasingly large camp of theorists who believe that computers will not only be able to reproduce human-like intelligence but also consciousness. Computer chips are considered to be analogous to brain cells and both intelligence and consciousness are thought to result from their networks. On this matter we have to agree with Searle (1997) who writes that computer programs, "...deny the real existence of the conscious states they were supposed to explain. They end up by denying the obvious fact that we all have inner, qualitative, subjective states such as our pains and joys, memories and perceptions, thoughts and feelings, moods, regrets, and hungers."

40 Hertz Rhythm of Neurons

Crick and Koch (1990) have postulated that the 40 cycle per second coordinated rhythm of brain cells (neurons) may be responsible for consciousness. Electrical activity of the brain, reveals that such a rhythm is widespread. "Brain waves" of various frequencies have been known for over fifty years. Whether or not frequencies of about 40 Hertz are responsible for consciousness remains to be proved. However, it may be impossible to prove for theoretical reasons to be explained in a subsequent chapter.

Quantum Mechanics

Penrose (1989), Clark, J.C.S. (1995), and Hameroff (1996) are among a growing number of those who believe that the answer to the origin of consciousness lies in the area of quantum mechanics. Quantum phenomena are those exhibited by the smallest known particles of matter, particles of which atoms are composed. The subatomic world of quantum mechanics exhibits unexplained physical phenomena which are still quite puzzling and lend themselves to theoretical explanations of consciousness. Some physicists point particularly to microtubules, discovered within the last two decades, which are cylindrical structures within cells of the body, and which are regarded as important in maintaining the physical shape of the cells. The structures are composed of proteins and are thought by the physicists to be responsible for consciousness. Zohar (1990) pointed out analogies between quantum phenomena and mental phenomena and it remains to be seen whether or not the quantum phenomena are merely analogous or are truly causative.

Critics of quantum theories are inclined to feel that a relationship between quantum mechanics and consciousness depends merely upon the fact that both phenomena are so completely puzzling and unexplained. It is interesting that quantum theory is considered to have considerable implication for panpsychism by some well respected authors. If quantum size particles have consciousness or proto-consciousness, then all substances may contain proto-consciousness. As strange and as unlikely as this sounds, the authors point out that it is conceivable. Pylkkanen (1994) states: "The idea is that *if* we want to understand how brains cause minds, then panpsychism must be taken seriously as a *possible* view." But he also quotes Nagel (1986):

If any two hundred pound chunk of the universe contains the material needed to construct a person...then everything reduced to its elements, must have proto-mental properties...But what kind of properties could atoms have (even when they are part of a rock) that could qualify as proto-mental; and how could any properties of the chemical constituents of a brain combine to form a mental life?

Identity Theory

This theory in its simplest form is not new and again has its roots in ancient Greece. However, in recent years it has been updated in several more specific forms. *The view to be developed in the remaining chapters of this book is a form of the identity theory.*

The theory is monistic: it holds that *the mind is a function of the brain* and that the mind and the brain are one. The bare statement itself seems evident to most people. It also means *that consciousness is identical with brain activity.* Injury or removal of the stomach or the spleen, etc., does not destroy consciousness but a relatively intact brain is essential to it. Even though the statement seems obvious and it is now the most popular theory of consciousness, "the devil is in the details." Explaining how consciousness can result from brain activity has seemed totally insurmountable. Very few authors have offered plausible suggestions and many, in what seems to result from desperation, turn to non-scientific, explanations. It is our intention to offer a mechanism and suggest known physical entities to explain consciousness.

Other Theories

There are a fair number of serious authors who believe that the mysteries of consciousness are "too profound for humans to plumb, scientifically or otherwise" (Horgan, 1994). McGinn postulates that the human mind is based on the appreciation of space and since the mind is non-material and does not occupy space, it is outside the limitations of human comprehension. "The human epistemic system has a specific structure and mode of operation, and there may well be realities that lie beyond its powers of coverage" (McGinn, 1995). There are also those who think that consciousness is a fundamental, similar to mass, and the charge of subatomic particles, in that, at the present time at least, it cannot be reduced to anything more elemental; that it simply has to be accepted and cannot be understood in any simpler terms. This view is currently fairly well accepted in different forms (Chalmers, 1995a; T. Clark 1995a; Velmans, 1995b). Velmans (1993) proposed a "dual-aspect" theory in which "consciousness and its correlated brain states may be thought of as dual aspects of a particular kind of 'information', which is in turn, a fundamental property of nature." Velmans related his theory to "an early version of...the dual-aspect theory of Spinoza (1677)—the view that mind and matter are manifest aspects of something deeper in nature..." His view could be considered to be a version of the identity theory. Chalmers, in the article cited above, also proposes a dual-aspect theory but he moves away (T. Clark, 1995a) from considering "information" to be the same as consciousness. Libet (1996) proposed the theory that a "consciousness mental field...emerged from the appropriate neural activities or the brain." (See also Libet, 1994.) Whether consciousness is regarded as a fundamental of one sort or another, these concepts seem to fall short of being a satisfying explanation of consciousness. This is not a fault, however, as the theories do not claim to be a full explanation.

Many theorists consider the mental to remain in a category distinct from the physical and none of the many authors who present their views on identity "go all the way." Feign (1958) does present an argument for the identity theory but only in general terms. T. Clark (!995b) argues for a form of identity theory in which he attributes consciousness to "certain sorts of physical, functional, informationally rich, and behavior controlling (cybernetic) processes." Macdonald (1992), in her relatively authoritative and much quoted book entitled *Mind-Body Identity Theories*, in which she critiques the various theories stated, "Since it is not part of the essence of any physical phenomenon...that it be rational, no [theory of consciousness]... can be identical with any physical phenomenon..."

In the Journal of Consciousness Studies, a leading journal on the subject of consciousness, Hut and Frassen (1997) make a rather strong statement:

> Yes, conscious experience correlates with brain activity, but by measuring and mapping those correlations, have we come any closer to an understanding of what many scientists would like us to believe, that somehow consciousness emerges out of (oozes out of?) (sic) nerve cells? If I've ever seen an incompatible pair of concepts, it's a configuration of molecules and a conscious experience!

Also, Dalton (1997) stated, "Can we understand conscious experience? It can seem that the answer is 'no'."

However, some authors have made significant contributions which do not explain consciousness but which can be applied to an explanation. Dennett (1991) and Searle (1996) are among them but Searle (1997) stated in a widely read book, "The neuron firings cause the feeling, but they are not the same thing as the feeling."

The above theories are more or less scientific. There are many others, which are current, but are often mystical. The theory we shall present allows for actual or complete identity of the physical and the mental. It makes the identity theory understandable and credible by filling in the substance behind the mere definition. It bridges the conceptual "gap" between the physical and the mental and does this in a way which is thoroughly legitimate as a scientific hypothesis.

We combine the identity theory with what we might call "developmental representationalism." Unfortunately attempting to state the theory briefly does not make it understandable, much less credible. It is very much like a chain. There are a number of links and without any one of them the theory hardly holds together as an intelligible whole. We begin, in the next chapter, with inherited "core elements" of consciousness and proceed with their development in the psychology of the individual until the consciousness of the adult is reached.

The Unconscious (Subconscious)

Before leaving the theories of consciousness we should mention the relationship of the unconscious to consciousness. Throughout history and to this day there is a strong tendency to consider consciousness to be the entire mind. Most serious thinkers, however, say that the mind is much more than consciousness, that in addition to consciousness there is an unconscious. Indeed psychoanalysts, psychiatrists, psychologists, and many philosophers agree that consciousness is only a small part of what constitutes the mind.

Freud is credited with having discovered the unconscious, with having been the first to recognize its extensiveness in the functioning of the mind. However, Leibniz, as well as a number of philosophers prior to Freud (1856-1939) speculated about the unconscious. Leibniz arrived at his concept of the unconscious mind through his theory of monads. Since the monads included or comprised ideas waiting to be brought out, the ideas were not conscious until the evocation occurred. Freud wrote in 1925 (published 1950, b), "...the overwhelming majority of philosophers regard as mental only the phenomena of consciousness...For them ...the mind has no contents other than the phenomena of consciousness." Very few philosophers accepted the concept of the unconscious and were at a great disadvantage as far as understanding consciousness and the mind were concerned. Philosopher, Daniel Dennett wrote (1981, p. 11):

> For John Locke and many subsequent thinkers, nothing was more essential to the mind than consciousness, and more particularly self-consciousness [introspection]. The mind in all its activities and processes was viewed as transparent to itself; nothing was hidden from its inner view. To discern what went on in one's mind one just 'looked'—one 'introspected'—and the limits of what one thereby found were the very boundaries of the mind. The notion of unconscious thinking or perceiving was not entertained, or if it was, it was dismissed as incoherent, self-contradictory nonsense. For Locke there was, indeed, a serious problem with how to describe all of one's memories as being continuously in one's mind when they were not continuously 'present to consciousness.' The influence of this view, together with 'common sense' was so

17

great that when Freud initially hypothesized the existence of unconscious mental processes, his proposal met widely with stark denial and incomprehension. It was not just an outrage to common sense, it was even self-contradictory to assert that there could be unconscious beliefs and desires, unconscious feelings of hatred, unconscious schemes of self-defense and retaliation. But Freud won converts. This 'conceptual impossibility' became respectably thinkable by theorists once they saw that it permitted them to explain otherwise inexplicable patterns of psychopathology.

In very recent years the acceptance of the unconscious has begun to change. In the fourth quarterly issue of the 1997 Journal of Consciousness Studies, Underwood, Peterson, and Chapman argue for the acceptance of the unconscious:

> Studies of implicit memory and implicit learning are typical of demonstrations of the effects of unconscious knowledge (see Underwood, 1996). Unconscious influences are particularly evident in language comprehension. There is the now classic finding that readers are faster to identify words that have a high frequency of occurrence in the language than words that have a low frequency of occurrence...it appears that current processing decisions are strongly influenced by unconscious knowledge that is based on our prior experiences of language use. Unconscious knowledge can also influence the interpretation that we assign to sentences.

The philosophers of the past have labored, not only without the benefit of having knowledge about the unconscious, but also without the benefit of advances in neurophysiology which the past one hundred years have brought about.

Even with a knowledge of the unconscious, many if not most authors still greatly underestimate the role it plays in daily living. We simply take for granted the myriad of functions that our brains perform for us at the *unconscious level.* An easily accepted example is the experience of the persistence of melodies in consciousness for hours or days after the melody has ceased to be heard through the ears. This may continue to the extent that it actually becomes somewhat annoying. The experience makes it clear that the internal music stems not from volition but from an unconscious source. Another common but unconventional example is the way people remember physical skills they have learned, such as how to ride a bicycle, without attempting to commit the procedure to conscious memory. They deliberately learn the movements but remembering them happens "automatically." Almost all memory is installed without conscious effort to remember, but which obviously implies that consciousness is involved.

There are an unlimited number of such activities. Our brain knows how to tie our shoes. But it is quite difficult to tell someone how to accomplish the task without actually doing it at the same time. It is a common experience to most physicians that if patients have been confined to bed for a few weeks they complain that they "forget" how to walk. There are those who would consider physical activities to be worthless examples of the unconscious because they involve so-called "motor memory." Teachings in medical schools imply that "motor memory" is in a different category from intellectual memory, a placement for which we know of no real justification even though motor coordination is mediated largely in the cerebellum rather than in the cerebrum, that is, in a different part of the brain. This does not necessarily mean that the essential processes of motor and intellectual memory are different.

What about the intellectual area? We do not have to make any conscious effort to remember that we particularly like a certain food. Nor do we have to make a conscious effort to make the decision to keep a safe distance from a growling dog. Such trivial examples are numerous but these are enough to be convincing that much of what the brain does is at the automatic, or unconscious, level.

We have not even mentioned the kind of things which concerned Freud. Common examples of the unconscious mind, more appropriate to psychoanalysis, would involve unconscious motivations or emotions. These involve internal conflict (hostilities, guilts, anxieties, and so forth), elements which the conscious mind does not wish to recognize and succeeds in "repressing." There are several other major psychological activities of the brain or mind which take place at the unconscious level and which are at once very common and directly relevant to the understanding of consciousness. These will be discussed in later pages.

Summary

Theories of consciousness that are currently popular include artificial intelligence as produced by computers, 40 cycle per second rhythm of brain cells, and quantum mechanics. The identity theory, that consciousness simply *is the same phenomenon as certain brain activity,* seems obvious on the surface yet is quite counterintuitive when one tries in any depth to explain consciousness and how it comes about. The aim of the succeeding pages is to accomplish that goal in a systematic manner.

Chapter Three

Consciousness Cores

The Consciousness (or Qualitative) Cores

There is an implication of elementary components of consciousness in John Locke's use of the word "sensation" (1975, p. 105). He maintained that all ideas come from "SENSATION" or "REFLECTION". First, in regard to sensation, he believed that the mind was blank at birth and that items from the external world entered the mind through the senses. *The senses supplied the building blocks for the mind.* He was certainly indicating that he regarded sensations as primary, elemental forms of mental processes. He also thought that ideas come from "REFLECTION." Reflection was viewed by him as an additional process. It was entirely internal, nearer to what we would know as introspection in which the mind obtains ideas "by reflecting on its own Operations within it self (sic)." We would consider reflection to be a process involving recombination; the mind combines and recombines the arrangement of the original ideas or "building blocks" (Brooks, 1995a) to develop new structures which can then be built into still larger structures, and so on.

Locke was basically correct. Pursuing his beginning we will introduce the concept of a theoretical "consciousness core" (Brooks, 1994, 1995b) or "qualitative core" as being fairly similar to Locke's "sensation." *We conceive of the consciousness core as sensory in nature.* The term "core" is used because it implies the heart or *essential element* of a sensation. Also, we will use the term "qualitative" since the experience of a sensation has a *unique quality* totally peculiar to that sensation. Further, we will use the terms "perceptual core" or simply "core" depending on the linguistic suitability.

Exactly what is a consciousness core neurologically? Neurons (nerve cells) are generally divided into three classifications: sensory, motor, and internuncial. The sensory neurons are those which carry impulses from the sensory receptor organs, such as those within the skin, through the spinal cord and to the brain. The motor neurons are those which carry impulses in the reverse direction, from the brain through the spinal cord to the muscles. The internuncial neurons lie between and carry impulses from one type of neuron to the other. Internuncial neurons may also connect to other internuncial neurons as in the brain. It is with the sensory neurons that we consider the consciousness cores to be primarily mediated. We cannot state that the cores are the same as sensory neurons or sensory neuronal impulses.

We regard these as possibilities but sensory impulses are processed on their way to the brain and within the brain. It is quite possible or even quite likely that the cores do not become *consciousness elements* until some amount of change or processing has occurred. The processing of the sensory neurons would largely involve internuncial neurons.

At this time we therefore do not have enough knowledge of neurophysiology to exactly delineate or define the consciousness core. We can, however, state the principles which are inherent in the concept. The concept of the consciousness core is based on the presumption, first, that the basic function of consciousness is the reception of *sensory inputs* or information from the environment. A second presumption is that consciousness can be subdivided into component parts. The consciousness cores then are conceived *as purely hypothetical and as the smallest, simplest components of consciousness.* For the moment, consider the primary colors or the theoretical primary tastes to be consciousness cores. They are combined to become all the colors and tastes which are known, that is, become conscious to us. They are processed to become sensory inputs.

We may regard the consciousness core as analogous to the atom. The atom was defined in principle about 400 BC by Democritus essentially as the smallest part of a substance which, *if cut any smaller, would no longer be that substance.* The atom was an entirely theoretical entity which conveyed a clear implication that materials could be divided into lesser substances. The concept eventually led to alchemy and then to chemistry with all of the marvels of chemistry which are now familiar. The atom therefore, even though it was only a theoretical notion, served a most useful purpose. We assume and hope that the idea of the consciousness core will also eventually be highly rewarding.

The ancient Greeks had no idea, of course, of the atomic elements as we know them today—oxygen, hydrogen, carbon, and the like. But in principle the definition such as the Greeks had would still stand today even though their definition is no longer fully correct according to today's understanding of the atom. Their definition is in keeping with the principle known as *reductionism*—the reduction of something to its component parts. It is the same principle that still underlies all scientific theory and which has resulted in the explosion of scientific progress in the past three centuries. In this book we base our theorizing on science. One might say that the history of science is the history of reductionism.

The Greeks did not have the knowledge needed to be specific but the principle behind their reasoning was right on the mark. According to today's definition, the smallest division to which most substances can be reduced and still be that substance, is a molecule. Actually atoms would result from dividing *molecules* into their still smaller component parts. For

21

example, a molecule of water (H_2O) is made up of two atoms of hydrogen and one atom of oxygen and if it were cut into its component parts the substance would no longer be water. The remaining parts would be the gases of hydrogen and oxygen.

$$H_2O \text{ (molecule)} = \text{Hydrogen (two atoms)} + \text{Oxygen (one atom)}$$

So the idea of the Greeks is not totally correct according to today's knowledge. Nevertheless, it is most important to recognize that their basic approach, the reductionist principle, was correct and that we should apply the same principle to the study of consciousness. It is unfortunate that this has not always been the case.

The consciousness cores are not being postulated as being full consciousness, only the primary elements of consciousness—the atoms if you will. Even though we like to think of ourselves as being very knowledgeable and sophisticated in all areas of science, we are roughly in the same position relative to consciousness vis-à-vis the consciousness cores as were the Greeks relative to substances vis-à-vis the atom. On the matter of understanding consciousness, in the last few years we are beginning to make progress—perhaps. It depends on the extent to which our basic theories are beginning to focus on the matter as it actually exists. It seems unmistakable that we are at least moving in the correct general direction.

In attempting to reduce consciousness to its simplest elements, to limit as narrowly as possible what constitutes a consciousness core, a second consideration is that, in the extremely complex systems of the human brain, *the processing is multistaged.* There are levels in the processing of a perception before the neurological development reaches the stage of consciousness and we do not know at which level the initial elements of consciousness begin to fit into place. For example, in the sensory mode of vision, let us divide the neurophysiology into three rough stages: (1) cells which are located in the retina, (2) in the intermediate aggregates of brain cells called nuclei (not to be confused with the nuclei of individual cells), and (3) in the cerebral cortex (the uppermost level of the brain). Each of these stages has component stages within it which are integral parts of the visual system. It is therefore difficult, or actually impossible at the present time, to determine where one should draw the line to exactly designate the most elementary components. To compare the visual system to an automobile, supposedly we could say that the explosion of the gasoline inside the cylinder is the most elementary component of the power which moves the vehicle. Since the main purpose of the automobile is locomotion, it is the initial force that we might call the "core." But the electrical power from the battery starts the engine and furnishes the spark which ignites the gasoline. So the situation is not a simple one. In the eye, more specifically in the retina, there are receptor cells known as rods and cones. Should we consider the nerve impulses emanating from the rods and cones to be the most elementary components of consciousness? Are the individual nerve cells in the eye (and in the brain) the smallest components? At our present level of knowledge that would seem to be the easiest place to draw the line. But there is a problem with drawing the line at that stage. It is quite possible that actual consciousness elements may not exist at that level. We do not know at what level in the nervous system the initial elements of consciousness *begin* to appear. Accepted current thinking is that consciousness is at the highest level of the three stages, namely the cerebral cortex, and most likely *not* at the first level.

There is a possibility that the elementary consciousness components of the different sensory modalities or types may even be present at the first level. The nerve cell fibers of the various modalities other than vision are largely kept segregated within the spinal cord and brain stem on their way higher and continue to be separate to a considerable extent within the brain. The segregation of the modalities suggests that in addition to differences in their destinations there also may be variations in the compositions of their neurons. It is also possible that between unlike modalities the impulses themselves may have differences in timing or other characteristics. To complicate matters even further there is parallel processing. For instance, the color of objects may be processed at the same time as shape, motion, and other such details. It is usually believed that all of the different aspects must come together eventually as a single percept. However, it is clear that the "coming together" at what might be called a final perceptual level is not as complete as is generally thought, or further, that it may not be complete at all, even though on the conscious surface it seems to be so. (This involves synecdoche which we will discuss in a later chapter.) In short, the important point is that at this time we cannot exactly pinpoint the consciousness core neurologically. But we will adopt the theoretical concept of a simple core and, similarly to that of the early place of the atom, it will be very useful as an element in our theory of consciousness.

Even though in humans it is not currently possible to physically separate out "core" elements, in lower animals it might be much easier to isolate them. This could be true particularly of those organisms at the very earliest levels in the animal kingdom at which consciousness might be present. Research in this area might be very helpful in discovering the elementary aspects of the physiology of consciousness. We would probably find that there are degrees or types of consciousness, that consciousness as it is present in the human went through long stages of development in evolution. Memory is closely allied to consciousness in the human. How much and what sorts of things do animals remember? They seem to remember some things quite well, particularly things related to food. A hungry stray cat has no difficulty remembering where it was once fed.

It is quite certain that visual consciousness in the scallop is much less complex than in the human. The scallop has numerous eyes or visual sensors all around the edges of the shell opening and we have to assume that it has some degree of consciousness. It is known that the eye of the fly, being compound, is more primitive than that of the human. Therefore its conscious vision must be different from that of the human. How should we look upon pain in the earthworm? Any fisherman knows that when an earthworm is cut in half, it wiggles furiously for a moment. It certainly looks as if there is some consciousness of pain. While still relatively complex in comparison to even lower animals, its physiology must be somewhat closer to the level of our putative consciousness core. Even the flatworms *(Planaria)*, which are the lowest animals in the phylogenetic chain to have a head containing nervous tissue, react to a mild electric shock. This seems to be akin to pain. Assuming that consciousness in the human resembles that in lower animals, the question then is, at what phylogenetic level does consciousness begin and where should we draw the line as to what constitutes the most elemental components of consciousness? The proper answer is that we simply do not know enough to clearly answer the question. However, it is not necessary for the theory of consciousness, which is being presented, to know exactly what are the most elementary components. *We merely need to regard consciousness as not being a unitary entity but as being composed of basic elements.*

Since many of the cores take their origins in the physiology of what are called the perceptual modalities, let us examine them, proceeding from a physiological standpoint. Conventionally the perceptual modalitites are those that are conveyed by the "five senses"—vision, hearing, touch, taste, and smell. The experiences resulting from them are fully subjective and are definitely unique. They are not only different from each other, they are completely different from anything else in nature.

The theory being propounded begins with the idea that the consciousness cores are the primary elements, the beginnings of consciousness. We have also called them the building blocks of consciousness. In chapter seven we will discuss our concept that consciousness is not a single entity but is composed of sensory inputs. The physical apparatuses (or the precursors for experiencing consciousness cores) are inborn. Some of them are present at birth or sooner. By a process of development, which will be explained within the remainder of this writing, *the consciousness cores become consciousness as it is known to the adult.*

#77   12-17-2014 2:54PM
Item(s) checked out to p19262619.

TITLE: The New religious consciousness
BARCODE: 441092000098074
DUE DATE: 01-07-15

TITLE: Reference and consciousness
BARCODE: 34213000032895
DUE DATE: 01-07-15

Clifton Fowler Library   303-963-3250
Renew at http://ccu.opac.marmot.org

#77   12-17-2014 2:54PM
Item(s) checked out to p19262619.

TITLE: The New religious consciousness
BARCODE: 441092000098074
DUE DATE: 01-07-15

TITLE: Journey into the realm of conscio
BARCODE: 34213000215128
DUE DATE: 01-07-15

Clifton Fowler Library   303-963-3250
Renew at http://ccu.opac.marmot.org

For this section and for our entire concept of consciousness, it is important that the reader be clear about the meaning of the word, qualitative. Is there any doubt that the taste of a banana has a completely different quality from the color of a blue sky; or that the sound of a bell has a quality which is totally different from the feel of sandpaper? Even within a single sense modality, for example smell, the aroma of cinnamon is completely different from the aroma of apple. Each odor seems to be an entirely individual core quality even though they are both within the same sense modality.

The particular redness of a red flag is a much used example of perception. It could also be considered to be a consciousness core and an isolable quality in the sense of being a raw, or bare, perceptual element, a "raw feel" as mentioned by Kirk (1994). As far as consciousness is concerned, the cores are not reducible to lesser components at the present time. Analogous to the role served by the concept of the atom in the history of chemistry, *we define the consciousness core simply as being the earliest sensory component of the nervous system which constitutes elementary consciousness.* Any smaller components of consciousness are beneath the conceptual levels of psychology.

Not only are the qualities quite possibly irreducible psychologically but they may also be distinctive in the way they are produced in the nervous system. In the retina, the cones distinguish between red, blue, and green colors (wavelengths). This is fairly strong physiological justification for considering these colors to be elementary and to be consciousness cores. The few types of rods and cones receive the light waves in various proportions and these account for the thousands of colors which the human being is capable of discerning.

Within the sense modality of smell, it is not known how the different odors are distinguished. There are various theories but they are beyond the scope of this writing. Whether they are physiologically distinct or whether they consist of combinations of more than one core, is yet to be empirically determined.

In the modality of taste, it is usual to classify the sensations as sweet, sour, salty, and bitter. However, efforts to find differences in the taste buds to account for these sensations have not been successful. Again, as in the sense of smell, it is not known whether four or five primary characteristics can account for the seemingly large number of different taste sensations of which the human is capable. In the modality of hearing, in the inner ear the cochlea has "hair cells" which are arranged along a membrane somewhat like the strings of the orchestral harp. These cells reverberate to different sound frequencies (pitches) and begin the process of discriminating between the frequencies.

Different tastes and odors may be a combination of "primary" tastes and odors. In this writing, for want of more exact scientific knowledge at the present time, we will refer to different modalities, such as vision and smell, in an inclusive sense to be qualitative cores. However, in order not to force the definition unnecessarily beyond our knowledge of neurophysiology, we will also consider each of the modalities, to have a number of core qualities within it. We do this advisedly but the indefiniteness does not detract from the usefulness of the consciousness core concept within our view of consciousness. They are the elements of which consciousness is composed.

It has been mentioned above that we should regard the capacity for having consciousness cores as innate. Of course, since the whole concept of consciousness cores is theoretical, we have no *hard evidence* for making the further statement that the capacities for them are innate. It is merely that it seems very reasonable since many cores are present at birth in the human and in lower animals. Another quotation from Daniel Dennett (p.55) will elaborate upon the point. The quotation also is supportive of some of the other points we have been making.

According to the still robust tradition of the British Empiricists, Locke, Berkeley, and Hume, the senses are the entry portals for the mind's furnishings; once safely inside, these materials may be manipulated and combined *ad lib* to create an inner world of imagined objects. The way you imagine a purple flying cow is by taking the purple you got from seeing a grape, the wings you got from seeing an eagle, and attaching them to the cow you got from seeing a cow. This cannot quite be right. What enters the eye is electromagnetic radiation, and it does not thereupon become usable as various hues with which to paint imaginary cows. Our sense organs are bombarded with physical energy in various forms, where it is 'transduced' at the point of contact into nerve impulses that then travel inward to the brain. Nothing but information passes from outside to inside, and while the receipt of information might provoke the creation of some phenomenological item (to speak as neutrally as possible), it is hard to believe that the information itself—which is just an abstraction made concrete in some modulated physical medium—could *be* the phenomenological item. There is still good reason, however, for acknowledging with the British Empiricists that in *some way* the inner world is dependent on sensory sources.

We are in full agreement that the purple cow is not purple. The purple is only in our minds. Our brains have created it. When we say "created it" do we mean it exists? Is there a purple pigment in our brains? Of course not. It is purely "mental." How the brain creates color for us, makes us see color, is really the crux of the problem of explaining consciousness and in subsequent pages we will make some approaches to the issue.

But there is a question concerning the first part of Dennett's statement. He mentions, "...by taking the purple you got from seeing a grape..." The question is, where did you get the purple from seeing the grape? From seeing a purple sweater? But where did you get that purple? Sooner or later, we realize that the purple had to originate in the mind itself. Perhaps it was there from before birth, waiting to be stimulated by the proper wavelength of light. In other words, purple is what we are calling a consciousness core (or possibly is composed of a mixture of them). Whether it is actually present at birth or develops a little later from predispositions is immaterial to our discussion. In either case the capability of seeing purple is inborn and the quality, the purple color, is originated by the brain.

Hume (1711-1776) (see 1978) made the clear statement in regard to the sensory sources of information that people, "are nothing but a bundle or collection of different perceptions, which succeed each other with inconceivable rapidity, and are in a perpetual flux and movement." Schopenhauer (1788-1860), agreed that all knowledge was acquired through the senses.

Distinctions Between Qualia and Consciousness Cores

"Qualia" is an older, well established and widely used term, while "consciousness cores", having been introduced in this book, are new on the scene. In actuality both concepts are theoretical and imprecisely defined. The term "qualia" has typically been used in relation to the representation of a face and to simple colors. The color red, for example, "as distinct from any source it might have in a physical object" (Webster's New Collegiate Dictionary) has been typically regarded as a quale (single for qualia).

In many cases the two terms, qualia and consciousness core, may have similar usage but there are also distinct differences between the concepts. One significant difference between the two terms is in the theories which support them. Recall that in representationalist theories, a representation such as that of a visual object, is formed in the mind and the mind then becomes aware of the representation. We shall not attempt to describe qualia in great detail at this time but they are supported by representationalist theory. They are entire representations and present sensations and objects for *appreciation* by consciousness. Confusion between "qualia" and "consciousness cores" can easily arise because both can be applied to perceptions such as colors, tastes, or sounds, etc. In practice "qualia" is most often used in relation to such simple perceptions apparently because its theoretical position has not been sufficiently elaborated for theorists to feel comfortable in using the term for complex perceptions.

On the other hand we regard consciousness cores as individual sensory inputs which serve to comprise either simple or complex perceptions. Unlike the concept of qualia consciousness cores are more apt to be *combined* to form perceptions. Theoretically they are the building blocks of consciousness comprising not only touches and colors or other simple sensations but also complexes such as memories, abstractions, and concepts. In this book "consciousness core" is used in conjunction with the version of the identity theory we are promulgating *that consciousness ultimately consists of consciousness cores.* We will often use "consciousness core" in contexts which differ from the customary use of "qualia."

Another difference between the two terms is in relation to the conscious vis-à-vis the subconscious. "Qualia" is most often used in relation to *entirely conscious perceptions whereas consciousness cores may or may not be conscious.* They are most frequently unconscious. In distinction to qualia we hold that a *conscious* touch or a color may be a consciousness core but a large *conscious* complex (a memory, concept, etc.) would be composed of consciousness cores which are *unconscious.*

"Qualia" are sometimes considered to represent whole external objects. Even though objects always have a number of aspects, qualia are customarily thought to represent them all at once. Bertrand Russell (1914) states, for example, "...*mountains, only become data [qualia] when we see them.*" (Italics ours.) In his description the mountain is a quale but we prefer to consider the color, size, height, etc., to be consciousness cores which comprise the larger concept of the mountain. The concept of consciousness cores which we are offering applies only to individual qualities. How we become aware of objects as wholes, according to our theory of consciousness cores, will constitute a substantial portion of the remainder of this book.

A further, very significant difference between qualia and consciousness cores is that *we regard emotions as consisting of consciousness cores,* while the term, qualia, is not used in connection with those functions. We consider emotions, "ideas" (exactly what the term includes is debatable), and memories to be inputs to consciousness just as are sensations from the external senses or from the body organs. This is not the customary way of regarding emotions but, as perceptions, they arise consciously in the same subjective manner that other inputs arise. All inputs have to enter the same door of consciousness, so to speak, and in our view ideas, emotions, and memories should not be set aside as being different from other inputs in relation to consciousness.

Bridging the Gap Between Mind and Body

The qualities of the consciousness cores, of which we have been writing, have two sides to them. They have a physical side since they are nerve cell activity. They also have a mental side, a psychological side, since they comprise qualitative experiences. They are experiences in consciousness. Thus *the consciousness cores bridge the gap between the physical and the mental.* This is the same gap which has been an enigma since ancient times and which was heavily reinforced by Descartes. It is the same gap which has been called the mind-body problem, the mind being the mental component and the body being the physical component. The bridging between the physical and the mental results, in our theory, from the identity of nerve cell impulses with consciousness. The identity theory will be elaborated upon in chapter sixteen.

Having made the above statements, let us support them with some simple examples. There are few who would question that colors result from physiology, that they have a physical side. There are also few who would doubt that to see colors involves psychological experiences. The mind has to "interpret" what the retina detects and what is relayed from the retina to the cerebral cortex. The same principal applies for sounds, touches, pains, and all the other sensations. They all involve both a physical and a psychological aspect.

Notice that at this point we have made no claim of explaining how the physiology and the psychology manage to become intertwined. We merely say that they do so and we postulate the consciousness cores as the elementary components involved. Even though at this time we are unable to define the consciousness cores in exact physiological terms, we can say that the psychological modalities definitely have physical origins. It is difficult to understand how anyone can doubt that the mind and body are one.

However, let us hasten to point out that the various theories which claim to explain consciousness, even if they turn out to be correct, still leave a huge explanatory gap between the elementary level and the level of consciousness as we are acquainted with it. This is true whether the theories are in terms of quantum mechanics, neural networks, electron tunneling, intercellular transmitter substances, or anything else at such an elementary level. The gap is between the physical and the mental as well as between the physical or physiological level and the level of consciousness. Such theories do not explain the consciousness of the adult much less the possible consciousness of the late term fetus or the newly born infant. The consciousness of the adult not only consists of consciousness cores but also has complexes of them such as loves, hates, ambitions, desires, motivations, creativity, memories and the numerous other functions which interest psychologists, psychiatrists, and psychoanalysts.

Location of the Consciousness Cores

What can be said of the location of the physical or physiological substrate of the consciousness cores? It is generally assumed that perceptions, whether of qualities or of other items of consciousness, take place in the cerebral cortex or definitely within the brain. This has been a long standing assumption and is usually taken for granted. However, within the concept of the qualitative cores (Brooks, 1994) it is *quite possible* that the original elements of consciousness, the rudimentary elements of which consciousness is constructed, are present from the beginning or near the beginning of the sensory nerve pathways in the body long before they reach the cerebral cortex or even before they reach the brain. To state it more specifically, the elements are possibly present within the nerve cells at the periphery of the body, that is, in the skin, the eye, the ear, in muscles, internal organs, etc. (By "periphery" or "peripheral nervous system" we mean outside the brain or spinal cord, that is, outside the "central nervous system.") Emotions have no receptor organs at the peripheral levels of the nervous system and would therefore be exceptions. Let us be clear that we are not stating that fully developed consciousness is possibly present in the periphery of the body; only the initial elements of consciousness, which then require processing.

Particularly in the case of the retina, where the types of receptor cells differ for the different primary colors, it is highly suggestive that a consciousness producing element (chemical substance—molecule) is contained in incoming nerve cell impulses from or near the beginning of the neural chain and that the cellular pathways actually contain and extrude equally specific molecules all the way to the cerebral cortex. Not only might the molecules be present in the cells of the retina but comparable ones might be present in the nerve fibers of the receptors for touch, which are located in the skin, or in the fibers where pain is discriminated, and in the sensory fibers in general. To make the point emphatic, even though it is only a possibility, *any sensory nerve cell could contain the elements of consciousness.* If such is the case, then we can state that sensory nerve cells are the sources of consciousness cores. (The reader may be assured that this is not meant to suggest a form of panpsychism. The scheme mentioned is limited entirely to the body.)

To continue the scheme, different tastes and odors may be a combination of "primary" tastes and odors. If there are different molecules, for example, those for red and others for blue in the nerve cells of the retina and if related molecules finally reach the cerebral cortex, it is possible that the color purple comes about by an actual combination of the two types of molecules.

Nervous System, Brain, Nerve Cells, and Nerve Cell Impulses

Simply in order that we may not be misunderstood, let us be clear about our use of the terms, brain, nerve cell, and nerve cell impulses. It is not known exactly which of these nervous components are responsible for consciousness. As a consequence, in our writing, when we use these terms, particularly in relation to the origins of consciousness, we will often not attempt to carefully discriminate between them. We believe that the nervous system is undoubtedly responsible for consciousness, but this is not true of all parts of the nervous system. Some parts are involved primarily in motor activity, other parts in coordination, and so on. Therefore it is correct to state that the nervous system is responsible for consciousness. The same reasoning applies, in somewhat smaller dimension, to the brain. At a still smaller dimension, we believe nerve cells and their impulses, particularly sensory nerve cells and their impulses, are even more directly responsible. It is at smaller dimensions such as these, where we wish to be clear that we use the terms fairly interchangeably and that we have no solid justification for insisting that one of the terms is more applicable than the other. There are theories which reduce consciousness, or features of consciousness, to the coordination among nerve cells, to intercellular substances, and to structures within cells but these are all very tentative and will be discussed in later pages.

Summary

The consciousness cores are viewed as the simplest elements of consciousness, analogous to the historical position of atoms in the field of chemistry. The cores are sensory in nature and are qualitatively different from each other. They are processed and combined to become both memory and consciousness. The physical substrates of the cores apparently are within nerve cells, or perhaps are molecules which are transmitted between nerve cells, or something which is as yet unknown. The consciousness cores differ from qualia in several respects. They have both a physical and a psychological aspect and bridge the mind-body gap. We have essentially equated the terms, consciousness, perception, awareness, and sensation. Their differences are largely semantic rather than neurological. We use the term "sensory" to refer to any inputs to consciousness, including "thoughts", emotions, memories, and bodily sensations as well as the products of the "five senses."

31

Chapter Four

Equivalence of Terms

Let us again bring up the subject of reductionism, the reduction of objects or concepts to more elementary terms. We somewhat defined and defended the concept of reductionism earlier in this writing in connection with the reduction of substances to atoms and with the reduction of consciousness to "consciousness cores." It is also important to indulge in a verbal sort of reductionism. Not only have we attempted to reduce consciousness to simpler, physiological terms but we have equated terms which have customarily been treated as disparate. Our doing so has not been coincidence. The various terms overlap greatly in meaning or have the same underlying mechanisms even though they have been used (and are still useful) in different contexts. Velmans (1995c), too, mentions that terms related to consciousness are often used interchangeably.

We have largely equated the terms, sensation, perception, and awareness with consciousness. Such terms have somewhat different linguistic uses but they overlap considerably and are probably the same neurologically. Because they are different superficially they have the unfortunate effect of causing the philosopher or scientist to regard them as also being different at the neurological level. This tends to obscure the underlying mechanisms and to postpone their discovery.

The progress in science in the past two hundred years has been the story of looking beneath the appearance of phenomena to the discovery of the underlying facts. Until relatively recent times, because there was no knowledge of an unconscious, almost all observations regarding the mind were made from the perspective of consciousness. From a deeper perspective, that of the neurological level, the observed phenomena are the result of nerve cell activity. Such processes take place at an unconscious level. In the entire sphere of concepts related to consciousness, concepts and their terminologies have historically been taken from folk language based on surface appearance instead of physiology. In ordinary experience things which appear on the surface to be different are regarded as different before their structures beneath the surface are known. When the subsurface structure is discovered, the different surface appearances are often understood to be but different presentations of the same things. If we did not have the experience of seeing liquid water change into ice, snow, and steam, we would consider them to be completely different substances. Only now is the physiology of the mind beginning to become available. There are still many terms pertaining to psychology which are considered to be different from each other but which, from the neurological perspective, are the same phenomenon. While it is probably the fault of no one in particular since there was no knowledge of an unconscious, the prestige of Descartes is considered to be largely responsible for the persistence of the concept of the mind as separate from that of the brain.

Let us consider the terms perception and consciousness in particular. We have been using the terms perception and consciousness as if they are two separate functions. Some philosophers make definite distinctions between them. Since the two terms have not historically been regarded as the same, in common usage they are not entirely interchangeable. In their usual contexts the terms are still useful as parts of our language but they undoubtedly produce confusion in the attempt to understand their underlying neurological mechanisms. Because this has probably been responsible for some delay in scientific progress, we need to examine the terms and to compare them. The difference between "perception" and "consciousness" is that perception is given a more limited meaning. For example, we could refer to the loss of vision as a loss of a form of perception but not as a loss of consciousness. Consciousness is generally regarded as involving all forms of perception, as an overall state of mind. If a person has lost all forms of perception he has lost consciousness. Nevertheless, it is safe to say that consciousness occurs within any single mode of perception; what we see or hear is seen or heard consciously. In a later chapter we will delve into the time relationships of consciousness. These relationships leave little doubt but that consciousness and perception are the same. This also applies to the terms "awareness" and "sensation."

The whole matter of perceptions, whether from outside the body or from within, is much more varied than is ordinarily taken into account in most writings on the subject of consciousness. Previous to this point, we have mentioned only the five senses. They are, of course, the senses by means of which we perceive the external world; yet not all of those. Sensations of pain, cold and heat, vibration, itches, and tickles, for example, can also come from the external world. We leave ourselves open to serious omissions if we consider almost exclusively the modalities of vision and sound. Not only are there innumerable combinations of tints, shades, and colors, but there is also intensity. In the auditory sphere, in addition to a range as far as pitch is concerned, there is loudness and timing or rhythm. The variety of tastes, smells, touches, pains, etc., also seem innumerable. In addition, we may include as perceptions those sensations which arise from within the body. These have been entirely omitted from most philosophical writings possibly because it was considered to be unnecessary to include them. Vision and hearing were probably thought to be sufficiently representative. However, it is clear that there are also perceptions which arise from within the body—those sensations or perceptions arising from the stomach (including hunger), bowels (including the rectum), urinary bladder, and occasionally from the lungs, heart, etc. Further, let us not overlook the sexual or erotic sensations. Without attempting to be thoroughly specific, we should also note that many of the different types of perceptions would have to be included among the consciousness cores.

There is another point regarding perception which is important to the understanding of consciousness and about which we should be clear. *The term "perception" should cover all forms of awareness, including those from within the brain itself, such as thoughts, memories, and emotions.* Thoughts, memories, and emotions are definitely perceived and there is no reason to believe, as far as consciousness itself is concerned, that these mental processes are essentially different from those of vision or hearing. Emotions have always been considered to be in a category by themselves. Apparently this is so because they have no peripheral sense organs and are not consistently connected with any external objects. We will include them among the consciousness cores since, like the other cores, they are perceived and are qualitatively unique. To what extent there may be primary cores which are combined to form the myriad of "feelings" is not known. Freud considered anxiety to be a basic emotion and even wrote of unconscious anxiety. He segregated fear from anxiety on the basis that fear felt like anxiety but was connected to something conscious while anxiety was faceless.

The matter is much more than a question of simple definition. *It is essential to the theory being presented that consciousness be viewed as being present within any single mode of perception.* Whether we visually perceive an object, perceive a sound, or perceive the import of a statement, it becomes apparent that we may regard perception as normally implying consciousness. Anything fully perceived is consciously perceived. Conversely anything which becomes conscious is perceived. One would suspect that perception and consciousness are produced by the same mechanisms physiologically and can be regarded as one and the same process. Certainly without perception there is no consciousness. From the perspective of consciousness the customary meanings of the terms "perception", "consciousness", and "awareness" have differences but from the perspective of the underlying neurology there seems to be no reason not to regard them as the same. We will therefore equate consciousness with perception and will use the terms consciousness, perception, and awareness interchangeably. Many authors would not agree with such usage but it seems to us that the interchangeable use of consciousness and awareness, at least, is becoming fairly common in recent years. Chalmers (1995,b) distinguishes between the two but mentions a "direct correspondence" between them.

"Sensory" and "Sensation"

We will engage in further verbal reductionism in connection with two other words, "sensory" and "sensation." This time we will not merge the two but will treat them individually. In the section entitled "Location of the Consciousness Cores" we mentioned that any *"sensory"* nerve cell could theoretically contain the elements of consciousness. Also in the section prior to this one we stressed that thoughts, memories, and emotions as well as sensations from within the body are inputs to consciousness. (Later on we will have to discontinue using the term "inputs to consciousness" because it will not be in agreement with our theory, but for the moment we will continue using it.) The term "sensory" has previously referred, at the level of consciousness, to the five senses and, at the neurological level, to nerve impulses which traveled upward from the body toward the brain. We now need to include as "sensory" not only the customary "sensory" sources of consciousness, but *any* sources. Impulses from within the body as well as thoughts, memories, and emotions are also "sensory", as far as consciousness is concerned, in the sense that they are inputs to consciousness. Day dreams and sleep dreams are also sensory. For the purposes of this writing, we have to expand our understanding of the word "sensory" to include any such inputs irrespective of their sources. We will regard sensory sources from the perspective of consciousness rather than from the anatomical position of the brain.

While we are in the process of altering conventional terms, it does not appear to be necessary to make a basic distinction between sensation and perception. Sensation, is often used in connection with what are regarded as physical feelings, such as a sensation of cold or of sexual sensation. It is clear, however, that sensations, in both popular and technical usage are perceptions. A distinction between sensation and perception is made by many authors on the basis that they consider sensations to be simpler and that perceptions involve integration at higher levels (Kelly, 1986, pp. 44-80). We will make it clear that both involve integration at higher levels and we will therefore not make such a distinction. Both processes are regarded as involving consciousness which, for our purposes, is the defining ingredient of perception. It should also be noted that we are simply grouping day dreams, conceptions, anticipations, and numerous other mental processes, as "thoughts."

Preperceptual Processes

Consciousness involves the processing of nerve cell impulses. For example, they are processed beginning with the impingement of light energy on the cells of the retina. The processing continues in the cellular connections in subcortical centers and in the cerebral cortex. The cellular pathways are intermingled in many ways, only some of which are known. However, it is known that much processing takes place before final consciousness or perception occurs. We will refer to such processing as "preperceptual." It could also be called "preconscious" but the latter term could be confused with the psychoanalytic usage of the term.

There are many indications that it is the relatively rare preperceptual process, rather than the common one, that becomes conscious. Most preperceptual processes are screened from consciousness or simply allowed to wither on the vine and do not reach consciousness. For example, we are aware of only a few at most of the items in our visual fields at any one moment. Yet all of the items must project their images through the lenses of our eyes and onto our retinas. This is not to mention the items in our auditory fields or proprioceptive fields or the sensory impulses from the skin, all of which are impinging on our nervous systems at the same time. Proprioception is another type of sensory input which often does not reach consciousness. By "proprioception", we refer to sensory impulses from the muscles, tendons, and joints. A commonly used example which occurs during walking, is the proprioceptive stimulation which is being integrated at a preperceptual level. Such stimulations includes those from the feet, legs, and arms, etc., which are unconsciously coordinated.

A very interesting demonstration in which preperceptual processes are fairly well developed without reaching consciousness is given by what is known as blindsight, first reported by Weiskrantz (1974). This involves patients who are totally blind on *one side* of their fields of vision as a result of injury in a particular small area of the brain. Despite the blindness the patients can report about visual stimuli which are presented to them in the blind field with much greater accuracy than can be accounted for by random guessing (Zeki, 1992, p.73). It means that these patients receive visual input but it does not become conscious. The visual receptive apparatus is intact but a part of the brain which is necessary for complete visual processing and consciousness has been destroyed.

Kolers and von Grunau (1976) point out that there can be a reaction by the ego even before there is consciousness of an event. There are also some very interesting experiments by Libet (1985) which demonstrated that in the performance of voluntary actions, the brain begins the process *before the person has any consciousness of the intention to perform the action.* Subjects were asked to move a finger and to notice the exact time at which they decided to initiate the movement. It was found that the electrical activity in the brain began more than three tenths of a second before there was consciousness of the intention. This experiment is contrary to what we would expect according to our usual view that our voluntary actions are consciously initiated (!). Yet, should it be so surprising? In order to make a decision, there would have to be some processing, conscious or unconscious, which would lead to the decision; some processing has to precede and result in (cause) the decision. The ramifications of Libet's experiment have wide reaching implications both for the role of the unconscious and, as Valentine has pointed out (1994), for the concept of conscious will.

Perception in Representationalism

The inclusion under the term perception of those sensations arising from within the body raises some damaging questions in addition to those we have already raised, about the theory of representationalism. Remember that in the theory of representationalism a representation is formed of the object and the representation is perceived by the mind. The purpose of any representation would be to serve as an intermediate step in bridging the gap between the object and the perception of the object. This would be so, according to theory, regardless whether the object is inside the body or outside. In the case of vision there is an object which would have a clear relationship to the theoretical representation; the representation would be some sort of likeness of the object. But in the case of pain, which is entirely inside the body, the situation becomes much less clear. There would be a representation of what? A representation of the knife which inflicted the pain would be irrelevant. A knife is not a pain. On the other hand, one might consider the representation to be formed, not of the knife, but of the cut made by it. One might think of the pain as coming from the cut and not from the knife. Even so, a representation of a cut is not the same as the sensation of pain. The pain actually arises from nerve fibers which have registered damage. Would the representation be of those? But that is not in accordance with our observational powers. Our consciousness does not inform us of damage to nerve fibers as such. Even if it did, the damage is within the nervous system in the first place. Would there be any need for a representation to bridge a gap between one part of the nervous system and another part? It is possible, but if so, it would be redundant and, furthermore, it is not part of the representationalist theory.

We might examine a different answer to the puzzle, that the putative representation depends upon the *concept* that one has of the source of the sensory input. If one thinks of the knife as causing the pain, then the representation would be of a knife. Or if one thinks of the cut, or even the nerve fiber as causing the pain, then the representation would be of one or the other of those. As in the case of a "pain in the shoulder", mentioned previously in relation to qualia, the representation would be present in whatever way one happened to conceptualize it. The same with a "stomachache." Also, how would an emotion be represented? Since it is completely unlike any object, and entirely from within the brain, it would be represented as an emotional quality, that is, in the same way that it was represented in the first place, a situation which seems to make for an absurdity.

One might counter the idea that a representation depends upon the concept a person has of the thing represented: In such a scheme the representation originates too much from within the mind. It is provoked into being by the stimulus from the object but the representation need not resemble the stimulus. It can therefore fail to be a representation of anything. There is not sufficient contact with reality and this suggests idealism. In this connection, but falling considerably short of anything approaching pure idealism, Freud stated (1948) that attention, which is closely related to consciousness, meets the object halfway. His statement seems to be correct even though it was made in a different context. According to the statement, *perception results partly from the stimulus coming from the outside and partly from within the mind.* Perception rests on two feet, one being planted in the environment and the other in the mind. In succeeding pages, this will be explained more completely. The statement is justified by the physics and physiology of the situation.

There are other perceptions from within the body itself for which cases it is even more difficult to conceive of a representation. These include the lightheadedness, which many people feel upon changing from a horizontal body position to a vertical position (called "postural hypotension"), as well as vertigo, a severe form of dizziness from spinning around too quickly. It is true that a person tends to assign such sensations to something; but the "something" can be quite far from correctly representing the reality of the situation. There are also "spontaneous" perceptions such as tinnitus (ringing in the ears) and a different kind of vertigo (due to a condition of the inner ear called "vestibulitis"). Hallucinations and dreams are also "spontaneous" perceptions and for these there is no immediate external object to be represented. (This does not mean, however, that external objects are not involved at all. It was also offered by Freud that dreams and hallucinations utilize external objects ultimately stemming from memory. When one thinks about it, where else but from memory could dream elements originate if a person is asleep?)

Let us consider a more common stimulus such as a sound. In order to represent a sound, a representation of a bell or a sound wave would be irrelevant. They are not sounds. In our incorrect way, we do generally think of the object, such as the bell which produces a stimulus, rather than the stimulus itself (the sound wave), as the cause of a perception. This reasoning may be agreeable to those advocates of representationalism whose theory would require that the representation is of the object and not of the stimulus. Such a scheme, however, ignores the fact that it is the stimulus which our sense receptors detect rather than the object itself. We can offer a definite answer to the problem of representations but first we will have to present a considerable amount of background information. Therefore we will leave the subject of representations but will return to them in a later chapter.

Summary

We have essentially equated the terms, consciousness, perception, awareness, and sensation. Their differences are largely semantic rather than neurological. We use the term "sensory" to refer to any inputs to consciousness, including "thoughts", emotions, memories, and bodily sensations as well as the products of the "five senses."

Chapter Five

Creations of the Brain

In attempting to answer the question of how perception takes place we should proceed from a solid, empirical foundation. We will broach some concepts which will probably be new to the reader and which the reader may find difficult to accept at first. We shall begin with an explanation of the origin of the sensations which our senses reveal to us. It would be well to present quotations from John Locke and Johannes Muller. Locke stated that, "...*Qualities*...in truth are nothing in the Objects themselves, ... [except] Powers to produce sensations in us..." This was a powerful statement by Locke and is somewhat radical and difficult for many people to accept, even today. About two hundred years after Locke, the physiologist, Johannes Muller, (1801-1858) made a statement which has a similar meaning and which is regarded as being seminal. It is paraphrased in a textbook of general psychology (Gleitman, 1981a) as stating that "the differences in experienced quality [sensation] are caused not by the differences in the stimuli but by the different nervous structures which these stimuli excite, most likely in centers higher up in the brain."

These statements undoubtedly represent a fundamental principle. We will examine the meaning of the statements and fully corroborate them; but first let us make plain the physics and physiology of the senses. We will examine vision and hearing the most thoroughly since they are the best understood of the sensory modalities. Also they are traditionally treated in writings, which are mainly philosophical, about perception and consciousness in general.

Light waves consist of electromagnetic vibrations. They can also be in the form of photons which can be considered to be particles (or "packets" of energy). Sound waves consist of vibrations of molecules. In the case of light the vibrations stimulate the receptor cells in the retina, while in the case of sound the vibrations stimulate the receptor hair cells in the cochlea. Both types of receptor cells then send nerve cell impulses to the cerebral cortex. Neither light energy nor sound energy proceeds inward any farther than the first receptor cells they encounter. *Only nerve cell impulses proceed from that point.* The same principle applies for touch, taste, and smell. This is well known and fully accepted physiology. What is generally not accepted, or at least not stated, despite the fact that it seems obvious and unavoidable, is that the nerve cell impulses, together with brain activity, produce the qualities of color, sound, etc. It should be emphasized that the brain produces the qualities as a result of the incoming nerve cell impulses and not directly as a result of the light or sound vibrations. To further emphasize the import of that statement, let us say that the *qualities, light and sound, etc., do not exist in the environment. They exist only in the mind.* The qualities themselves are purely mental phenomena. This has to mean that the nervous system itself actually *creates* the perceptual modalities; it *originates* the "light" and the "sound." However, we must not lose sight of the fact that the nervous system does this in reaction to stimulation from the environment. To give a concrete example, the tree we see as green is not green at all. It has no color. This is the import of the statements made by Locke and Muller. The matter is both physical and physiological fact and not theory. The trees reflect electromagnetic radiations. These give our minds the impression of color.

Remember that we must make a clear distinction between light rays and perceived light. Light rays are electromagnetic vibrations in the environment but perceived light results from nerve cell impulses and exists only in the mind. Now there is a second step which we can take and which we consider to be very logical. *It is reasonable to believe that a brain which can "perceive" nerve cell impulses as being pain or hunger should not find it difficult to "perceive" nerve cell impulses as being light.* We do not think of light as being nerve cell impulses. Nerve impulses are entirely different from our concept of light. "Light is something we see and we do not see nerve cell impulses." That is exactly the thinking that we would like to alter. We see light only by means of nerve cell impulses. Our brains do not register electromagnetic vibrations directly. One might also argue that light is significantly different from pain or hunger. Light is initiated from outside the body, and pain or hunger from the inside. In both cases, however, *consciousness has to result from nerve cell impulses.*

Light, similarly to the other sensations, is an entirely unique, elemental quality, a qualitative core. Its electromagnetic vibrations are transmitted to the brain via nerve impulses where fully processed consciousness is attained. Again, *a brain which can perceive nerve cell impulses as light, vivid dreams, hallucinations, and thoughts should have no difficulty perceiving impulses as sound, touch, taste, or smell.* Such a concept constitutes a psychological hurdle for most people. The statement is quite true; but it involves a different understanding of light—what it is, where it is. The statement is of major importance for the "identity theory" and will be elaborated upon when we discuss the theory at length in a later chapter.

Color is an aspect of light. All of our lives we have been thinking of color as being part of the objects we see. We have not even considered that the color is in our minds. We have had no reason to think in such a manner. Our manner of thinking has worked perfectly well for us. It has produced

41

no contradictions. Most people, medical doctors and scientists in general, who know the physiology of light and sound, do not normally think of light and sound, etc., as being internal. They readily accept the statements of Locke and Muller when the statements are called to their attention even though they are unaware of, or do not realize, the implications of them.

As strange and counterintuitive as the above reasoning may sound, it does not mean that the world around us exists only in the mind. The reasoning actually subtracts nothing from the real world "out there." It does not imply that objects in the environment do not exist or that they are figments of our imaginations. Objects are "out there." People are there. Trees are there and the trees still look green. Furthermore, this is neither a contradiction nor an instance of trying to have it both ways by saying that objects are both "out there" and "in here" or that they do and do not have color. To state it in philosophical terms, it is not trying to be both a hard-core realist and a hard-core idealist. What is being stated is that the trees and people are in the environment but their colors and sounds are only in the mind.

A clear example of the brain's ability to create sensation is in the case of erotic sensibility. Stimulation, which under non-sexual circumstances is felt as touch, under sexual circumstances is felt erotically. The "pain" felt upon the death of a loved one is also impressive. There can be no doubt of the brain's ability to create sensations or perceptions.

Ultimate Reality is Unknowable

We now come to a corollary concept. Despite our subjective impression to the contrary, strictly speaking, one has to think that Kant (1965) was correct in stating that what is in the environment is, in a sense, "unknowable." Whether or not we understand Kant correctly is actually immaterial but, as we understand him, he meant this in an ultimate sense; not that we cannot know the tree or the rock but, as we explained in an earlier passage, we can know them only as our senses detect them. For instance, we cannot see the individual atoms of which they are composed. As Kant phrased it, we do not know them as they are "in themselves" but only as we perceive them.

In a similar vein, the sensory qualities we normally perceive as being in the environment are not in the environment at all. If light and sound are not in the environment, what is it like "out there?" It would not be correct to say that since there is no light out there, only light waves, that everything is dark. It is true that, conceptually, dark is the opposite of light but we must remember that light, as we know it, exists only in the mind. It is not easy to imagine but the situation must be that "out there" neither light nor darkness exists. As we have stated, the light that we "see" is produced for us by our brains. Light is actually nerve cell impulses. Light is nothing else. It is totally different from the light rays which reach the retina and which stimulate the production of light. This may be a difficult concept to believe and even harder to become accustomed to. However, if put into perspective, it is not as strange as it seems. A person who was sightless from birth would probably not find it difficult to accept.

It may help in understanding this view to consider the magnetic forces of the earth—something else which is "unknowable" to us. Homing pigeons have an appreciation of the earth's magnetic fields and it is possible that it is a conscious appreciation. If so we, of course, have no way of knowing what magnetism feels or seems like to the pigeons. We do not carry in our peripheral receptor organs or in our brains the mechanism for perceiving magnetism; we have no such consciousness cores. There are a number of other forces which we cannot appreciate—ultra high frequency sound, ultraviolet light, X-ray, etc. This does not disturb us because we are not accustomed to perceiving these forms of energy and we do not attempt to imagine what they would be like.

As for sound, there are sound waves in the environment but no sound. It is well past the time when we should put to rest the old philosophical question of, "When a tree falls in the forest and no one is there to hear it, is any sound produced?" To be emphatic about it, the answer is clearly, "No." The science of physics forces us to recognize that what we ordinarily call sound is actually incorrect. It is a misnomer. The air vibrations are not sound any more than the electrical vibrations in a radio, from which the speaker has been disconnected, are sound. One has to clearly distinguish between the sound waves and the perception of the sound. There simply is no sound other than that which is within the mind. We had better add, to avoid misinterpretation, that if we held a stethoscope to someone's head and only heard what came through the stethoscope, we would not hear the sounds that the person was hearing. There is no physical sound "in here" either—only the perception of sound which consists of nerve cell impulses.

Infants have to learn from experience that an area outside themselves exists and that the objects which they perceive are located in that area. One way infants corroborate the location of objects they see is by touching them (Piaget, 1963). This knowledge, acquired in infancy, serves us in good stead when dealing with reality but not when attempting to comprehend the mind. A change in our *understanding* of the location of the perceptual qualities is in order. They are not located in the object. They are in the mind. The brain is induced to produce the qualities by the stimulation originating from the object. This is one of the points which we had in mind when we stated in the section entitled "Perception in Representationalism"

43

in chapter four that perception rests on two feet, one in the mind and one on the object.

Summary

Physiologically, sensations result from nerve cell impulses and are not derived directly from external stimuli. We can therefore say that the tree is not green. Electromagnetic energy is reflected from the tree but the brain originates the color. Perception rests on two feet, one in the brain and the other in the environment.

Chapter Six

Directionality

In this chapter we will discuss the so-called primary and secondary qualities of John Locke and the way in which directionality makes for a distinction between them. The secondary qualities correspond substantially with our consciousness cores and are therefore important in our understanding of consciousness. The primary qualities are also perceptions which depend upon the consciousness cores. This chapter becomes fairly technical and can be skipped by the non-professional reader.

The seeming contradiction in what we are stating, that objects are in the environment but their colors, sounds, and so forth are in the mind, is further explained by the fact that there is more to perception than the traditional raw qualities alone. *There is also directionality and it is this, together with the traditional qualities, that keeps us in touch with the objects in the world around us.* By directionality we mean the direction from the observer to the observed object, or more correctly, the mind's interpretation of that direction. It is the direction to the object that the brain unconsciously uses to extract properties such as size, shape, motion, and solidity. The philosophically informed reader will recognize these properties as the "primary qualities" of John Locke. (Also, before Locke, of Robert Boyle, who was a friend of Locke and is best known for Boyle's Law, which formulates the relationship between gases and pressure.) The primary qualities are almost as elemental in relation to perception as are the consciousness cores. They are basic perceptual interpretations which depend upon consciousness cores and are a small physiological step above them in complexity. We shall elaborate upon the directional component of perception after discussing Locke's primary and secondary qualities, an understanding of which is needed as background information.

Primary and Secondary Qualities

In the previous chapter we attempted to make clear that the *qualities* of our experiences were not in the objects which we see or hear, but instead the qualities were in our consciousness. We used the illustration that there was no sound when a tree fell in the forest unless there was a mind present to produce sound from the vibrations. Statements made by Locke (1975) in the seventeenth century clearly imply such an understanding.

In regard to Locke's primary and secondary qualities there is much confusion in the minds of people interested in explaining consciousness. If these contain the elementary building blocks of consciousness, as believed by Locke, it is imperative to be as clear as possible about them. The secondary qualities, but not the primary ones, may be the qualitative or consciousness cores with all of the implications, described in the previous chapter, of sensory uniqueness and of being inherited. The primary qualities also have sensory uniqueness but they depend upon the secondary qualities and may be learned rather than inherited as a fully developed capacity.

The ancient Greeks recognized that some perceptions such as temperature and taste were subjective. What is warm to some people (corpulent people as a rule) is cool to others (thin people). What is sweet to some people is bland to others, and so on. Locke analyzed such differences in perception in an organized and concerted manner in his defining and describing the primary and secondary qualities. He did the same with the word, idea. His language on the subject is informative and well worth our close attention. His writing is also quite interesting as an example of his clear headed, precise manner of thinking (if one makes an allowance as described below) and as an example of the style of his seventeenth century language.

A number of well respected authors have felt that Locke was unclear and confusing in his statements about primary and secondary qualities. Bruner (1973, p.8) dismissed them altogether with the reference to "...the contradiction of Locke's distinction between primary and secondary qualities in perception."

Joad (1957) similarly observed that there is no real distinction between them. He pointed out (p.42) that Berkeley, who was Locke's successor, "abolished the distinction between primary and secondary qualities." Joad also added his own view that, "So far as the qualities are concerned, the distinction between primary and secondary qualities is clearly arbitrary." In contrast to these views, we offer that directionality, which we will discuss below, does make for a clear distinction based on physics and physiology.

We will not review the details of Kelly's arguments (1986), which are influenced by and interwoven with his general realist position on perception. He concluded (p.115, citing the reasoning in Jackson's "Locke's Distinction") that "the distinction between primary and secondary is at root a distinction between macroscopic and microscopic qualities." This distinction is flawed by the fact that at the microscopic level objects still have primary qualities, as mentioned by Locke (1975) himself, in the quotation below. The flaw was even mentioned by Kelly but was considered to be irrelevant, apparently because of Kelly's concern about *whole* physical objects (p.116). In other words, to Jackson and Kelly, the macroscopic/microscopic argument is correct. However, it does not describe the difference at a level sufficiently basic to make a distinction between the two kinds of qualities. When Locke wrote of "motion" or "mobility" he did not have in mind only the motion of whole objects. His concept also included the motion of "insensible particles" which would probably correspond with what we now call molecules. (Locke, p. 135)

It is evident that Locke was intuitively aware of the concept which was stated by Muller about 200 years after Locke. The implications of Muller's ideas, that color and sound are not in the object but are in our minds, as we mentioned in the previous chapter, are well known but little appreciated even today. In that chapter we used concepts of modern physics in the expressions "electromagnetic vibrations" in reference to light, and "vibrations of air molecules" in reference to sound. These are the physical means by which the corresponding objects produce our perceptions. The vibrations were not known as such by Locke. He therefore explained sensory perceptions as resulting from what he called "powers" of the object. In this he was correct as far as the knowledge of physics of his day would allow. Whether he used the term "powers" of the object or the more modern terminology "vibrations stemming from the object" does not alter the import of his statements. In fact, how much more do we really know today about light vibrations than that they are "powers"? We call them "energy", "electromagnetic waves", "vibrations", and photons but the terms are quite incompletely understood.

At this point, we will first present a key quotation from Locke and then further interpret his use of language. For ease of reference line numbers have been added to the quotation.

1) Whatsoever the Mind perceives in it self or is the immediate object
2) of Perception, Thought, or Understanding, that I call *Idea;* and the
3) Power to produce any *Idea* in our mind, I call Quality of the Subject
4) wherein that power is. Thus a Snow-ball having the power to produce
5) in us the *Ideas* of *White, Cold,* and *Round,* the Powers to produce those
6) *ideas* in us, as they are in the Snow-ball, I call *Qualities*; and as they are
7) Sensations, or Perceptions, in our Understandings, I call them *Ideas:*

8) which *Ideas*, if I speak of sometimes, as [being] in the things
9) themselves, I would be understood to mean those Qualities in the
10) Objects which produce them in us.

In lines 1 and 2 Locke mentioned perceptions and quite understandably referred to them as ideas in the mind. We no longer refer to perceptions as ideas but to do so is clear and is not incorrect. Some confusion enters where Locke uses the word, quality. As in line 6, paraphrasing him slightly, he stated that, as the powers are in the snowball, he calls them "Qualities." This is different from where we now locate the qualities. We place them in the mind rather than in the snowball. But this is really a matter simply of language rather than a point of disagreement with Locke. To people who are unfamiliar with Muller's concept, or who simply ignore its implications that the qualities are in the mind, it is common usage today to place the qualities in the snowball—"The snowball is hard and cold." In the previous chapter we found fault with that language and attempted to refine the concept behind it. The important point is, as Locke said, the *source* of the power is in the snowball and the "Understandings" or perceptions are in our minds.

Now let us consider the next paragraph of the quotation. In this paragraph he explains his "original or primary" qualities (see especially line 17) as being "Solidity, Extension, Figure [shape], or Mobility." As mentioned in the paragraph immediately above, it is more accurate to think in terms of the "powers" of the object to produce perceptions ("ideas in us") rather than that the "qualities" of the object produce the perceptions.

11) ...Take a grain of Wheat, divide it into two parts, each part has still
12) *Solidity, Extension, Figure*, and *Mobility;* divide it again, and it retains
13) still the same qualities; and so divide it on, till the parts become
14) insensible, they must retain still each of them all those qualities. For
15) division (which is all that a Mill, or Pestle, or any other Body does
16) upon another, in reducing it to insensible parts) can never take away
17) either Solidity, Extension, Figure, or Mobility from any Body, but only
18) makes two, or more distinct separate masses, reckon'd as so many

19) distinct Bodies, after division make a certain Number. These I call

20) *original* or *primary Qualities* of Body, which I think we may observe

21) to produce simple *Ideas* in us, viz. Solidity, Extension, Figure,

22) Motion, or Rest, and Number.

23) 2dly, Such *Qualities, which* in truth are nothing in the Objects

24) themselves, but Powers to produce various Sensations in us by their

25) *primary Qualities*, i.e. by the Bulk, Figure, Texture, and Motion of

26) their insensible parts, as Colours, Sounds, Tasts, etc. These I call

27) *secondary Qualities*. (p. 134-5)

In line 23 Locke, himself, clarified the confusion between qualities and powers by placing the "powers" in the object and by placing the qualities in the mind: "...Such Qualities, which in truth are *nothing in the Objects themselves,* (italics mine) but Powers to produce various Sensations in us..."

In a further passage Locke explained more succinctly and pointedly that primary qualities (powers) are "really in them [the objects] whether any ones senses perceive them or no." In today's understanding of physics, these statements would not be entirely correct and can still be confusing. The powers, as far as light is concerned, are not *in* the objects as Locke stated. The light vibrations are reflected *from* the objects. Even so, the powers are in the objects in the sense that it is the objects which determine which colors will be reflected. In the case of solidity of objects, it is correct to say that the powers are in the object; there is no intermediate element between the object and the finger which touches it. Of secondary qualities he said, "Take away the Sensation of them; let not the Eyes see Light, or Colours,..." and they "vanish and cease." (p. 137-8) If allowances are made for the insufficient knowledge of physics, Locke's statements make it quite clear that the *primary qualities* (powers) are in the objects and the *secondary qualities* are in the mind.

The primary qualities were so named by Locke (p. 135) in the sense that they are the first or "original" aspects of the objects to influence perception. Again, they consist of features such as *solidity, extension, shape, number, and motion.* (We agree with Locke's listing of the primary qualities with the exception of number. We regard it as a concept rather than a quality.) The important point from our point of view is that such features are *capable of being objectively observed,* even measurable. They do not change from one observer to the next and are not dependent on external conditions such as lighting. The secondary qualities, on the other hand, are aspects such as *colors, sounds, tastes, odors, etc.* Contrary to the primary qualities, secondary qualities are *subjective* and variable. They depend on the individual and on the lighting conditions, etc. What is seen by one person as red can be seen by another person, who is color blind, as brown. This is a definite distinction between the primary and secondary qualities. It is clear that by the secondary qualities Locke meant the sensory qualities which we know as the five senses—vision, hearing, touch, taste, and smell. They are not in the object; they are "Sensations in us."

Locke's language is forceful and appealing. But let us further clarify the confusion about the primary and secondary qualities in terms of physics.

Explanation of Directionality

For a further clarification considered to be particularly relevant, we propose a concept which we will call directionality. It involves only the primary qualities and separates them from the secondary qualities. We would like to offer that the primary qualities squarely depend on the mind's evaluation of direction—which is the meaning of directionality. The recognition of directionality makes for a definite distinction between the two kinds of "qualities." The primary qualities are mediated by the nervous system with the aid of the senses. That is, they are *detected* by means of vision, hearing, etc., just as the secondary qualities are. *However, unlike the secondary qualities, they require two or more observations which are then unconsciously subjected to interpretation.* Directionality justifies in physical and physiological terms the difference between Locke's "primary" and "secondary" qualities.

To provide specific illustrations, we will begin by considering those primary qualities which are mediated by vision:

Distance. We will first consider the perception of distance perception because it is the most familiar of the primary qualities. Distance perception was not mentioned by Locke but being measurable, it is objective and this places it among the primary qualities. As with the other primary qualities we will consider it in terms of physiology. It is often called depth perception and it is well recognized that it depends mainly on the mind's automatic interpretation of the minute difference between the directions in which each of the two eyes point. (See illustration number 1.) The closer the object is to the face, the more quickly the lines of sight converge and meet. The instrument known as a stereoscope utilizes the discrepancy between the lines of sight, the directionality, to obtain three dimensional pictures. Each of the two eyes receives a different picture which together comprise two observations. That the observations are different from each other is unconscious. What comes to the individual's awareness is a perception of distance. That the perception results from an interpretation by the mind is well established in the field of psychology. (It is incidental to our discussion but, in addition to directionality, distance can also depend upon judgments based on haze, and/or the presence of intervening objects or terrain features. When looking at a distant mountain, for example, the intervening haze causes the mountain to appear blue. This adds to the interpretation of distance.)

Illustration No. 1

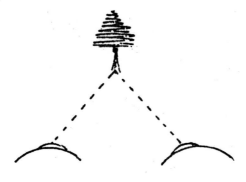

Distance

Size. This would be categorized as a "primary quality" because, first, it is measurable and to that extent is not subjective. As for the factor of directionality, it is clear that the impression of size resolves into a usually unconscious interpretation of the difference between two directions. The directions are the two lines of sight, one extending from the eye to the top of the object and the other from the eye to the bottom of the object or from side to side. (Illustration number 2.) The mind has to unconsciously interpret the difference between the directions—the angle between the two lines of sight. (An interpretation of distance also is taken into account, as mentioned below.) In this, and in all of the following examples, the sensory interpretation is generally accomplished on a completely unconscious basis. However, a judgment can also be applied consciously.

Illustration No. 2

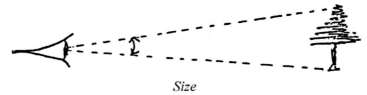

Size

Shape, a second of Locke's "primary qualities", involves the various directions from the observer to the object. The interpretation of the differences in the directions, that is, the differences between the lines of sight, are the physical and physiological bases for the judgments which determine the shape of the object. Shape is not only determined by vision but also by proprioception. Proprioception is the sensory information received from the muscles, joints, and tendons, and gives us the position of our limbs. Proprioception is actually a secondary quality not mentioned by Locke. It would be considered to be a secondary quality because it is a unique sense and is subjective. In those regards proprioception is similar to the "five senses." If an object, such as a book, is felt with the hands while the eyes are closed, its shape is mediated by proprioception. The perception is a matter of the location of the surfaces. Whether the determination of shape is determined by vision or by proprioception, a judgment is made from the difference between two or more observations.

Motion is perceived from the changing of direction in the lines of sight. Two or more fixes on the object are required. In both shape and motion, the angle between the directional lines unconsciously gives the clue to the mind. (See illustration number 3.) (In the case of motion, an estimation of time is also involved—the time interval between two positions of the object.) Incidentally, memory would be involved in the perception of any primary quality, since the perception of the changing of direction would require remembering the beginning position and its comparison with a later position.

Illustration No.3

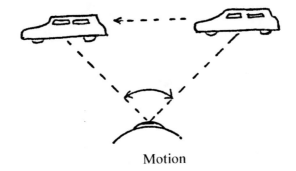

Motion

Solidity, also a primary quality, is determined by the judgment of one's ability to indent an object. Two ways of determining solidity are by means of proprioception and by vision. We will consider visual detection first as its explanation is the simpler of the two. As with the previously described primary qualities, the visual detection of solidity depends on two or more directions. Suppose that we indent, with our finger tip, a relatively soft object, such as a pillow or a piece of soft clay. (See illustration number 4.) As the finger moves, the amount of indentation is a matter of the change in direction of two lines of sight, one at the beginning of the indentation and one at the end of it. Once again, this is clearly a matter of directionality. The primary quality is detected by an interpretation involving directions obtained by means of a secondary quality, the quality resulting from vision or proprioception, or both.

Illustration No. 4

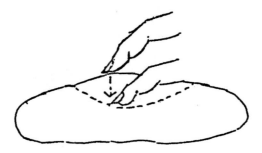

Solidity

Eugene M. Brooks, M.D.

There is a case in which it seems at first that directionality is not involved in the perception of solidity. If a surface is hard and cannot be perceptibly indented, there is no perceptible change in the location of the finger tip between the beginning and the end of the application of pressure. The perception of solidity in such a case is simply the proprioceptive appreciation of static force (muscle tension). It might be considered that static force does not involve directionality since there is no movement, no change of direction. On the other hand one is justified in saying that directionality is involved in the interpretation of static force since it is the interpretation of the *absence* of the change of direction. The ability to notice a change in direction or the lack of a change, as determined by the inability to produce a pitting of the object, such as when a physician presses the ankle of a patient to see if there is swelling or a baker lightly presses on a cake with his finger, would often involve both proprioception and vision. The absence of a change of direction does result from a change in muscular pressure between that which exists just prior to the beginning of the attempt to pit the object, at which time there is no pressure, and that which is exerted later in the attempt.

If it seems to the reader that the angle between two lines of vision is too minute for the brain to use in making interpretations such as those mentioned above, there is another example in which the brain uses extremely minute differences from which to produce an interpretation. We are referring to the awareness of the direction from which a sound originates. In that modality, direction is extracted from the difference in the time of arrival of the sound waves at each of the two ears. If the sound is to one side of the listener, the sound reaches the ear nearer the source sooner than it reaches the ear which is farther away. The difference in time that the sound takes in reaching each of the two ears is *less than one thousandth of a second.* (Sound travels in air at about 1125 feet per second.) Yet the brain is able to utilize the interval to determine the direction from which a sound comes. To extract directions, so-called stereo sound utilizes the discrepancy between the times of arrival of the sound vibrations at each of the ears.

There are other examples of the rapidity with which the brain operates, examples which would be unbelievable if they were not every day occurrences which we take for granted and easily overlook. The brain extracts different colors from light wave vibrations and different pitches from sound wave vibrations. 256 vibrations per second account for the difference between middle C on the piano and the next higher C. Each of the twelve notes which are included between the two C's accounts for an entirely different perception. The brain is able to distinguish between the clearly different tones by detecting the difference of time between vibration cycles of less than five hundredths of a second. The difference between the two highest notes on the piano is less that five thousandths of a second! The rather amazing rapidity with which the brain operates is very significant in relation to the concept of the "multiplicity of consciousness" which will be discussed in chapter seven.

We can now summarize that, from the standpoint of physiology, a difference between the primary and secondary qualities is that the primary qualities require an extra step in the process of their perception which is not required for the secondary qualities. The primary qualities require at least two observations of the object. Based on the two observations, an interpretation is made. (See diagrams below.) In addition to directionality, a difference between the two types of qualities is that *the secondary qualities are subjective* while the primary qualities, being measurable, are *objective*. With Locke's "secondary qualities"—sight, hearing, touch, taste, and smell—the direction to the object is not necessary for the perception.

The relationship can be diagrammed as follows:

A) Secondary Qualities (Color, also sound, touch, taste, smell)
    (One observation)

    Object—>Light waves—>Retina—>Nerve impulses—>Perception

B) Primary Qualities (Solidity, size, shape, motion)
    (Two observations)

1) Object—>Light waves—>Retina—>Nerve impulses\
                                    Interpretation—>Perception
2) Object—>Light waves—>Retina—>Nerve impulses/

It is also worth noting that the interpretations involved in the perception of primary qualities are learned by the infant (Faction and Reynolds, 1975) while the secondary qualities are inborn. The child has to learn to detect distance, and motion. He has to learn to interpret the directions (directionality) to the object which are the cues to that distance. This requires experience. The perceptions of secondary qualities by the developing infant, no doubt, also quickly become related to and benefit from experience but this is more basic and occurs prior to the learning of the interpretations needed for the primary qualities. The secondary qualities require a less complex order of learning, the learning being acquired directly from hereditary core elements rather than from both hereditary elements and the additional aid of interpretation.

Because they result from interpretations, the primary qualities are creations of the brain, just as are the secondary qualities. One does not have to make a conscious effort to form a judgment about size or distance, etc. The judgments take place automatically. However, *the primary qualities depend upon the senses, that is, they depend upon the secondary qualities* for the detection of objects. Because they utilize the senses they must utilize the same nerve cells and fiber pathways as the secondary qualities for part of the transmission to the cerebral cortex.

Therefore, in the sense that they are qualitatively unique, the primary qualities are similar to the secondary qualities but in the sense that they require an additional process, an interpretation, they have a distinctly different mechanism. It is the directions obtained from the senses of the secondary qualities, that play a necessary role in the segregation and interpretation of the primary qualities.

We do not regard the so-called primary qualities to be qualities in the same sense as the secondary qualities. The primary qualities are judgments or interpretations of consciousness cores. It is colors and sounds which are genuine qualities or sensations, both unique and inborn. We interpret Locke's "*Sensations* in us" as being *consciousness cores* while the primary qualities are directional *judgments* of two or more observations.

(*In a strict sense* the primary qualities are not entirely objective. Since they are mediated by the secondary qualities which are subjective, the primary qualities also have a subjective component and this undoubtedly adds to the confusion about the two types of qualities. Judgments of size, distance, etc., are variable. Nevertheless, being measurable, the primary qualities are objective in the ordinary sense.)

Size and Shape Constancy

The terms, size and shape constancy, are used in the field of psychology and we will explain them briefly so that they should not be confused with the distinguishing of the primary and secondary qualities. When a person is looking at an object, the image of the object which is projected onto the retina is smaller when the object is farther away than when the object is closer. Nevertheless the object is recognized by the observer as having the same size in both locations. For example, we are aware that an automobile which we see from a distance of ten feet, is the same size as an automobile which we see from a distance of one hundred yards. This recognition is known as size constancy.

Shape constancy relates to the same principle. The shape of an object, for instance, a picture hanging on a wall, is perceived as rectangular, even though it is viewed from different angles and the images on the retina are not rectangular. (See illustration number 5.) We need not go into detail but should simply point out that both of these constancies depend upon the interpretation of directions from the viewer to the objects, that is, upon directionality. (Even though they depend upon directionality and involve interpretations, size and shape constancy do not determine the difference between primary and secondary qualities.)

Illustration No. 5

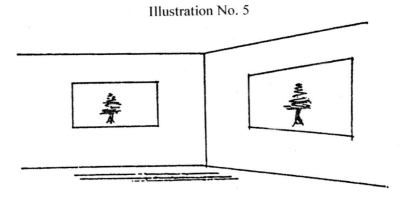

Size and Shape Constancy

Interworking of Primary and Secondary Qualities

To be completely clear about the primary and secondary qualities, it would be well to consider some brief concrete examples of the perception of objects. First, let us test the concept with an example we have used before—a tree. How is it that we visually perceive a tree? We perceive its shape and size from the direction of our eyes to its outlines. Size and shape are primary qualities. We perceive its color as a secondary quality. If the tree's branches are moving in the breeze, the perception of movement is based on the change of direction—a primary quality.

Second, consider a barking dog. We perceive it both visually and by sound. The size, shape, and movement of the dog, we designate as primary qualities. The color of the dog we detect as a secondary quality. The sound of the barking comes to us also as a secondary quality or, as we have termed it, a qualitative core.

Lastly, consider the taste of a cinnamon roll. This, as is well known, actually utilizes both taste and smell, both of which are secondary qualities.

Once again, we wish to stress that in the appreciation of reality in general, the suggestion is not being put forward that perceptions are entirely from within the brain. We are not espousing a form of pure idealism. Perceptions are stimulated by energies (light waves, sound waves, etc.) coming from the outside. The nerve impulses which result in perceptions correspond to the energies stemming from outside objects and are relatively accurate results of them. Without the objects, there would be no nerve impulses and no perceptions of those objects (except in the case of dreams and hallucinations to be dealt with later). *Perceptions correlate with outside objects as to size, location, etc., and are thus rooted in reality, but the qualitative aspects of perceptions (colors, sounds, etc.,) stem from within the brain.* In other words, the secondary qualities together with interpretations of direction, that is, the *combination* of the primary and secondary* qualities initiate our appreciation of reality. This concept of perception requires only an alteration in the usual understanding of how perception happens. It attempts to make no change in the appearance of the object.

Secondary Qualities and Consciousness Cores

We stated at the beginning of this chapter that the secondary qualities are roughly equivalent to consciousness cores. Let us attempt to be more concrete in our description of the consciousness core in order to make the concept more definite. We have to caution the reader to understand, however, that any concrete description is moving ahead of scientific discovery and is entirely hypothetical. Prior to this point in our description of the consciousness cores we have described the cores in very tenuous terms as being a useful concept to build upon in our further theorizing. We have stated that they are sensory in nature and that the capacity for them is inherited. Beyond that we have regarded them more or less as an X factor in the development of consciousness.

To be somewhat more definite let us suppose that the consciousness cores consist largely of what Locke called the secondary qualities—meaning mainly the five senses. Also let us suppose, in further agreement with Locke and other British Empiricists, that consciousness itself is composed of sensory inputs. We might consider them to be touch, pain, and the like. Touch, for example, stems from sense receptors located in the skin. The nerve fibers from the receptors go to the spinal cord. In the spinal cord they transmit impulses to other nerve cells resulting in impulses being sent to the brain. In the brain they reach the stage of consciousness.

Recall that we have defined "sensory" and being considerably more inclusive than the "five senses." But for the moment let us consider the cores to be sensory nerve cell impulses introduced at the level of the skin. It is very clear that there is processing of the impulses before they reach the level of consciousness. The exact forms of the processing and the locations at which it occurs in the nervous system are little known. We therefore cannot be definite as to the stage at which the impulses begin to function as consciousness cores. Even if we knew more about the stages of their processing, to define the cores as beginning at a particular stage would probably be arbitrary.

The consciousness cores can be compared to the bricks which are being used in the building of a house. The bricks themselves do not constitute the house. Similarly, the cores themselves are not consciousness. We must wait for empirical research to answer the question of the exact definition of a consciousness core. But we do wish to postulate that *consciousness is composed of component parts and that the components are sensory in nature.* To force an attempt to be specific, the cores could conceivably consist of the nerve cell impulses of different sensations, which are passed from one impulse to the next, all way to the cerebral cortex where consciousness obtains.

The concept of consciousness, as consisting of component parts, requires a considerable alteration in the thinking of those who regard consciousness as a single complete entity. But perhaps a second analogy to the consciousness cores will help to further clarify what is intended by the term. Consider an abstract painting which is composed of blocks of color arranged in an almost random appearing form. An artist might object to the wording of the painting's being "composed of blocks of color," on the grounds that the painting is a unit and is not composed of separate parts. The entire painting must be observed as a whole to have the desired esthetic value. Breaking it into parts completely destroys the essence of the painting, that which makes it a painting and not a simple collection of colors. On the other hand there are those people who are inclined to be particularly impressed by certain ones of the blocks of color. These blocks are beautiful to them. Some people will even describe the colors in terms of taste. "It is such a beautiful color, I can almost taste it." Regardless of which side of this argument one might wish to take, we merely intend to state that the blocks are analogous to the consciousness cores. Each consciousness content is composed of a combination of them. Each content is like a separate painting. The entire content is not in the cores any more than the entire experience of the painting is in the separate blocks of color. Yet the *elements* of the consciousness are already present in the cores. The content is composed of them. We wish to be clear that the consciousness cores are not a full consciousness in any sense. (To say that the blocks contain consciousness would suggest a form of panpsychism. Just as in the section above we were not espousing a form of pure idealism, we are not now promulgating panpsychism or anything approaching it.) The consciousness is the final amalgam of the cores, but the cores contain the elements. In the subsequent chapters we will have considerably more to say about the role of the consciousness cores in the development of consciousness and their functional definition will be determined by that role.

Eugene M. Brooks, M.D.

Summary

The "secondary qualities" of John Locke are, as far as he enumerated them, the equivalent of consciousness cores. They are inherited and are both subjective and unique. As named by Locke they consist of color, sound, touch, taste and smell. Only a single observation of any of them is required for their perception. "Primary qualities" are also unique as far as their conscious qualities are concerned. They consist of solidity, size, shape, and motion. For their perception they require a minimum of two observations of objects. The observations consist, in the visual mode for example, of two lines of sight, two directions between the eye and the object. Having the observations, the brain then makes a judgment; it perceives the two directions (the directionality) as a particular quality. The primary qualities are objective in the sense that they are measurable. However, they can be considered to be partly subjective in that they are mediated by the sensory mechanisms which are associated with secondary qualities. Our "contact" with the physical reality of the world around us results from the appreciation of primary and secondary qualities.

The consciousness cores correlate with Locke's secondary qualities but are more inclusive. They comprise the elements of which consciousness is constructed. The functional relations of the cores will emerge as their role in the development of consciousness is described further.

Chapter Seven

Multiplicity and Dynamicity of Consciousness

Multiplicity of Consciousness

At least since the time of the ancient Greeks the concept of a single or unitary consciousness has been entertained fairly exclusively and was given authoritative sanction by Descartes who assigned the pineal gland in the center of the brain as a probable location of consciousness. Instead of one location in the brain, Crick (1994) has broadened the conception of the location with the suggestion that there may be "multiple Cartesian theaters" where consciousness is experienced. In our discussion of the identity theory in subsequent pages we shall extend the concept of the location of consciousness much further with the postulation that the *initial elements* of consciousness may be present within the peripheral sensory nerves.

The fact that consciousness has been looked upon as a single entity would appear to be one of the principal problems with understanding it. Because of that view researchers as well as philosophers have until recent decades generally followed in the footsteps of Descartes and have expected to find a single location for consciousness in the brain. We are now fairly certain that consciousness is diffuse within the cerebral cortex if not at a lower neurological level as well. In this chapter we will explore the present indications and the possibility that consciousness consists of a series of rapid occurrences rather than a unitary enduring phenomenon, that consciousness is a sequence of separate events rather than a single entity which receives inputs from the senses. *There is considerable suggestion that while consciousness appears to be a single phenomenon it is nevertheless composed of multiple occurrences.* As an analogy consider the motion picture. It is a series of individual still pictures which only appear to be a single, moving phenomenon.

Common language reflects the supposition that consciousness is unitary, that there is a single consciousness. The term "consciousness" is used almost exclusively in singular form. It is interesting that the term "awareness", which has essentially the same meaning as "consciousness" is frequently used in the pleural form. Our language refers to many awarenesses but not to many "consciousnesses." William James (1842-1910), regarded consciousness as being a single entity. Nevertheless, he occasionally used the expressions "pulse of consciousness" and "pulse of subjectivity" (1950, b), terms which can suggest separate instances of consciousness.

61

That consciousness is not unitary was suggested by us in 1994. It was also suggested by Valentine (1994): "Because we are aware of only one consciousness, it is difficult to throw off the illusion of unity." Consciousness *appears* to be unitary upon introspection but such is not likely to be the case. This is not only important for the concept of consciousness we are developing, it has many implications for science in general and particularly for the development of conscious or pseudoconscious robots. In our theory we will regard consciousness to be an imperceptibly rapid succession of discrete occurrences rather than a single entity.

In the development of our theory of consciousness, we applied, as an analogy to our concept of the consciousness core, the role of atoms in the historical development of chemistry and physics. The atomic theory began with atoms as purely theoretical entities which served as beacons for scientific thought but which are now confirmed as hard science. We discussed the principle of reductionism and its success in science in general, and while adhering to this principle we developed our theory. Continuing to utilize the parallel with atoms, we proposed, in the chapter previous to this one under the section heading of "Secondary Qualities and Consciousness Cores", the concept of the consciousness cores as the basic building blocks of consciousness, that consciousness is composed of the cores as *component parts*.

In chapter three we stated that we could not delimit consciousness cores in exact physiological terms. There is a likelihood that the cores consist of numbers of sensory nerve cell impulses and that the excitations comprise primary components of consciousness. It is the consciousness cores, or aggregates of them, which would constitute the individual contents of consciousness. Pursuing this concept, there is the possibility, if not the requirement, that consciousness is multiple rather than a single entity. Since complexes of cores constitute consciousness contents, as the complexes of cores change, consciousness changes. There is hardly any doubt that consciousness results from nerve cells or nerve cell impulses, whether the impulses remain simply as volleys of impulses or whether they are processed into something more complicated, which we have designated as consciousness cores. In either case, in our theory *the nerve cells or their activities comprise consciousness* and the arrangement strongly suggests that consciousness is multiple. Nevertheless, one could still regard consciousness as an entity which receives information and perceives images, the images being in the form of nerve cells or their activity.

Let us be explicit at this point, as we have touched upon before by "nerve cells or their activity" we intend to be as broad as possible in our meaning. We use the term to encompass intracellular substances such as microtubules, intercellular transmitters, the timing or coordination of impulses, the creation of "fields", internuncial nerve cells which relay sensory impulses, or particular nerve cells which as a whole constitute consciousness components.

The view of consciousness as consisting of consciousness cores has enabled us to develop further our unique theory of consciousness. As will be brought out in later chapters, the conception of consciousness as multiple lends itself to each stage in the construction of our theory. Such is the case in relation to memory, attention, the denouement of consciousness and finally to our understanding of the self and of reality. We acknowledge that we do not prove that consciousness is multiple, but in our estimation it dovetails much more parsimoniously with our theory than does the view of consciousness as an entity.

In the usual representationalist approach to consciousness there is a need for a central observer to perceive the representations. Considering consciousness to be unitary, places it squarely in the role of being such an observer and has the result of putting consciousness in the position of the homunculus with the intractable problem of a "reduction to the absurd": If consciousness is an observer of sensory inputs, a second consciousness is needed to observe the first, *ad infinitum*. The avoidance of regarding consciousness as a central observer is of the utmost importance for explanatory theories. To ignore the problem with an observer seems to render the scientific explanation of consciousness impossible and has been a major stumbling block for all theories which disregard the problem or attempt to gloss over it. Also, a central observer is often thought of as a single entity residing in a single grouping of brain cells or "center"; but considering consciousness to be multiple aids in relieving the burden of finding such an entity. Current theories of consciousness, including the more recent ones of networks, coordinated rhythm of brain cells, quantum mechanics, and others, all treat consciousness as if it is unitary.

Evidence that consciousness is multiple is provided by lesions in the brain, to be reviewed later in some detail. These lesions cause loss of discrete perceptual functions while leaving others intact. This evidence leaves no doubt that the processing toward consciousness of the different functions is, at least to a considerable extent, handled separately and in different areas of the brain. These and other neurophysiological findings of recent years are more finely detailed examples of what has been known since ancient times, that the loss of a perceptual modality, such as vision or hearing, does not eliminate consciousness. This is true not only when there is the loss of peripheral receptor organs, such as the eyes, but also when there is a localized lesion in the brain.

In our thinking consciousness should be considered to be a collective term similar to the word, traffic. One can look upon the traffic on a busy highway as a single group of moving vehicles and the word has a unitary meaning. But if one is considering the individual automobiles, then the word has a meaning involving multiplicity. It would appear to be absolutely crucial, if we are to understand consciousness, to explore it not only in the overall sense, as has been done in the past, but from the standpoint of separate components.

Another point favoring the concept of multiplicity is that such a view is in accord with neurophysiology. It is strongly indicated and generally assumed that consciousness consists of nerve cell impulses, and individual impulses are not continuous. As in dreams, they may last for only a fraction of a second but consciousness persists throughout one's waking hours or longer. Even though impulses can occur in very rapid sequence and in volleys, each impulse is a separate event. This fact lends itself to the likelihood that consciousness itself is not a single entity, that it is composed of impulses and that its appearance as an entity is an illusion.

If we maintain that consciousness is a series of events rather than a single entity then in the pages previous to this one we have been using terminology which, according to our theoretical understanding, is technically incorrect. We should not be using the phrase "inputs to consciousness." Such phraseology treats consciousness as a receiving entity rather than as a collective term which refers to many separate neurological events. Instead it is preferable, where language permits, to speak of "nerve cell impulses which become conscious" or "impulses which become consciousness." In our view each consciousness content, each perception or thought, is its own instance of consciousness. Each content has a duration of less than a second, as explained in the next section. They occur continuously, one after another, but we become aware of them as if they are a single ongoing entity.

Physically we are one—one body—and it is quite natural for us to apply this concept to consciousness. We feel that we have one consciousness but this appears unlikely in view of our understanding of neurophysiology.

Time Relationships of Consciousness

The rapidity with which the content of consciousness changes does not, of course, provide proof that consciousness is composed of multiple events. It could still be possible that consciousness is like a moving light beacon which illuminates continuously but moves from one item to another. Whether consciousness is unitary or multiple, if it is composed of a series of perceptions, how fleeting would each of them be? According to two psychologists (Pillsbury, 1913; Boring, 1933) cited by Ebb (1980) the duration of a single content in perception lasts for about half a second. Actually the time required for an idea to flit through an individual's mind may be considerably less. It has even been reported that some nerve cells are capable of being stimulated thousands of times a second. The time interval between hearing a tone and pressing a button is only about one tenth of a second and this involves both becoming conscious of the tone and then pressing the button.

The shortest duration of a consciousness content may be the shortest duration of time directly perceptible to a human being. An example of the rapidity with which consciousness changes contents would be the process one goes through in trying to recall a particular name while speaking: One might say to oneself, but with each phrase conscious and deliberately voiced aloud in order to let the listener know what one was doing, "Let's see. What was his name?...I can't think of it!...Oh, yes! It's John Doe." The quotations represent the stream of consciousness only in small part. While saying, "What was his name?", one consciously tries to search for some memory cues such as the individual's appearance, where he was last seen, etc. Intermingled with those thoughts, one also notices whether or not the listener is paying attention. When the speaker is conscious of being unable to find the desired answer, he says, "I can't think of it!" He is conscious of saying those words and then is aware that the listener is still waiting. When the sought for name becomes conscious the speaker then says, "Oh yes! It's John Doe." All through the process, the many ideas, memories, voice inflections, and facial expressions, etc., may be fleetingly and separately conscious and consciously controlled in an appropriate manner. The different contents could persist for only very short intervals of time.

An indication that a single content of consciousness requires only a small fraction of a second for its entire occurrence is present in motion pictures. The physical fact is that when individual frames are viewed in succession they appear as individual pictures until they are viewed more rapidly. They then "merge" and are perceived as smooth motion. The usual way of regarding a motion picture when the motion begins to become disjointed is that the film is moving too slowly which causes the motion to begin to *fail*. However, it is equally valid to consider the failure from the opposite perspective: When the pictures are presented faster than about twenty per second, the perception of the still pictures "fails" and they are seen as depicting smooth motion. If we can regard the situation with the motion picture as indicative of the case with consciousness, a twentieth of a second would be a maximum length of time for a single consciousness content to persist without its merging into another content. Since only twenty picture frames can be seen as individual pictures in a second, this is an indication that discrete consciousness contents can remain discrete only if they each occupy *no longer than* one twentieth of a second. The situation in the case of sound is approximately the same. If a sound is presented which has a frequency of less than about fifteen or twenty vibrations per second, one can hear individual pulses, but if the frequency is raised beyond twenty vibrations per second only a tone is heard.

Of shorter duration than either of the above two forms of perception is the blinking which can sometimes be seen in a fluorescent light bulb when it is beginning to burn out. These blinks occur at sixty per second. The same rate is encountered when one feels an electric shock from an ordinary house current. And faster yet is the detection of vibration from a tuning fork when the fork is struck and the shank of the fork is placed against the knee cap or against the skull behind the ear (the mastoid bone). One can easily feel the individual pulsations of the vibration at the rate of 512 per second.

In the previous chapter (under the explanation of solidity as a primary quality) we mentioned that in determining the direction from which sounds arise, the brain discriminates between sounds arriving at each of the two ears at intervals of less than one thousandth of a second. This perception of direction affords a suggestion of the speed of brain function. All of the examples presented seem to provide a clear indication that at least some types of consciousness events can occur at a very rapid rate and they provide for the possibility that consciousness consists of a rapid series of individual events which give the illusory impression of a unitary, persisting entity.

Multiplicity and Evolution

The many activities which are carried out concomitantly give an impression that a person is conscious of several things at the same time. One can be walking, talking, looking about and so on. It appears, however, that many activities, once initiated, are continued "automatically" thereby freeing attention or consciousness to focus elsewhere.

That there is only one content of consciousness at a time is compatible with both our concept of multiplicity as well as the concept of consciousness as a single entity. In the multiplicity concept each content is a separate instance of consciousness. This is very straight forward. With consciousness as a single entity, as in the moving beacon analogy, there is also one consciousness content at a time. The single beam illuminates each content in sequence. Even though multiplicity is somewhat counterintuitive, evolution has not excluded the possibility of multiplicity and further, it seems as plausible, if not more so, than a single consciousness.

Whether or not consciousness has a value to the human being (of which some writers actually express much doubt), its origination by the process of evolution is of much interest. There are many who would question that only one content (or possibly two) is conscious at any particular instant but certainly attention is limited. If there is only one content at a time why would nature have arranged the brain to function in such a manner? We can only speculate as to the answers. Considering the tremendous survival value of the various senses, and the millennia over which nature has had the opportunity to refine consciousness, it seems safe to assume that the development of consciousness has been adaptive in the process of evolution.

Further Arguments Favoring Multiplicity of Consciousness

A reason for the occurrence of consciousness contents as separate from each other is suggested by computers. Since the advent of computers, it has been found to be advantageous to handle processes by digital rather than by analog methods. Digital processes are in discrete units, all of the same size, which resemble nerve cell discharges in the regard that individual nerve cells either send an impulse or do not. There are no partial impulses or degrees of them. They act according to what is known as the all-or-none principle. Contrary to the digital process in computers, the analog process utilizes continuous degrees of change rather than discrete units. The difference is like that between the digital clock, in which the minutes or seconds change abruptly, and the earlier electric clock, in which the second hand moves continuously. The nervous system therefore is basically a digital system. The digital system has been found to be easier to control and is the more accurate of the two.

An additional reason that there may be only one conscious content at a time is found in the functioning of vision. Vision is generally credited with being our most valuable sense in relation to survival. Even though we have two eyes they can focus on only one point at a time. Also, the eyes do not move smoothly but jump from one fixation to another. The objects between fixations receive little or no attention. All of this seems to correspond best with a digital, discontinuous system. Such a system also tends to support the concept of a multiple consciousness consisting of rapidly changing, discontinuous contents.

If there are two perceptions in any single instant or even several perceptions, there can be much mental conflict and confusion. Perceptions which are unrelated result in the loss of the time needed for their comprehension and for the selection of the most important one. Perceptions also require time for a decision to be made as to the action required. Consider attempting to view a television screen which displays two separate pictures superimposed upon each other. Neither can be clearly perceived. Additionally, in the human sensorium, there are hundreds or thousands of stimuli impinging at all times from both external and internal sources. It is highly questionable whether one can even select the single most important perception or make a single decision if there is more than one item of consciousness at a time. A further argument is that while the body can do more than one thing simultaneously, such as walking and eating, an extremity in any one moment can move in only one direction, that is, it can react without delay to only one perception. To make a selection between two or more perceptions would add to the time required for a reaction. Such a condition would lessen the chances of survival in any life threatening situation. That there has to be some mechanism for shielding consciousness from the myriad of sensory inputs which are potentially impinging at all times has been presented by Freud (1936) and others.

It also may well be the case that there can be only one content of consciousness at a time because physiologically consciousness, utilizing parallel processing, occupies so many brain systems that only one conscious content at a time is actually possible. Such appears to be the situation despite the tremendous number of neurons and the tremendous powers of the brain. The powers of the brain are not, after all, unlimited. Alzheimer's disease, strokes, and other conditions which reduce the number of neurons in the brain reduce the fullness, or at least the range, of consciousness. That the range is reduced, is obvious in advanced stages of such conditions. The range of consciousness is also reduced when one is under the influence of various drugs, including alcohol, or when falling asleep and during sleep.

One would think that for items to be conscious separately and consecutively, would require more time than if the same number of items were present concomitantly. Regardless, it appears to be more economical in the overall consideration of time, energy, and particularly clarity, for the brain to have a single item in consciousness rather than to have more than one item at the same time.

Dynamicity of Consciousness

For the purposes of this book, a highly important factor supporting the concept that consciousness is best viewed as being multiple, is the element we shall regard as the dynamicity of consciousness. The dynamic nature of consciousness is also of great importance to an understanding of consciousness aside from the matter of multiplicity.

The realization that much of mental functioning takes place at an unconscious level is particularly necessary for the dynamic concept. According to this concept, *the various nerve impulse volleys are competing with each other to become conscious. Only one volley becomes conscious at any one instant.* Searle (1992a) refers to this volley as the "winner" of the competition. From the neurological standpoint, at each instance of consciousness, the winner is the volley which has the greatest number of favorable factors and the least number of unfavorable factors (Brooks, 1994). The favorable ones include having arisen from stronger stimulation in the beginning (as in the case of a sudden, loud noise) as well as from having more facilitation (by interests, etc.,). We feel that a volley of impulses militates in favor of the multiplicity of consciousness. In keeping with the identity theory, to be elaborated upon later, it is nerve cells or their activities which become consciousness. There is no need to postulate that impulses are apprehended by a separate agency.

It is well known and the mechanism is well understood, that nerve cell discharges regularly facilitate or inhibit the discharges of other nerve cells. Such inhibition would appear to be very important in the competition for consciousness. This may contribute to the circumstance which is suggested by introspection that the "thoughts" or contents of consciousness are present only one at a time. The exclusion of competing "thoughts" could be accounted for physiologically if impulses, as they reach higher levels in the nervous system, have a greater capacity to inhibit their rivals. The greater net strength in cellular impulses would determine the final outcome, that is, which cellular discharge or volley of discharges inhibits all others and becomes conscious. Such a system would fit Searle's conception. However, while it is known that nerve cell impulses do have facilitative and inhibitory influences on other nerve cell impulses, something would have to cause the impulses to inhibit or facilitate their neighbors. We prefer a scheme in which ultimate control would stem from "higher centers" rather than simply from nerve cell discharges at "lower" levels. The control could be effected by interests or anxieties, that is, by the net conscious and subconscious emotional configuration at each moment. We shall discuss the subject of such control further under the headings of "Peripheral Selection" and "Monitoring", as well as under "Interests and Anxieties."

The psychological/physiological concepts of Hebb (1980) as well as those of Dennett (1991) and Crick (1994) are clearly dynamic in character. Also Bruner (1973, p. 23) mentioned, "Accessibility [to consciousness] then must have something to do with the resolution of competing alternatives." And of course, psychoanalysis is replete with concepts of the dynamic character of the unconscious conflict between the Ego, Id, and the Superego. This dynamic character is probably nowhere better exemplified than in The Interpretation of Dreams written in 1900 (Freud, 1913). Preperceptual nerve impulses undoubtedly have numerous sources and there can be little doubt that these compete for consciousness.

Summary

We view consciousness as consisting of separate contents occurring in imperceptibly rapid sequence. It is regarded as being multiple rather than a single, continuously functioning entity. There appears to be a "competition" between nerve cells for access to the conscious level. Apparently only one content can be conscious at a time. It is known that nerve cells regularly inhibit or facilitate the action of other nerve cells. The reaching of the level of consciousness is probably controlled by facilitations and inhibitions under the influence of interests and anxieties of the individual.

While we cannot rule out the possibility that consciousness is a unitary entity, we suggest that multiplicity is a more parsimonious and a more likely concept due to several considerations:

- No single location has been found for consciousness.
- Awareness, which is synonymous with consciousness, is often used in the plural form and understood to be multiple.
- A unitary consciousness seems to be inevitably subject to a *reductio ad absurdum.*
- Multiplicity accommodates our theory of consciousness as consisting of nerve cells or their activity and of consciousness cores.
- Since brain function is based on nerve cells and their activity, it is more parsimonious to regard consciousness as similarly based rather than on an unknown mechanism even if the unknown mechanism also involves nerve cells. In keeping with the identity theory, there is no need to postulate that impulses are apprehended by a separate agency.
- The concept of competing impulses—dynamicity—is compatible with consciousness as simply consisting of nerve cells or their impulses.
- Certain brain lesions eliminate some forms of consciousness while leaving others intact, thereby suggesting that consciousness is not a single entity.

Chapter Eight

First and Third Person Perspectives

It is clearly relevant to the understanding of consciousness, to know that there are two perspectives from which consciousness can be considered. From one of these perspectives we can *experience* consciousness; from the other perspective we can *observe* it in others. These are the first and the third person perspectives.

For those who may have forgotten their English grammar lessons, let us remind you about the declension of pronouns. You recall that they are as follows:

	Singular	Plural
First person	I	We
Second person	You	You
Third person	He, she, or it	They

When speaking or writing from the first person perspective we use the first person pronoun, "I": "I am aware", "I think", "I see", etc. The important point is that the first person perspective is subjective. It relates to consciousness from a position inside one's mind.

In the third person perspective there is the consideration of consciousness from an "outside" position. In this case the consciousness is the object of observation either by oneself or by another person. The consciousness of oneself or of the other person is referred to as "it."

One importance of being aware of the two perspectives is that in the observance of other people, their consciousness can only be inferred. The other person's consciousness can only be viewed from the third person perspective. It cannot be experienced by us. The other person appears to be conscious to us because he says he is, and he looks and acts as if he perceives and feels the same way we do. However, his consciousness cannot be examined directly. This fact imposes a great handicap in the attempt to explore consciousness. We can learn what the other person is thinking or feeling only from what he or she tells us which may not be entirely accurate or complete.

In the case of animals, the study of consciousness is even more limited than in humans. One has to conjecture as to whether the behavior of animals results from consciousness or whether it stems from so-called instinct or reflex. For example, the cells in the retina of the frog's eye are arranged in such a way that the frog can see a small object such as an insect

71

much more easily than anything else. Does its behavior in snapping up a fly result from conscious volition, from mindless instinct, or from simple reflex? Removing or anesthetizing an area of the frog's brain would not tell us whether or not we had affected its consciousness directly or whether, for example, the frog was merely blinded.

Similarly to lower animals, small children, much less infants, cannot tell us what is in their consciousness. This is of crucial importance in the case of children. Consciousness is well developed as an instrument before a child has the ability to describe his consciousness. We cannot learn from the infant what he can or cannot see, what he understands of what he sees or how his earliest awarenesses take shape and develop. It seems certain that consciousness develops from preadult stages. Perhaps we could even say prehuman stages, in the same sense that the body of the human embryo develops through stages during which it has gill clefts like a fish, looks like a pig, has a tail, and so forth. Consciousness could not, like Athena, who was born fully grown when she leaped from the head of Zeus, begin its functioning in the adult form. A number of philosophers take the contrary view, that consciousness is "emergent", that is, that it appears on the evolutionary scene all at once or as a new development without precursors. It would seem that such a view would stem from conceiving of consciousness only as we know it in the older child or adult.

The view that consciousness appears all at once is also in keeping with the idea of not a few theorists that consciousness is the soul. The soul is generally not conceived of as having developed in stages but as having become incorporated into the body at a particular time.

Philosophers point out the fact that it is impossible to completely prove that someone else is really conscious. Of course, it seems perfectly reasonable to assume that other people beside ourselves are conscious and that their consciousness is much the same as our own. In fact most animals seem to demonstrate some sort of consciousness. Nevertheless the fact that someone else's consciousness cannot actually be proven has raised many questions for philosophers in connection with the attempts to logically be certain that the other person is real and not imaginary. As already mentioned, it also results in great difficulty for scientific research regarding consciousness.

Appreciate Consciousness Only from the "Inside"

To further consider the "inside" perspective of consciousness, it is perhaps easier to think in terms of looking at objects. Ordinarily the way we thoroughly examine an object, for instance a spring powered mechanical watch, is to observe it from the outside and then open it to determine from the inside how it is put together or functions. We can even do that with the brain. We can see its shape and convolutions from the outside and then cut it open to inspect the gray matter and larger tracts on the inside. We can also scrutinize cells of the brain through a microscope. But there is no way we can accomplish the equivalent inspection with consciousness. *There is nothing to see from the outside.* We can see nerve impulses in the form of electrical traces on an oscilloscope, but that does not help. *From the "inside" perspective the nerve impulses, with all of their vividness and variation, are appreciated as consciousness* From the "outside" perspective they are viewed merely as nerve cell impulses, "action potentials", transmitter substances, etc. Even knowing which nerve cells or structures within nerve cells, are relevant to consciousness, merely moves the problem of understanding consciousness to smaller entities but does not change the problem. For the foreseeable future at least, we cannot know consciousness from the outside. From the outside we can know only the effects of consciousness—speech, bodily movements, etc. We can know consciousness itself only in the form of its various "contents", and to be aware of the contents we must know them from the inside perspective.

It seems counterintuitive but the difficulty with the outside perspective applies to seeing one's own behavior. In playing a piano we see our hands moving but our hands are outside consciousness, outside our "minds". We are still an outsider making observations. The actual act of seeing is inside consciousness but the behavior is outside. This is probably more easily conceptualized if we observe ourselves "making faces" in a mirror. What we are seeing is clearly outside. The volition or intent is inside.

Furthermore, it is important that technically it is impossible to view even our own consciousness from both the "inside" and "outside" perspective at the same time. Either we are thinking about our consciousness, in which case we are considering it from the "outside" perspective, or we are *experiencing* from the "inside" perspective what is taking place in our consciousness. One might challenge the latter statement on the grounds that, in "thinking about our consciousness", we are experiencing our thinking and consciousness at the same time. However, our rebuttal is that in the process of introspection we experience what we are thinking but not the *original content* of our thinking. To illustrate this let us say that we see an object, a pencil. The pencil is the content of consciousness; we will refer to it as the first experience. Introspection involves a second experience, an experiencing of thought about the first. Introspection, according to our definition of memory as a recovering of the past, is placed as a reexperiencing. This will become clearer when we discuss the "inside" and "outside" perspective and the observance of memories further in a later chapter.

The difficulties encountered in examining consciousness in the laboratory was reflected in the approach of the behaviorist school of psychology. The behaviorist philosophy, which dominated the thinking in psychology for the first half of the twentieth century, was strictly to observe behavior and to ignore or even disclaim consciousness. Consequently, little or nothing was contributed to its understanding. The behaviorists made the deliberate decision to eliminate consciousness from their consideration since it was both unfathomable and subjective. They preferred to be thoroughly scientific and to use strictly empirical methods.

What might be looked upon as a step toward bridging the gap between the first and third person perspectives, is the experimental work of the neurosurgeon, Wilder Penfield (1975). The brain itself does not have pain receptors and patients can be conscious during brain surgery. Penfield's patients reported what was in their consciousness when their brains were electrically stimulated at discrete points on the brain's surface, the cerebral cortex. For example, some heard sounds or music, while others felt themselves to be reliving experiences from the past. The experiences were quite real to them, yet at the same time, they knew they were in the operating room being operated upon. Such studies, as interesting and valuable as they may be, are nevertheless quite limited as far as explaining consciousness is concerned. One reason for the limitation is that the surgeon cannot know whether the experience is produced by a single cell, a widely dispersed number of cells, or by cellular sub-structures. Obviously, the tremendous complexity of the brain and its processes means that at best there is much need for further development of the technique.

Summary

From the first person perspective (the "inside" perspective) we can *experience* consciousness. From the third person perspective (the "outside" perspective) we can observe only memory of consciousness or the effects of consciousness, such as behavior or reports, etc. We will discuss the observance of memories in a later chapter.

Chapter Nine

The Self. Preliminary Considerations

Some of the concepts of the self give it direct relevance to the understanding of consciousness. It has usually been considered that it is the self which does the perceiving. This has the effect of equating the self with consciousness, that is, the self, frequently expressed as "I", perceives the object. And, of course, we are using the term, object, not only in the sense of something which can be seen or touched, but also as the "object" or target of perception. The idea that it is the self which does the perceiving, that consciousness is appreciated by the self, is a widespread conception. One must take issue with this view as in this regard the self is similar to the homunculus, the imaginary little man in the brain who is needed in the representationalist theory of consciousness. As explained in chapter one, he is needed because something has to "see" the representations of objects for us; but a severe disadvantage of a homunculus or even a more scientific sounding "central observer" is that it results in a reduction to the absurd.

The word, self, as it is used alone without a connected pronoun, apparently came into use at least as early as the time of Socrates (Gallager, 1997). The term and concept obviously had no basis in empirical fact but apparently resulted from thinking based more on common intuition than on logic. One seldom sees the term employed in modern English except when used in philosophical discussion. The concept has been pondered at great length and there is still much disagreement regarding it. Webster's dictionary defines it as "the identity, character or, essential qualities of any person."

The following is from the introduction to a recent widely read article by Strawson (1997) which indicates the extent to which the word is unusual:

The substantival phrase 'the self' is very unnatural in most speech contexts in most languages, and some conclude from this that it's an illusion to think that there is such a thing as the self, an illusion that arises from nothing more than an improper use of language...It is too quick to say that a 'grammatical error...is the essence of the theory of the self' or that 'the self' is a piece of philosopher's nonsense consisting in a misunderstanding of the reflexive pronoun' (Kenny, 1988, p. 4).

In the literature other examples exploring the "problem of the self" are numerous and extensive. A question regarding the "self", either used alone or combined with a pronoun, is whether or not the "self" refers to the mind or to the body. A person might say, "I enjoyed taking a walk by myself." If the person enjoyed the physical exercise we might consider that he was referring to his body. But was it not his mind which was enjoying his body? And is the mind separate from the body?

There is an interesting and entertaining short story by Dennett (1981, p. 217) which illustrates the situation particularly well. He described himself as a fictional person who was selected by the Pentagon to recover a highly radioactive atomic warhead which had been placed deep in the earth. The radioactivity would "cause severe abnormalities in certain tissues of the brain." His brain was therefore removed from his skull and kept alive in a vat. All of its connections to his body were preserved by replacing them with "elaborate radio links." He, or his body, then went below ground to accomplish the mission of recovering the warhead. But he was continually puzzled by the question, Where am I? Was he in the vat or deep in the earth? In other words, where was his self? In some of his musings, the "I" referred only to his body. But even then, it was *his* body, (which actually must have meant his mind/brain's awareness of his body).

Assuming for the moment that there is such a thing as a self, what is its nature? Questions which are often explored include: Is it something physical? Is it a separate part of the brain? If it is mental, is it the nebulous entity one is "aware of when one is aware of oneself" as mentioned by Brook (1998); and if so does the self exist only when one is aware of oneself or is one always aware of oneself? Further, does it change over time as one's opinion of oneself changes ("I am an honorable person" or "I am despicable.") These questions indicate only a few of the ambiguities about the self.

Some of the confusion about the self, among those who give it serious thought, results from treating it as a sort of nebulous entity. One thing which seems to be clear about the word is that its meanings depend upon the presuppositions which one brings to its use. Since basic presuppositions about the self are usually simply taken for granted by individual authors, the self is often in conflict with the underlying concepts of the reader. It is quickly found to be very ambiguous. We are in agreement with Dennett who regards the self as an "abstraction." We would add that it helps in describing the meaning of the self to consider it to be an abstract *concept*, an understanding. It is not a physical entity or even an entity which is separate within the mind. In other words, the self is what the individual user of the term considers it to be. The term does not have a single, specific meaning and its meaning at any particular time depends upon the context. In turn the context implies presuppositions about mind and body, concepts which are also apt to be unclear and ambiguous. Considering the self from the first person perspective, as a concept of oneself, it can include all of oneself—one's body, as well as one's mind, thoughts, sensations and memories. In short *it can include anything or everything of which one can be conscious and can consider to be one's person. In this sense the self is one's image or understanding of oneself.* It is simply a content of consciousness.

In philosophical literature, "self-consciousness" is often treated as being the meaning of self. However, self-consciousness is probably best considered to have the popular meaning of the term—to be overly conscious of oneself or embarrassed in the presence of others. The term, introspection seems much to be preferred if one means the examination of one's thoughts or feelings.

Some philosophers regard self-consciousness, awareness of oneself, to be the same as consciousness. This concept gives the impression of too severely limiting the meaning of consciousness. Consciousness certainly involves much more than awareness of oneself. There are other philosophers who feel that through the practice of meditation one can become aware of one's self as being "pure consciousness." One can consider the self as being an entity separate from the remainder of the mind, or a separate function, almost as if it is located in a separate area of the brain. But in regarding the self as merely a concept, it becomes very doubtful that one can be conscious of one's own self as an isolated entity.

Popper and Eccles (1977), and a number of other authors, believe that it is the capacity for introspection or self awareness (which they term as "self-consciousness") that makes man unique among the animals. They feel that lower animals have consciousness but not the self-awareness that is present in the human. They also believe that the human awareness of death, with a termination of the self, is absent in lower animals. As an abstraction the intellectual concept of death probably requires more intelligence than lower animals possess. Some philosophers, those who consider the soul to be immortal, regard it as a way for the self, as the essence of the person, to escape termination. These presumptions suggest religious views which are not the particular concern of this book.

The psychoanalytic term, ego, is often used in the sense of the self—"His big ego (his exaggerated concept of himself) stood in the way of his receiving a promotion." However, the ego also has a much broader meaning, one in which it is the integrator of the personality.

Summary

The self is a concept and not a nebulous physical entity. The exact meaning of the term depends upon one's preconceptions of mind, body, and consciousness.   To regard the self as the perceiver of the contents of consciousness is to render it similar to the homunculus with the attendant problem of a reduction to the absurd. One's image or concept of the self (in the sense of oneself) has different meanings at different times.

Chapter Ten

Underlying Philosophical Problems

There are several topics relating to consciousness which have been debated at length by philosophers and which need to be included in this writing (in addition to those regarding the self). As is usual with philosophical topics, they have an important underlying bearing on the subject. One such topic is whether representations of objects are passively received by the brain or whether they are actively formed by some brain process. The philosophical question of whether the brain has an active or passive role has a direct bearing on the concept of hierarchical development of mental processes to be discussed later in detail. An active process would be a requirement for hierarchical development of perception, and hierarchical development is a pillar in our theory of consciousness.

Activity versus Passivity of Perception

The question of activity versus passivity of perception extends back to the early Greeks but was intensively renewed by Galileo, Locke, Berkeley, Hume, and Kant. One would think that if objects are outside the mind and if representations of them within the mind are to be accurate, then the mind most likely receives its impressions passively. If the mind were inventive in the formation of representations then representations of objects would hardly be true to the objects. We would not be in touch with reality. And the notion that we are not in touch with reality is strongly opposed by common sense. Yet the mind can be deceiving and common sense is often misleading when dealing with matters of the mind. The mind definitely has problems when attempting to objectively understand its own inner workings.

It is obvious that if the acquisition of perceptions were a purely passive process, the perceptions would have to be entirely supplied from the outside. This was clearly considered to be the case by the modern philosopher, William Earle (1955): "Cognition is and must be absolutely non-creative." In other words, Earle reasoned that the very end stage of perception, the final act of becoming conscious, is necessarily receptive—that it is passive. This view of consciousness implies that the reception is of some sort of image of the object. Such images are generally called sense-data or qualia. But seeing the images requires an infinite series of homunculi; all of which is a familiar story. Earle's statement was made in support of the realist approach to consciousness—that there is no inference or judgment involved. He further stated that an observer is a "pure spectator...Apprehension is

79

transparency." That is, the mind sees directly through to the object. His view squarely confronts any idealist approach. An idealist approach states that, in our perception of the world, the mind is creative to a very large extent, if not exclusively. The representationalist approach, as usual, is in the middle ground. Its representations of reality, the sense data, are considered by some philosophers to be produced by the objects, in which case the brain is relatively passive. Other philosophers consider the representations to be produced by the brain, in which case the brain actively produces the images in reaction to sensory stimulation.

In a theoretical system in which perception is totally passive, perception would be like a mirror reflecting reality rather than an individual's interpretation of what he saw or heard. There would be no process of selection, alteration, or addition to the stimulations received from the outside. Perception would be isolated from the other functions of the mind until the perception was completed. This is not in accord with well accepted views of perception in which individuals may receive quite different perceptions depending upon their backgrounds. For example, after an automobile accident the details of the accident, such as the colors of the cars involved, their speed, whether or not one vehicle traveled through a stop signal, and so forth, will differ according to different witnesses. Yet each witness is "certain" of what he or she perceived. From the neurophysiological standpoint, any change or increase in knowledge of an accident would have to result from processes which occurred after the events of the accident and would necessarily require an active process.

On the other hand, if meaning came from the brain alone, then all knowledge or perceptions would have to be inborn and merely triggered by outside stimulations into becoming conscious. Such a concept would mean that knowledge is innate, or "a priori" and this was propounded in essence by Plato, Augustine, Descartes and others. The fact that there is processing involved in an act of perception indicates that the mind is able to be active in receiving stimulations. In both the receiving of perceptions and in the building of knowledge, the mind utilizes material from within itself. In the case in which one comes upon new knowledge by reasoning alone, it is obvious that the mind performs actively.

These statements presume that the receiving of perceptions and the building of knowledge, for the most part, utilize the same mechanisms. The acquisition of knowledge would have to involve perception. In later pages we will elaborate upon the mechanisms.

There is another arrangement by means of which the brain could build knowledge or receive perceptions. Instead of one receptive system, there could be two separate systems. It is possible that representations are formed in a receptive system and that there is then a second system in which the representations are integrated. In such an arrangement the receptive system could be totally passive and the second system could then be active in integrating the representations. While such an arrangement is possible, it seems quite unlikely. In the first place, the whole idea of representations, formed either passively or actively, is strictly hypothetical, as we have discussed more than once, and begs for explanation. In the second place, to assume that the first system operates passively and, in addition, to invent a second system, which is separate and operates completely differently, is stretching the matter even further. The indications that the mind is very active in the formation of perceptions completely outweigh the arguments favoring passivity.

In the final analysis, the philosophical argument has been rendered largely moot by the advance of science. Psychology today would hardly give a second thought to the idea that perception is entirely passive. Let us be somewhat specific: Light energy falling upon the retina is subjected to processing even in that initial location. What we call "attention" is brought into play, presumably by the cerebral cortex. The attention may be directed by a strong stimulus such as a loud noise, or it may be directed as a result of one's internally stimulated interest, such as in looking up a word in a dictionary. In either case most of the light energy falling upon the retina is of no interest and is ignored, particularly the part which falls upon the peripheral areas of the retina. The remainder of the "light" is actively selected for further processing. There are three layers of cells in the retina which are involved in the reception and processing of light energy and which give rise to nerve cell impulses. After leaving the retina, the nerve cell impulses are known to go through several stages of further integration, both before and after reaching the cerebral cortex. Before consciousness occurs, these stages at the very least involve timing and rearrangement of the impulses. (To be generous toward the idea of passivity, we could assume that the chemical transformations which constitute the "reception" of the light energy by the cells of the retina, are a passive process in the sense that they are "automatic." This is particularly true of the peripheral areas of the retina where attention and consciousness are involved but considerably less so than in the central area.)

Illusions as Indicators of Activity

There are examples of perceptions which are relevant to the question of activity versus passivity and which are also relevant to the theories of both realism and representationalism. They apply whether or not representations are involved in the process of perception. Such examples include illusions, such as optical illusions, with which we are all familiar, and with some related phenomena.

Illusions are instances of perceptions which can be experienced in two different ways, each of which is correct. Such experiences have been used by philosophers to challenge many of the versions of realism. The illusions indicate that the mind is highly active in the formation of perceptions and that the concept of realism—that the mind perceives directly from the eyes and ears with an unavoidable implication of passivity—is not correct.

One instance of such perceptions is the type of optical illusion in which each of the two perceptions appear to change back and forth fairly easily. Since the object is the same in both cases and since the light energy reaching the eyes in each case is identical, it is clear that the differences in perception are not due to differences in the object. The differences in perception also cannot be due to differences in *representations* produced solely by the object. The differences must be due to cerebral processes, an interpretation which seems unassailable and is the accepted one in the field of psychology (Gleitman, 1981, b). Another example would be the well known illusion in which the foreground and background alternate as to which is the object; the foreground in one of the perceptions appears as a vase and in the other appears as two faces.

Examples such as the above have led philosophers to agree that if we cannot trust our senses in some cases, we cannot be sure they are trustworthy in any case. This doctrine has been applied to cases which have become standard fare. In one way or another, they are "misperceptions" and, similarly to the cases mentioned above, they can also be explained as the achievements of "higher" processes. They often include the following: When one hand is warm and the other is cold and they are both placed in a container of water, the temperature of the water feels different to the two hands. The temperature of the water could not be the cause of the perceived difference. Also, a straight stick appears bent when it is immersed in water; objects appear to be smaller when viewed from a distance; an object such as a penny is perceived as round even though it is observed at an angle from which the light rays emanating from it actually form an ellipse. Finally, an object such as a cloth which appears white in daylight is still interpreted as white in artificial light of a different color. We should make it clear, however, that even though the "misperceptions" can be explained as the interpretations of "higher" processes, this does not explain the mechanism by which the interpretations are made. We shall have more to say about the mechanisms later.

There are also perceptions that stem entirely from the brain or are greatly influenced by the brain. Examples of these perceptions include not only illusions but also dreams and hallucinations as well as many sensations involving sex. Various emotions such as joy and grief, while connected to an external situation, are largely from within. Emotions greatly influence perceptions of all kinds. Anxiety exacerbates pain. If one is frightened, the enemy appears larger. On the more pleasant side, if one is hungry, food tastes much better. These statements can probably be generalized to include any physical or psychological need—the greater the need the keener the gratification is felt to be.

A second instance indicating activity on the part of the mind in forming perceptions is the experience of total darkness such as is perceived in a deep cave. It is striking to be completely unable to see the movement of one's hand directly in front of one's face. This experience occurs with no stimulation of the retina. There is no object in the usual sense and no outwardly produced representation of an object and yet there is a distinct perception of darkness. The darkness itself becomes an object but since there is no visual stimulation the perception of darkness would have to be an interpretation of the *absence* of stimulation. An interpretation being the product of activity on the part of the mind, the perception of darkness puts a heavy burden on realism with its emphasis on the idea that perception is "direct"—without interpretive activity. The perception of darkness also puts a burden on theories of representationalism, which subscribe to the idea that a representation (sense-datum, quale, or otherwise) is produced entirely by the outside object.

Idealism goes far beyond the consideration of illusions in indicating that the mind is active in the formation of perceptions. One form of idealism, known as solipsism, asserts that "reality" is entirely a matter of the mind. According to Kantian idealism, we should consider it impossible to be aware of *any* objects as they actually are "in themselves", that is, apart from human observation. Strictly speaking, Kant's view of this matter seems fully correct. However, for practical purposes, the "primary qualities" (size, shape, etc.,) being measurable, are sufficiently accurate, stable, and verifiable to ordinarily impart great confidence in their portrayal of reality. The emphasis here is on the terms "ordinarily" and for "practical purposes." The accuracy of primary qualities is only relative and fails miserably as one reaches the limits of perception. In these areas, it becomes very apparent that our perceptual mechanisms mislead us greatly. For example, water which appears "pure" to the naked eye, can be seen to be full of living organisms when seen under a microscope. Under an electron microscope, even more than under a light microscope, "straight" edges are no longer straight but are grossly irregular. Theoretically, at much greater magnification, atoms would appear to be mostly empty space. And so on, presumably *ad infinitum*.

At no level would our perceptual mechanisms, even with the aid of instrumentation, reveal objects to us as they are "in themselves." As explained earlier, "secondary qualities" (color, sound, etc.) are creations of the mind and exist only in the mind as perceptions. Furthermore, perceptions of the primary qualities are interpretations of direction, mediated through the receptor mechanisms of the secondary qualities and limited by the acuteness of those mechanisms. Therefore, when we ask what objects are "truly" like we can properly mean only what they are like to the human mind. That is our only perspective. As indicated by Kant, what objects are like intrinsically ("in themselves") is unknowable. What they appear to be like depends on the sense receptors and the brain. The brain under consideration, of course, could even be other than human. As we know, bees react to light in the ultraviolet range, while dogs and bats react to sound frequencies higher than humans can perceive, and so on. The next section should help to make it clearer that the mind plays a very active part in the production of consciousness.

Directness versus Indirectness in Perception

The reader will remember that realism regards perception as being "direct." Kelly (1986) examines the concept of directness thoroughly and distinguishes between direct and indirect perception on the basis of whether or not the mind employs inference. He gives the example (p. 149) of knowing that there is a package on the table downstairs because he hears the delivery van and he knows where packages are always put. Such knowledge or perception, he calls "indirect" because it is arrived at by inference from other things of which he is aware. His hearing of the sound of the delivery van, on the contrary, is "direct" because it came to him through his senses; it was not an inference. Yet perceiving the sound of the delivery van also involves an inference. How else would he know that the sound was not that of a motorcycle, an army tank, or some other engine? In fact Kelly, himself, in the same discussion (p.147), mentions (and with this we fully agree and consider it to be most important to an understanding of consciousness), "We bring to perception an enormous fund of background knowledge..." He also mentions and accepts that, "...any conscious activity must be interpretive or constitutive." We have to think that Kelly, and to the considerable extent that his view represents that of realists in general, is being inconsistent in this instance and is underestimating the extensiveness of cerebral processing. He considers hearing the delivery van to be direct, that is, without inference, but knowing that a package is on the table he considers to be an inference. In our estimation it is a matter of where one wants to draw the line between inference and non-inference. Both hearing the van and knowing a package is on the table involve "an enormous fund of background knowledge" from which he utilizes inference. We are forced to conclude that perceptions are built, not simply received.

An example of my own, not too unlike Kelly's, may be of some help. I walked into the kitchen and said to my wife, "What is that smell? Oh, you must be cooking mushrooms", which turned out to be correct. The odor came to me through my sense of smell but it took prior knowledge and inference to perceive it as mushroom. Otherwise it would have been an entirely unfamiliar odor to me.

Perhaps the best illustrations of the shaping of perceptions by previous experience, including emotional experiences, are those in which the perceptions can be regarded as indistinct. Almost every year in Michigan one or two deer hunters are shot when they are mistaken for a deer. Such instances can be considered to be partly the result of the wish to discern the desired target. Another illustration is that of a lady who turned a corner inside her house and was startled by a relative who was standing there and with whom she was well acquainted. She screamed in horror. She later said, "He looked just like a rat!" This was apparently related to a fear originating in some previous experience. Also, common examples include the images people see in clouds, the faces of religious figures on the outside walls of churches, the perceptions obtained from Rorschach (ink blot) tests, and so forth.

Summary

Philosophers have long debated whether or not the brain has an active part in the formation of perceptions. The philosophical position of realism requires that the brain is passive and reflects reality like a mirror. To the contrary, psychologists now agree that perception indicates an active process on the part of the brain. A mechanism for the brain's activity will be discussed later under the topic of hierarchical development of perceptions.

Chapter Eleven

Location of Consciousness

Background

With the preceding material as background, we can now consider the matter of the location of consciousness. Historically, not only the brain, but the heart (Aristotle) and the liver were the suspected organs of conscious. Considering the anatomical knowledge of those times, the organs mentioned do not seem unreasonable since the elimination of them resulted in the elimination of consciousness. Descartes believed that the pineal gland, located approximately in the center of the brain, was where consciousness resided. The quest for the "seat" of consciousness has not been abandoned. In recent years, however, it is considered to be fairly certain that consciousness draws from many areas of the brain. This view has been given much support by positron emission tomography (PET scans). The instrument is able to make cross sectional color pictures of the brain while the subject is alive and conscious. Different colors indicate which areas of the brain are the most active at any particular instant. If a person is using her eyes and a conscious visual content is being experienced, the areas at the rear of the brain involved in vision are the most active—though not at all exclusively. An instant later, when an auditory content is developing, the areas on each side of the brain, which are involved in hearing, are more active. This indicates that the locations of consciousness are constantly changing and depend on which instant one is looking for them.

The question remains, however, whether or not all the sensory areas of the brain feed into a single area where consciousness occurs. The possibility that consciousness is multiple, that is, a rapid sequence which *seems* continuous, adds to the likelihood that there is no one location of consciousness, that instead consciousness occurs in numerous areas.

A compelling factor involved in the question of the location of consciousness is the dynamic character of *preconscious* processes. They consist of impulses approaching consciousness from various areas including emotions and memory. That these factors all contribute actively to the production of consciousness means that cell impulses adding to the activity would come from many parts of the brain.

Such considerations make it seem quite likely that many areas contribute in concert to consciousness and that these areas shift constantly and rapidly. It must even constitute a great oversimplification to take into consideration only the few mental functions which have been mentioned.

Consciousness, or at least elements which serve to make up consciousness, must occur at numerous sites at different instants all over the brain. These events may occur in diffuse multicellular, or possibly partly subcellular, interactions.

Consciousness Elements May Originate All Over the Body

There is another possibility as to why no "seat of consciousness" has been located, a possibility which we suggested in connection with consciousness cores. It would allow for the possibility of *consciousness elements* before the impulses complete any set course or reach any common final station where fully processed consciousness regularly results. The initial elements of consciousness may arise from peripheral levels of the nervous system instead of in the brain. In previous chapters we have already suggested that consciousness as we know it may consist of a series of contents, a concept we have called "multiplicity of consciousness." Now we wish to suggest that the elements of consciousness may originate in the periphery and not only in the brain.

We need to be clearer and more specific. It is nothing new that sensory nerves from the body go to the brain and contain the potential for information which becomes consciousness. For many years it has been assumed that the different sense modalities simply have different paths into the brain, that the brain processes each modality separately, integrates them and finally, at the end of the process, adds consciousness. For example, if the nerve cell fibers (actually the chain of fibers) originate in the retina, they proceed to areas at the rear of the brain which handle vision. If the fibers originate in the skin, within the receptors for touch, the chains of nerve cell fibers proceed to the areas of the brain which handle touch. The basic requirement for this system is the location of the fibers, both in the sense receptors at the beginning of the chain and in the brain. The fibers merely stimulate areas of the brain where consciousness resides. There are even maps drawn of the surface of the brain which show the correlation with the periphery of the body. The chemical and physical nature of the nerve fibers, whether they originate in touch receptors in the skin, in "light" receptors in the eye, or in any other receptors, are all considered to be essentially the same. The information provided to the brain is thought to depend on the destinations of the fibers and their processing in the brain. The fibers from the periphery carry impulses which merely stimulate areas of the brain which then produce consciousness.

If our postulate is correct, the arrangement would be different in that the *basic components* of consciousness would be present in the periphery. That is, the sensory elements would be in the system from the start of the sensory pathways (or in the chain of sensory neurons at some level prior to their reaching the brain). For example, the elements might be present in the form of specific molecules. Processing of these core elements, which would involve screening, arranging, registration in memory, etc., would take place in the brain where full consciousness is attained, but the actual elements of consciousness would be within the system in advance of the processing. In a very real sense then, consciousness would begin and be present in the periphery and not only in the brain. This is a radical departure from the usual thinking about the matter and we acknowledge that it is quite speculative. The whole of conventional thinking about possible mechanisms for the production of consciousness may need to be revised drastically. An immediate argument against the concept we have suggested is that the loss of a finger, an arm, or even an eye does not eliminate consciousness. There is a loss, however, of consciousness from the affected area.

We have said that consciousness is always "of" something, that there are always contents of consciousness. There is an implication that the converse is also true—that *there is no consciousness without inputs.* The "inputs to consciousness" (such language treats consciousness as an entity) are indispensable if there is to be consciousness. Hitherto the "inputs to consciousness" have been looked upon as supplying nerve cell impulses which are later converted into consciousness. But so far as we know there is nothing to exclude them from being considered to be an *integral part* of consciousness. Not only the sensory inputs from the "five senses" are an integral part of consciousness but the same would be true of the inputs from inside the body—pain, proprioception, emotion, memory, and so forth. *The raw elements of consciousness, then, may be located not only in the brain but all over the body.* It is possible that the brain is only the locus of the final processing.

Technically the eye is a part of the brain, having developed in the embryo as an outcropping of the brain. It is conceivable that in the case, particularly of the eye, a consciousness producing element is contained in incoming impulses from or near the beginning of the neural chain in the retina. What would be the nature of such an element? Since no such elements are known at this time, we should keep the field of consideration as wide as possible. In recent years it has become recognized that many different types of nerve cells emit different substances at the intercellular junctions where succeeding cells in the cellular chain are stimulated. If it is true that specific consciousness elements occur at the beginning of the neural chain in the case of vision, it is possibly true for other sensory modalities as well. It is then likely that the element is different for each of the different senses. In other words the molecules may be sense specific. This is all quite speculative, but it is not implausible.

Under the postulation we are making, information is still related to the location of fibers but *also* to differences within the fibers all along the sensory paths. Fibers from the eye contain elements, possibly in the form of molecules, which provide information about color; those fibers from the skin give information which provide for the quality of touch. The same would be true of pain or heat, etc. The brain's function would then be to effect the integration of the consciousness elements which originate in the periphery.

Location of Consciousness

As previously stated it has generally been thought that consciousness occurs as the final step of the sensory process, but it seems increasingly indicated as research develops that such a concept is too limited. Regardless, it is no wonder that the "seat of consciousness" has not been located.

Now let us elaborate. If consciousness elements do indeed arise "all over the body", then in a new sense there is no one location for consciousness. Warren McCullough, mentioned in the introduction to this book, interestingly compared locating consciousness to specifying a location for speech in a telephone system. In his plan the speech is located not only at the microphone end of the system where a person is talking at a particular moment. It is also not located only at the other end of the system where the sound waves are emitted and someone is listening. Nor is the speech located at any particular point in between. It is located throughout the system. To return to the comparison with consciousness, if the input, for example, is from the ear but it is not "interpreted" as sound until it reaches the "other end" in the brain, then consciousness is at neither location alone. It is at both locations and at all points in between. In such a scheme we could say that the process of consciousness is everywhere in the system but nowhere in particular. While McCollough's analogy is quite interesting, we would prefer, however, to regard the earlier stages as consisting of *prior elements* of consciousness and that those prior elements which are selected by the "higher centers" become consciousness.

There is no doubt that the brain has an integrating function but there is also some integration of sensory impulses (pain, proprioception, etc.,) within the spinal cord before the impulses reach the brain. It would perhaps be more accurate from this point forward for us to use the term, *nervous system,* in connection with consciousness instead of *brain* but we will usually continue to use the conventional term, *brain.* If we have not begun to sound mysterious or confusing enough, there may be even more fundamental reasons why a location, or locations, for consciousness have not been found, indeed will not be found for a number of years at the soonest. These will be discussed in later chapters and involve the relationships of consciousness to meaning and to the self as well as the idea, which will be elaborated upon, that consciousness occurs only "inside" nerve cells.

Mind-Body Problem

The discussion now brings us back to the age-old mind-body problem. Ryle regarded the mind-body problem as a "category mistake" (Michaels, 1981). By that he meant that the body, or more specifically the brain, was looked upon as physical but that the mind was *erroneously* regarded as being in an entirely different category. We are in agreement with Ryle's point and we view the mind as a collective term which refers to the functions of the brain, such as consciousness, thinking, and remembering. We can simply say then that the mind is a function of the brain or nervous system. The statement assumes that the nervous system functions within the laws of physics and chemistry and that somehow, whatever are its mechanisms, its functioning results in all of the manifestations we call the mind.

Such a statement would be disputed by some, perhaps many philosophers and even many scientists who regard the mind as entirely separate from the body. These people are known as dualists. Along with Descartes, some think of the mind as the soul or the spirit. The opposing idea, the regard of the mind as a product entirely of the brain (or body) has been called a "monist" (*monos*, Greek = single) and a "materialist" position. The remainder of this writing should help furnish background for the latter view. That the mind is a function of the brain becomes clearer the more the physiological substrate of the brain's "mental" functions become understood and are seen to underlie the actions of the mind.

Further Matters of Conventional Language and Concepts

As the reader is already aware, when discussing or writing about consciousness, there is a difficult problem with language. It would be well for the reader to be clearly cognizant of some of the problems in order to make it easier to give up erroneous, or questionable, outdated concepts. The language problem can be subtle but it is nevertheless important to examine it. Language, after all, is based on concepts and when the terms used are those which apply to former concepts, the situation not only makes it difficult to explain new ideas but also makes it easy to slip back into the old way of thinking. This is a very real problem when discussing or even thinking about consciousness.

The idea that consciousness is always "of" something has very wide acceptance: we are conscious *of* the tree or *of* the color. We agree that consciousness, as we experience it, is *of* something; it is difficult to conceive of consciousness without any content. Yet to say, as is frequently found in the literature, that consciousness is "aware of" something, that consciousness is "aware of the color", treats consciousness as if it is an entity distinct from the rest of the mind, an entity which does the perceiving, almost a thing occupying space. It implies that consciousness is separate from the color, something which observes the color. But let us not forget that the brain creates color, that consciousness is not a separate entity, not an object. It is part of the concept of the mind, a function of the brain.

Stating that consciousness is "aware of" color also tends to personify consciousness, treating consciousness as if it were the person who is "aware" or at least as if it were the person's entire mind. In addition it is within the idiom of the homunculus since consciousness is "aware of the object" but who or what is aware of the consciousness. The same can be said for the word "interprets", as in an expression such as, "consciousness interprets the nerve impulses as having color." Analyzing the terms further, they are anthropomorphic. They assign what we consider to be human attributes to entities which are not people. Consciousness, and even the mind as a whole, is a function of the brain but does not constitute a person. The terms are often equated with a person because they are central elements of what we regard as constituting an individual. Nevertheless, to think of consciousness anthropomorphically tends to make for treating it as an entity with no material basis but with mystical or practically magical properties rather than as a concept entailing various functions which need to be explored scientifically and understood in physical and chemical terms. It would be well to replace terms, which personify consciousness and the mind, with terms which are within the concept of the physiologically functioning brain.

However, it is still difficult and often clumsy to avoid using anthropomorphic expressions. We hardly have any other words to use. We will continue to use them but as sparingly as possible and often will put them in quotation marks to indicate that they are used knowingly. What has been called "the Cartesian myths" of images (representations) which the mind observes, as well as the conceptualization of the mind as some sort of non-material substance separate from the body, are indeed pervasive and enduring. The "myths" endure possibly because such ideas contain some element of truth or because they have not been clearly replaced by better concepts. As usual, such concepts began with the ancient Greeks, or earlier, and have persisted ever since (Popper, p.153ff).

Eugene M. Brooks, M.D.

Robots

We have now come to the edge of an even deeper problem. If the brain is a biological organ and the mind is a function of that organ, then they both lie within the sphere of the biological, the material. This often gives rise to the question, "How different are we from robots and in what ways?" The answer to which we are partial is that *we possess qualitative cores and consciousness, which robots do not possess,* at least not yet. Many of the sensory qualities can be simulated at the present time using cameras, microphones, and the like but we appear to be far from being able to reproduce emotion. The qualitative cores give rise to genuine sensations, sensations as we experience them, and not simply actions which *give the appearance* of stemming from sensations. Such appearances are all that robots would be capable of unless they possessed consciousness cores and what are apparently complexes of them such as love, hate, ambition, and so forth.

Researchers, who are trying to develop consciousness in computers and to have the computers operate human-like robots, need to remember that there is much more to being a human than merely having consciousness. The human infant requires decades of living and experiencing to become an adult with a full range of human sensibilities and to develop, in addition to everything else, what we call a mature personality and good judgment. The "brain" of the robot, in order to act completely like that of a human, would have to go through experiences (perhaps condensed) such as we all have in "growing up." Although, in order to save time in the development of such androids, the first "adult" robot "brain" could theoretically be copied. The copied "brains" could then have further experiences, beginning where the earlier one ended, thereby developing additional knowledge and new personality traits. The android would not have to die and its brain or mind development would not have to start over from the beginning as does that of humans.

Summary

Consciousness is clearly not located in any single area in the brain. In fact, the raw elements of consciousness, possibly consciousness cores, might be located in the nervous system peripheral to the brain. They would then be processed in the brain. Regardless, the ancient mind-body problem is no longer a complete quandary. The manifestations of consciousness and mind result from the activity of the nervous system. The mind is no longer considered to be a separate entity from the brain or composed of a mysterious separate substance as believed by Descartes. Robots differ from people primarily in that they possess only simulated consciousness cores. They do not possess genuine consciousness.

Chapter Twelve

Synecdoche

Synecdoche in General

There is another concept which is vital to the complex of factors resulting in consciousness. Recall that nerve impulses, before they reach the level of consciousness, are referred to as "preperceptual." Such nerve impulses might be those that arise, for example, in the visual system prior to their reaching the cerebral cortex.

It is often thought that the separate preperceptual aspects, such as shape, size, color, etc., are recombined in the mind to form a perception of a single, whole object. As discussed earlier, Locke (publication 1974, also Joad, 1957) held the contrary view that the separate aspects were not actually united. Berkeley and Hume agreed with their predecessor in maintaining that the separate aspects were not reunited. In their thinking the separate aspects were simply found to be together sufficiently often to become associated together in the mind. By extending their logic, however, Berkeley and Hume were forced to take extreme idealist positions. Berkeley (publication 1952) reasoned that objects existed only when being perceived. To explain why objects did not cease to exist when a human was not observing them, he invoked the mind of God. As long as God was observing the objects they would exist. Extending Berkeley's reasoning, Hume (publication 1974) eliminated God and ended at the idealist position that logically objects do not exist at all.

Yet common sense tells us unequivocally that we do perceive objects, that the separate aspects of objects are recombined in our minds. But this recombination could hardly be as complete as it appears in our consciousness. Let us turn our attention to a function which the brain regularly performs. This function is given specific recognition in the analysis of poetry. It is the figure of speech known as synecdoche and can be defined as that figure in which a part represents the whole. An example of synecdoche would be, "He got his wheels when he became sixteen years of age." "Wheels" refers to an automobile, not simply wheels; yet our minds understand or get the impression of a whole automobile. We can apply "synecdoche" to the general functioning of the mind. Suppose one makes an effort to mentally picture an automobile. One usually imagines only one or two aspects of the vehicle. One might recall a profile or some other feature but there are many features that are not pictured—the size, the color, the design of the hub caps, the front grill, the number of doors, or even the slight dent in the door panel. While one or two aspects that are pictured are the ones which are registered, there are many other features of the automobile which are available from memory. If one attempts to bring them into consciousness, these supporting details are available immediately and "automatically" so to speak. The "backup" aspects would seem to be very helpful or even crucial in the success which the synecdoche process has in giving the illusory impression that a whole object has been perceived. In short, only one or two features of the automobile suffice in "picturing" the vehicle. It is thus not necessary to recombine a complete complement of aspects. In fact, since the number of features observable in most objects is unlimited, to recombine all of them to form the perception of the object would be impossible.

An article by Fischbach (1992) states,

> A tennis player who wanders to the net from time to time will be alarmed to learn that the movement, color, and shape of a tennis ball are processed in different [cerebral] cortical centers. Separation of these information streams *begins in the retina* [italics added]; they remain segregated in … the primary visual cortex en route to the higher visual [areas].

(This statement is not only relevant to the way vision is processed. As we have discussed earlier, there is an implication, at least in the case involving vision, that since the segregation process begins in the retina the primary elements of consciousness may well be in the sensory nervous system from the beginnings of that system.) There is a suggestion that if the features are handled separately, they may well become conscious separately. They do not have to be recombined for one to become conscious of the ball. The "ball" may be an inference, a synecdoche, and is not perceived in any single instant in its entirety or anything near its entirety. The "alarm" of the tennis player indicates that he assumes upon seeing the tennis ball that he sees all of its features. It appears as if all of the features are somehow combined by the brain into one perception. However, we would like to suggest that the synecdoche process makes such a recombination unnecessary. It seems unlikely that the tennis player sees the "ball" coming toward him. He only gets the impression that he sees the "ball." He may see only two or three of its features and probably only one of them *in any single instance of consciousness.* To see as many of the features of the ball as he is capable of attending, he needs to see its shape and color, its trajectory, its speed, its location in relation to himself, to the boundary lines, and so forth.

A further point crucial to the idea of synecdoche, as in the example of the automobile, is that the tennis player would be able to *support his perception* of the ball from memory. He could recall any features of the ball, even without conscious effort if he had any need to do so, in order to complete his impression of the ball. If necessary he could also make further physical observations of the ball.

Other examples of the synecdoche effect will probably be useful: We walk into a room and walk out again. We then feel that we have seen the "room." Actually we obviously did not see all of the features in the room. Yet when we think we saw the room, we generally mean we saw most or all of it. When we recall the appearance of an individual we do not recall all of the features. Again, that would be impossible. We most likely recall one or two features, which gives us the impression that we remember the "person" more or less in entirety. We do not question whether we registered each and every feature of the person. We are satisfied that we saw the individual.

Synecdoche makes the perception of objects basically similar to the perception of concepts and memories. All three are interpretations. (As will be explained later, they are also meanings.) One merely has the *impression* of perceiving a whole object, a complete concept, or a whole item of memory. Hodgson (1994) mentions,

> In our conscious perceptions we seem to experience 'all-at-once' many features of what is perceived. In vision, for example, we experience all-at-once and non-sequentially shapes *and* colours *and* movement. This totality must be provided by myriad neuronal processes in different parts of the brain. These processes seem to be physically linked only by nerve signals propagating at less than the speed of light; so how can the processes combine to form a unified experience? I don't believe that either classical physics or the materialist consensus can give any answer. I contend that quantum non-locality offers the best prospects for explaining this unity of consciousness; and that this suggests that consciousness is associated with quantum level events in the brain, and thus with quantum indeterminism.

Quantum events are phenomena involving ultra small particles which have odd properties and some of which have notably resisted explanation even by physicists. While we are not ready to endorse Hodgson's opinion that quantum effects are needed to explain consciousness, his statement helps to support the need for an explanatory mechanism such as synecdoche. Further, synecdoche mechanisms involve much smaller theoretical leaps than do quantum effects.

The synecdoche principle applies quite generally in mental processes. Further examples will indicate its extensiveness. It is not only involved in the conscious perception of objects, it is also used in retrieval from memory. Indeed most recollections and concepts as well as "ideas" must also be handled as synecdoches. We are not in conscious possession of as many details as we think. The synecdoche represents a size much larger than its own length. This is occasionally exemplified when one attempts to express an idea and one finds that the idea is quite incomplete in consciousness. Similarly, it can be felt that a particular object's appearance is well known, but when there is the need to describe the object, only a very few features are actually available. On the other hand, a speaker may receive the opposite impression when words seem to come to mind immediately and without the slightest effort. On the surface this seems as if the words are all constantly present in consciousness. Nevertheless, words have to be retrieved from memory. This is made obvious when, in speaking, one has to grope to find them. The idea, which is a synecdoche, is present in consciousness, but the words and the details surrounding the idea are within memory.

The above examples are also indicative of another important aspect of synecdoche, a time saving feature. Since it is an abbreviated form of activity it contributes greatly to the rapidity of mental functioning. This aspect of synecdoche will be presented in the next chapter.

Synecdoches seem to serve essentially the same functions as symbols but we would give synecdoche a somewhat broader meaning. A most common example of a symbol is the flag which represents the United States. Words may also be symbols in that they represent ideas. But words are synecdoches as well as symbols in that the ideas behind words may be very extensive and the mind understands much more than is actually presented, On the contrary, the visualization of an object such as the tennis ball mentioned above, is not conventionally considered to involve a symbol but it is a synecdoche. In short, the concept of synecdoche applies to both the perception of objects and to symbols.

Ebb (p.46), who relied on psychological studies, made the observation that, "There is plenty of evidence in children's drawings, and in adult errors in perspective drawings, to show that a person looking at an object thinks that he sees much more of it than he does." Perhaps a somewhat trivial but common example which must involve a synecdoche process is the drawing which uses only the outlines of objects or the "stick drawings" of people which are readily understood to represent entire people.

Illustration No. 6

There once was a man

who had no hair.

It grew so fast

he wasn't there.

Synecdoche in Stick Drawings

The mind is in a sense misled. It perceives a mere part to be the whole. The enlarged impression is usually most fortuitous as it no doubt allows for tremendous efficiency in mental "work." Consider how it would be virtually impossible to visually perceive *any* object if we had to become conscious of every visual aspect that made up the appearance of the whole object. Every object larger than the smallest perceptible point reflects innumerable light "rays" which would reach our eyes and which would need to be registered as part of the object.

If we turn our attention from the perception of "simple" visual objects, to more complex perceptions, it becomes even more obvious that a part is taken to represent the whole. This requires a shift in the meaning of "perception" but the change is a legitimate one. Whether the perception is of a visual object, as we usually think of perception, or a more ideational one, in both cases the mind has to form an *understanding* which is broader than the sensory inputs alone. To "get the point" of a statement or of a joke is the *perception of a meaning.* (The italicized words suggest a very close relationship between perception and meaning and give an inkling of what we will have to say later about their relationship.)

If synecdoche is useful it can also be unfortunate. As is well known, first impressions of people can be very incorrect and influenced by prejudices. Preconceived notions and partial knowledge of subjects often result in misperceptions or hasty judgments. Consider racial prejudices, or misconstrued interpretations of statements regarding politics or religion. These examples generally involve considerable emotion but even calmer, more deliberate judgments, such as those supposedly involved in business meetings or committees are frequently based on quick or incomplete consideration of the issues. Indeed, to be exact about the matter, do we *ever* base our perceptions on *all* aspects of objects or on all matters which are relevant to issues? Compulsive people do so more than others but at the expense of delaying action. Synecdoche is both a blessing and a curse, but in any case it is the way the mind works.

Kelly (p. 144) states, "What we perceive are entities as wholes, as units possessing properties [aspects], not the properties themselves as units." The import of synecdoche is that what we *ordinarily assume* to be sensory input is in reality only a part. The rest is an impression supplied not by the object but by the mind itself. Perception is much more than the clues supplied by sensory input.

Synecdoche and Representationalism

For the mind to become conscious of a representation, the usual theory of representationalism brings into play the implication of a theoretical central observer or a homunculus which is needed to complete the consciousness. Then further central observers are required, *ad infinitum.* In contrast to this, because the synecdoche uses only a part to stand for the whole, we view the synecdoche as eliminating the need for a representation of a *whole* object.

The question can now arise, if the synecdoche process eliminates the need for representations of whole objects, can it eliminate the need for representations altogether? Does it eliminate the need of representations for parts of objects—the separate aspects? We would have to answer that synecdoche alone does not eliminate the need. The synecdoche process would still not answer whether or not representations are formed of the separate aspects. It merely means that *whole* objects are not needed for perception and shifts the problem of representations to the smaller dimensions.

It would be gratifying at this point to pursue the discussion of representations further. We cannot complete the matter, however, because in order for the reasoning to be intelligible we must first develop some other concepts. We will therefore defer the consideration of representations to subsequent pages. But we wish to add, to avoid any misunderstanding, that synecdoche does not explain how the final consciousness of an object occurs. It is only part of the process which leads to consciousness.

The synecdoche concept could evoke criticisms from many philosophers on the basis that synecdoche implies idealism, that the mind is not actually in touch with objects but is in touch with only aspects of them, and therefore is not in touch with reality. The answer to such a criticism is that the mind is in touch with what the perceiver normally regards as reality even though it is not in touch to the extent that the perceiver thinks it to be. The mind is in touch to the limits of our senses. The Kantian view that ultimate reality is "unknowable" helps to support the concept of synecdoche. We know only some aspects of objects, but feel that we know the entire object. However, as we had to discontinue our discussion in the matter of representations, we shall also discontinue the discussion of synecdoche at this point. We shall return to it later at which time we will suggest neurophysiological mechanisms which may underlie it.

Summary

It would be impossible to perceive all aspects of objects in a single observation. Synecdoche is the figure of speech in which a part represents the whole. A synecdoche mechanism is regularly used by the mind in the perception and recollection of objects and of ideas. It contributes greatly to the rapidity of mental functioning.

Chapter Thirteen

Extracting the Consistently Associated

"Shorthand"

As the writing of this book progressed it became clear to us that consciousness is actually a form of meaning—that the two are the same. We shall explain this in a later chapter but until then we shall treat them as separate concepts and in relation to meaning we shall use conventional language.

Meanings which enter consciousness from memory can do so in extremely swift succession. For example, in reading the prior sentence, each word has its own meaning and, even though it takes less than a second to read the entire sentence, the different meanings register in the mind. Judging from the speed with which this transpires, the meanings which are stored in memory must be retrieved in some *rapid or shorthand* form. One such form, synecdoche, was discussed in the previous chapter and will be mentioned again here in relation to the speed of mental functioning. Synecdoche is used not only in the receiving of information from the environment but also in the retrieval of meanings from memory.

Memory items very often become conscious in the form of a synecdoche. Some central or essential element is all that needs to be retrieved. It produces the impression of being a complete memory because more details are immediately and "automatically" present if sought for. The phenomenon of seeming to have been present all the time or "automatically" present is very common. Quite often in speaking, for instance, the words seem to come to mind immediately and without the slightest effort. Nevertheless, the words have to be retrieved from memory; they are not present in consciousness at all times. This is made obvious when, in speaking, the words are not immediately present and one has to grope to find them. Sometimes an association path is consciously used: "I think the word begins with an 'a'... Oh, yes! The word is 'automatically.'"

Psychologically meanings are apparently complex hierarchical structures which are developed from simple beginnings. The same must be true of their neurophysiological substrate. To understand the meaning of the word "consciousness", for instance, requires considerable prior knowledge. Despite the rapidity with which the nervous system functions, meanings could hardly be reprocessed and redeveloped from their earliest beginnings each time they are summoned into consciousness. In order to find and verbalize a commonly used word, the mind would be unlikely to take the time to trace the development of the meaning of the word through all of the related experiences back to childhood when the word was first learned. For example, in a current situation, the brain could hardly redevelop the knowledge that four is the square root of sixteen beginning with the learning of numbers and then append the concept of multiplication, the memorization of four times four, that the square of four is sixteen, the development of the concept of square root, and finally the square root of sixteen is four. And, of course, our statement of the development has been shortened greatly, mentioning only major stages in the learning process.

Since computer functioning is often regarded as being somewhat analogous to the functioning of the mind, we will describe the computer mechanism to illustrate both what we mean by "shorthand" and a method for the "shorthand" or rapid retrieval of items from memory. Let us caution the reader not to construe this illustration from computer programming as an indication that computers function to any large extent like the brain. There are probably similarities but they are limited. We use the computer example merely to concretely illustrate a process of "shorthand."

To those familiar with computer programming, the retrieval of meanings appears to be superficially akin to the way computers can combine and retrieve symbols which represent words. Several symbols can be combined and handled as a single symbol. The result is a great saving in the time required for manipulation of the symbols. For example, X can be designated by the programmer of the computer to equal the sentence, "I have a dog." Y can then be designated to equal, "His name is Spot." Finally, Z can be designated to equal X plus Y. If the programmer then has the computer print the content symbolized by Z, it does so as, "I have a dog. His name is Spot."

Printing the two sentences requires retrieval of the content of the symbols—what the symbols represent. In order to print the content of Z, the computer must actually search its "memory" and make connections to the physical locations where the contents of X and Y are stored and then combine their contents. In the example above, if the computer printed only the letter Z, the person seeing the Z would have no understanding of its meaning. However, the brain functions differently. It manages to use some method of "shorthand" in conveying meaning. As rapidly as the brain performs, it would not be fast enough to go back in time to locate, combine, and retrieve all the contents which comprise concepts. For example, in the sentence above which was symbolized by Z, a person would need prior knowledge in order to understand the meanings of "dog" and "name."

Extracting and Remembering the Consistently Associated

Learning involves the bringing of new material into consciousness. It also involves the extraction of particular items from overall experience and their retention in memory. The extraction of items from larger experience is a mechanism in addition to synecdoche by which perceptions are quickly acquired. Perceptions which are related or relevant to a purpose and which are *consistently associated* together may be readily and efficiently remembered. An example of such retention, which has been studied extensively by psychologists, is rote learning as in the memorization of poetry or the learning of a speech. In this type of learning it is generally recognized that repetition of items, which are related in meaning and are in conjunction physically or temporally, greatly enhances rapid memorization. By reading the words (and ideas) repeatedly, since they are consistently associated, they are committed to memory. Daily living is full of activities which are associated and retained in memory. Simply hearing a series of separate musical notes, particularly if they are heard more than once, is apt to result in associating the notes together and remembering them as a tune. Consistently seeing another person and hearing her name assists in retaining the association. Another common example is the relating and retaining together the dual elements of phrases such as the names of cities with their states. Such retentions are often accomplished with little volition or attention. Much, if not most, learning is accomplished either deliberately or automatically in this manner.

Pavlov's dogs (1927) furnish an excellent example from the laboratory of the effects of consistent association. Consistent association in this case has been called "conditioned response." Stimuli such as the sound of a bell, which are found by the animal to be repeated, are retained in association with the receiving of food. This results in salivation. Other stimuli, such as the color or style of the experimenter's clothes are not consistent. The memory of these is not retained and there is no salivation. It takes several repetitions of the experiences for the animal to accomplish the necessary extractions of the consistently associated elements.

Computers combine strings of words and numerals very efficiently and "remember" them perfectly. However, there is a very important difference between the theoretical process used by the brain and that used by computers. Unlike the functioning of computers, the memory items of a person are not simply added serially to each other to form larger, more extensive units. It seems clear that memories, to result in "shorthand" retention and to be quickly available, need to be extracted. This suggests that the essential, relevant elements of an item are the elements which are retained, while the non-essential elements are not preserved within the same neurological structure. For example, traveling a particular route in an automobile more than once or twice produces memory of the route without special effort.   One remembers the essential elements such as the appearances of buildings and so forth where one has to make turns.

The questions now arise, "How does the brain know to remember the particular buildings? How does the brain know which are the essential elements of an experience that should be extracted and remembered? If the brain has no homunculus within it, how does it know which elements of an experience it should retain?'   Information is very often acquired unconsciously, that is, without volition and without the realization that one is doing so. There are also intellectual and emotional indications as to what is relevant and important and, in addition, the consistently associated items are those which tend to be retained in memory.

Extracting and Motor Skills

The process of extracting essential elements as a result of consistent association would seem to be a fundamental process in mental activity not only in intellectual learning but also in the acquisition of physical skills. In a physical skill, such as in learning the series of actions in combing one's hair, playing a piano or riding a bicycle, the non-essential physical components of the activity are allowed to be lost, while the essential components are retained. The essential components are those which work the best, those which make the activity smoother, swifter, more accurate, and more efficient in terms of time and energy requirement. The selection of the essential components, with the elimination of the inessential ones, proceeds both at a conscious and at an unconscious level.

Experience also results in *greater specificity* as to the elements which are associated and retained. If a child feels frightened of a *brown dog which is barking*, the child extracts from the experience. She retains the memories of the *brown color* and the *barking* in connection with dogs. If she later sees a *white* dog which is *barking*, she remembers only *dogs* and the *barking* as the elements which are frightening.   The element of *color* is not consistently associated and, after several experiences, is not retained in connection with the fear. As she grows older, the child learns to eliminate barking, as fear producing (unless it is associated with other cues such as growling, baring of teeth, and so on). The memories are thus repeatedly *refined by experience* with the consistently associated (and therefore relevant) memories being extracted from earlier memories and the non-retention of the irrelevant ones. The repetition of the activity allows for further and further refinement of the process. In short, "practice makes perfect."

Infants in the first weeks of life generally require a few repetitions before they make the needed extractions and learn to recognize or become "accustomed" to the sound of the mother's voice. (This may be a large part of the "bonding" to the mother which takes place.) When they are a little older, on the other hand, they learn some things very quickly, as exemplified by their learning from a single visit to be afraid of the pediatrician in his white coat.

Not only in humans but also in the lower animals, activities which are consistently associated are often retained. Cows in a pasture quickly learn to go to the barn at milking time after being milked there a few times. Even birds learn to look for food in a particular feeder. The learning in such examples requires neither "intelligence" nor "judgment" beyond the level of association (experience). More complicated actions, such as teaching dogs to "sit" or "heel", require several associations and it is important that the associations be consistent.

Difference Between Extracting the Consistently Associated and Synecdoche

Let us be clear about the difference between extracting the consistently associated and synecdoche. There is actually an element of meaning involved in both of the functions but the meaning is central to the concept of synecdoche while it is secondary to the concept of extracting. As in the example of Pavlov's dogs, extracting presumes that the extracted item (the ringing of the bell) has meaning or relevance to the dog but the emphasis is on the consistent association of the observed element with another element which is within memory (the dog associates the ringing of the bell with food). In the process of extracting, an element is isolated from other elements with which it is associated in an experience. The extracted element is then associated in memory with a second item, as when a name is associated with a face, or as in an example mentioned earlier, separate notes are remembered and associated as a tune. In synecdoche a part is isolated from a larger context and given the meaning of the whole. In the example of the musical notes, several notes call to mind the tune. In our example of hearing, "He got his wheels when he was sixteen" a larger *meaning* of automobile was obtained from the mention of wheels. Nevertheless, in a sense a synecdoche can be an extraction of the consistently associated (wheels can be consistently associated with automobiles) but the essential element in synecdoche is that a meaning is derived, a part represents a whole. The synecdoche is more than simple association. Another example of a synecdoche would be a teacher's telling a room full of students "Take your seats please." This means more than "Sit down." It also means "Come to order. The class is beginning." Rapidity of function and mental efficiency is accomplished in both extraction of the consistently associated and in synecdoche but in synecdoche the efficiency is accomplished at a higher intellectual level. Extraction of the consistently associated can occur at a level requiring little or no intellectual involvement, that is, little or no understanding.

Extracting from Memory

The relationship between extracting and memory warrants further attention. The process of extracting the consistently associated must perform in the same manner for items which are brought from memory into consciousness as for items which are brought from the outer world into consciousness. Notice that in both cases there are inputs which become conscious. Furthermore, the inputs from memory are extracted and are often refined and given greater specificity just as are inputs from the environment. An example in support of this principle is the manner in which perceptions are sharpened by the acquisition of new information. Seeing a movement in the brush (the environment) turns out to be a deer upon closer observation. Seeing a woman might initiate the thought, "That is not Mary. Mary is shorter than that."

Each time one has a new input which becomes consciousness, the input is matched and combined with a preexisting item from memory. This reawakening of the memory item reinforces it, that is, the more a memory item is reawakened and used the more readily it is brought into consciousness. The more a child uses the multiplication tables, the better he or she remembers them. The more the child reads, the better he or she becomes at doing so. We wish to emphasize that the process described happens automatically. In the ongoing controversy over the best way to teach children, particularly arithmetic, it is well known that improvement can occur without the child's understanding the underlying processes by which the multiplication or the division is accomplished. We shall discuss a possible physiological mechanism for reinforcement after we have discussed memory hierarchies.

Summary

In addition to synecdoche, discussed in the previous chapter, the brain uses other methods of "shorthand", that is, rapidly registering information as well as retrieving it. Items which are consistently associated in experience tend to be retained. This is true both of perceptions and of motor activities. Each time a memory is made conscious, elements of it are extracted and recombined. This produces reinforcement of the memory as well as refinement.

Chapter Fourteen

Contributions from Physiology

Let us consider by way of speculation exactly what physiological mechanisms produce the consciousness cores. As we have said previously, we conceive of the consciousness cores as the elemental qualitative aspects of perceptions. What are they physiologically speaking? Are their fundamental mechanisms intracellular or intercellular? Are they chemical or physical? Zohar (1990) and Penrose (1994), if they were to accept the concept of such cores, might suggest that quantum effects are responsible. The thinking of Crick and Koch (1990) has been along the lines of a synchronized 40 Hz (40 cycles per second) rhythm of brain cells. The final answers are, of course, not known at this time but a number of suggestions from neurophysiology point the way.

Neuroanatomy

Before discussing the possible physiological mechanisms a brief description of nerve cells and neuroanatomy will be helpful. Brain cells and nerve cells in general are composed of a central, often globular "body" which has slender, root-like arms extending from it. (See illustration number 7.) The arms may be quite short or may be very long and may have many branches. They are called dendrites if they conduct impulses toward the cell body. If they conduct impulses away from the cell body they are called axons.

Illustration No. 7

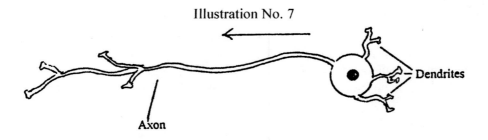

Axon

Dendrites

Nerve Cell

Such extensions make functional contact with other nerve cells, that is, they establish a chain of intercellular conductivity. The cell bodies of the sensory nerves, which supply the periphery of an individual's body are generally located in groups alongside the bones of the spinal column. From there they send their fibers to the skin, muscles, bones, and other tissues. They also send shorter fibers inward to the spinal cord where they stimulate other nerve cells which, in turn, send impulses to the brain. Nerve cells of all types number in the billions and each may have hundreds or thousands of fibers which carry impulses to or from other cells.

It is known that the different sense modalities have different types of receptor organs or organelles. These are microscopic bodies which are located, for example, in the skin at the ends of their respective nerve fibers. In the eye they are located in the "rods" and "cones" of the retina; in the ear, in the "hair cells" of the cochlea.

Illustration No. 8

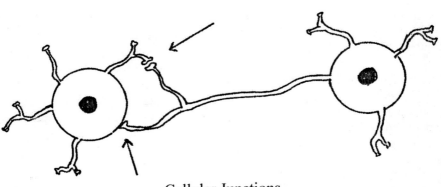

Cellular Junctions

Intercellular Transmitters

We have previously touched upon several possibilities as to the physiology of the consciousness cores. One possibility mentioned was that the consciousness cores may possibly be embodied in sensory nerve cell impulses. More specifically the cores may be related to molecules which carry messages between different types of nerve cells which send impulses to and within the brain. According to Fischbach in 1992 (p. 51) there were about fifty such substances which were known. The list of such molecules has undoubtedly increased considerably since then. Such substances are extruded at the junction of two cells, the junction being called a synapse. (Arrows in illustration No. 8.) The molecules are known as synaptic or intercellular transmitters. When a nerve impulse is conducted from the body toward the brain, the transmitters are extruded from the cell which is more distant from the brain and cause the stimulation of an impulse in the cell which is closer to the brain.

The differences between the various types of consciousness cores could result from differences in the internal chemical composition of the diverse nerve cells as well as from variations in their intercellular transmitters. In fact, since there definitely are distinct transmitters, the chemical compositions of the cells which manufacture and extrude these substances would necessarily be different, in at least some respects, from other cells of other types.

Do such molecules constitute "cores" of the perceptions? There is much evidence that such molecules are important in connection, for example, with emotion. One type of synaptic transmitter, called the enkephalins, is involved in depression. Another one is called dopamine. Antidepressant medications are designed to suppress the effectiveness of these molecules and the salutary effect of these medications provide a strong suggestion that intercellular transmitter substances correlate with consciousness cores or at least play a significant role in relation to them.

It is known that there are many types of nerve cells. This is quite apparent from the distinct differences in size and shape when seen under the microscope. Some are large, others are small. Some are round, others elongated or pyramidal. Some have many branchlike fiber projections from the cell body, others have few, etc. Different types are grouped together in different locations in the brain and other areas of the nervous system. Also, as mentioned, there are chemical differences. It would be compatible with the concepts of consciousness which we are presenting, for the qualitative cores to stem from some of the different types of sensory nerve cells, each type producing its own quality of consciousness. The explanation of the large number of different qualitative aspects of consciousness would not be problematical to this theory. The countless number of brain cells must contain a sufficient number of different types of cells to provide the needed variation. The synaptic transmitters, in many cases at least, do much more than simply carry nonspecific nerve impulses from one nerve cell to another. It is conceivable that they are involved in the specialization of consciousness cores.

We will speculate that there is even no need to conceive of the nerve cells, which produce the qualitative core elements, as being limited exclusively to the brain. It was previously mentioned that, in the case of the retina, which is an outgrowth of the brain, it is possible that potential consciousness producing elements, such as specific molecules, are contained in incoming nerve impulses throughout the cellular chain. Even the senses from the periphery of the body, such as touch and temperature appreciation, could be mediated by cellular chains which contain the elements for qualitative cores.

Emotion

We wish to emphasize that we consider the emotions to be consciousness cores. As with the other consciousness cores they consist of unique qualities. Also, as with the other consciousness cores, we do not regard the emotions as needing to be appreciated by a separate organ of consciousness. *They are a form of consciousness.* This will be explained further in connection with the identity theory.

We know our emotions, as we do the other consciousness cores, only from introspection, that is, from what is often called the first person perspective. We know the emotions of other people only from the way they appear or from the way they describe their feelings, but we cannot know their emotions first hand.

Similar to some of the sense modalities, particularly taste and smell, it is not known whether or not there are primary emotions which combine to produce the numerous shades of emotional feeling which we experience. Some of the emotions seem to be elemental and, if so, we would consider them to be consciousness cores. Depression has been considered to be a primary emotion and the specificity of the effect of antidepressant medications tends to support this view. Pleasure and anger might also be examples of consciousness cores.

According to Freud, love, although he leaves it somewhat ill defined, is considered to be a primary emotion. Anxiety would also be considered to be primary even though its workings are not always apparent at the conscious level. Freud considered anxiety to be the same as fear with the exception that he regarded fear as being related to something which was known to the individual, while anxiety was not connected with anything of which the individual was aware. He attributed the feeling known as guilt to an underlying anxiety about possible disapproval or punishment from other people.

The emotions are perhaps different from the other consciousness cores in that they seem to accompany or to be merged with the other cores. It is doubtful that any inputs to consciousness are completely devoid of emotion. They can, however, be repressed or not recognized as such by the individual undergoing the emotion.

Modules

Techniques have been perfected in the last several years by means of which pathways of individual nerve fibers in the brain can be traced (Fischbach 1992). This can be accomplished by using,

> ...a variety of molecules...[which] are transported along nerve fibers. Such transporter molecules can be visualized under a

microscope once the tissue is properly prepared. Connections have also been traced by fine tipped microelectrodes positioned close enough to a nerve cell body [or nerve fiber] to detect the small currents generated as an impulse passes by.

These techniques have shown that cells and small columns of cells in the brain and the retina, called modules, are interconnected functionally and act as a unit in responding to specific visual features. To simplify the neurological functioning of the modules we can consider them to be like boards containing holes through which pegs fit. Let the holes correspond to the modular nerve cells. The pegs correspond to nerve cell fibers. The fibers bring impulses, for instance from the retina, to the modular cells which in turn relay the impulses onward toward the cerebral cortex. If the holes are arranged in a vertical line and the pegs have a similar arrangement, then the pegs will go through the holes (the impulses will stimulate the cells which will relay them further). If the pegs are arranged in a horizontal or diagonal manner they will not fit through the holes (impulses will not be relayed onward).

The physical arrangement of the modular cells thus have the effect of being like a screen. They allow impulses which have the proper pattern to pass through and screen out impulses which do not have the proper arrangement. To leave the analogy and to return to an actual neurological situation, let us assume that light energy striking the retina has a particular arrangement; let us say it is arranged in a vertical line. The rods and cones of the retina upon which the energy impinges then have the same physical relationship and the nerve cell fibers leaving the retina reach the modules still retaining that arrangement. The modular cells, having a similar arrangement, relay the impulses onward where they eventually become consciousness as vertical lines. Now let's assume that the retina is stimulated by a horizontal line. The impulses would extend *across* the line of the vertically arranged modular cells and therefore would not be transmitted farther. Impulses which have a horizontal arrangement are allowed to pass through by different modules.

The overall concept of modules is that various aspects of sensory stimulations are segregated and allowed to proceed. The remainder of the sensory stimuli are screened out. This is a process of selection and filtration. Supposedly, modules which transmit different features are involved in simultaneous processing of the impulses associated with each of the features. In the cat and monkey, and most likely in humans, such modules react to edges of solid bodies as well as the orientation of edges in space—vertical, horizontal, or diagonal (Hubel, 1962). Similar mechanisms apply to some shapes. Certain modules react to the impulses which result from particular "colors" (that is, result from particular wavelengths of light). There is also evidence that motion is separately discriminated.

It has been thought that the outputs of modules may be regrouped or recombined at a higher level to become consciousness (Blakemore, 1979; Penrose, 1989; Restak, 1991). The putative reintegration is frequently referred to in the relevant literature as "where it all comes together" to form a single percept. The mechanism by which it happens is not known and has been called the "binding problem." Nevertheless we believe the "coming together" may not be as complete as it seems to the perceiver. For instance, if the outputs of the modules are not recombined, or if only a few of them are recombined, instead of being reconnected they may become consciousness in rapid succession thereby giving the impression of a single perception. It is also possible that the outputs of the modules may be one of the neurological bases for synecdoches: The outputs which are individual features may be interpreted by the mind as the whole object.

The knowledge of modules is of recent vintage but it seems reasonable to speculate that the principle involved in modular filtration might have a much wider application than the mere segregation of vertical and horizontal lines and the like. The principal of filtration possibly extends to even the highest levels of organization, to the level of the recognition of objects and the grasping of ideas and so forth. A hypothetical neurophysiological system for such complex levels will be developed further in the next section and in later chapters in connection with "matching" against levels of memory hierarchy.

Plasticity

Neurophysiology has certainly barely scratched the surface of what there is to be known about perceptual processes. Nevertheless enough is known to give some hints of the picture. A brief review of selected physiology is in order.

There are various indications that many cells of the brain become permanently interconnected according to the stimulation they receive. This occurs in a major way at different stages during development in early life. There is considerable evidence for this.

Modules react to the outlines of familiar faces such as the face of an infant's mother. This reaction involves what is known as "plasticity." It is accomplished by the actual physical growth of new connecting links between brain cells or by the retraction of existing links (Penrose, 1989). Such extensions are known as dendritic spines or synaptic knobs. The spines are small outgrowths on the arms of the brain cells.

Apparently plasticity is involved in the formation of modules as they develop in response to the pattern of environmental stimuli. It is thought to be involved in a mechanism of learning. It constitutes evidence that learning can result in neurocellular growth or change, that is, a change in the physical "wiring" of the brain. Such a process was long suspected before it was verified. It means that the brain literally wires itself in response to some experiences, at least those which are often repeated and occur early in life. This would be equivalent to a computer's programming itself in reaction to the use made of it. Common experience teaches us that if a human is to learn to play a musical instrument or to develop various other motor skills well (skills involving muscular movement and coordination), she must develop them largely in childhood. Even the more intellectual skills such as the learning of language and reading are much more easily developed in childhood.

Observations of animals are also applicable. The mechanism is probably involved in the way human infants and many baby animals learn very quickly to recognize their mothers. Baby zebras learn to recognize the individual stripe patterns of their mothers and baby giraffes learn to recognize their mothers' spot patterns. According to Ornstein (1991), "Kittens raised so that they see only horizontal lines can never develop the capacity to detect vertical lines to the same degree as horizontal lines." Also, "...when kittens are raised in the dark. Without the opportunity to use both eyes together, in the critical developmental period, the kittens can never develop the capacity to overlap the visual fields of the two eyes."

Experiments with birds indicate that baby birds which, in the first week or two of life, are prevented from hearing their parents sing, never learn to sing. It has long been known that newly hatched ducklings will "imprint" upon the mother duck. If, instead of the mother duck, a human is present at the time that the ducklings hatch they will "imprint" upon the human. They will then follow the human as if he or she is their mother. In the laboratory, brain cells have been seen to grow their wire-like arms in order to connect with other cells according to the type of message which is being carried. There are many other indications that the interconnections of many of the brain cells depends upon the stimulation they receive.

Association

It was Locke and Berkeley who enunciated the extensive role of association in mental processes. Also, as mentioned by Gleitman (b),

'...other philosophers dating back to Aristotle believed that the associative principle was demonstrated by the chain of thought. We often jump from idea to idea until we arrive at a point that seems altogether different from where we started.' Basically 'association' means 'connection.'

> Associationists believe that all learning can be described as the establishment of associative bonds and all remembering as their appropriate evocation. (Gleitman, c)

While many memory traces are permanently present in storage, access to them and bringing them into consciousness requires a path or connecting link—an association. The connecting links are similarities or relationships between two experiences. These may be several and any one may result in a recollection. Examples of this abound: a name suggests a face and vice-versa; a first name produces recollection of the last name; the sound of a voice reminds one of a certain person; a song brings an experience into consciousness.

There are undoubtedly relationships which do not result in consciousness as soon as a new perception is registered but which become consciousness later, depending upon the configuration of interests and anxieties at the later moment. For example, we meet a person whose face is somewhat familiar and later recollect the incident in which we met the individual. There are also associations which do not become consciousness at all. For instance, it has been found that students perform better on an examination when the examination is held in the same room where a course is taught. We may fail to recognize people when we see them in unfamiliar settings but recognize them when we see them in familiar surroundings. In short, similar or related aspects often result in associations and it is well known that there are unconscious associations. Apparently lack of associational access to memories often renders them unavailable, not the total loss of the memories. We will discuss *random access* of memory after we have discussed hierarchies.

How associations are bonded together is not known. However, it would not be surprising if, in the workings of the brain, the process of *association of ideas* occurs in a manner more complex but similar in principle to that of the module: Cellular impulses have to correspond to particular cellular arrangements in order to succeed in passing through one level to a higher level. The same system is used in computers where a series of signals has to match a preexisting series in order to be transmitted farther. For instance, a computer locates a desired word in a page by finding the series of signals which comprise the desired word in a matching series within its "memory." It then prints the matching series on the monitor (the television screen). In a subsequent chapter we will discuss the "matching" of sensory inputs, including ideas and perceptions, with preexisting items in memory. The matching process can be viewed as a form of neurophysiology underlying association. In the process of matching sensory inputs, the matches become connected.

Carbon Monoxide Poisoning

In humans, carbon monoxide poisoning, by damaging very localized areas of the brain, can cause loss of various discrete perceptual (consciousness) functions. Such damage compellingly indicates the respective functions of the involved areas. A patient may be unable to visually recognize objects as a whole but be able to recognize and describe their color and their form. A different lesion can cause the color or the form to be lost while recognition of entire objects remains intact (Livingston, 1988). Certain lesions cause the perception of form to be lost if the objects are in motion but not if the objects are stationary (Zeki, 1974). Further, the perception of form by means of vision can be lost, while form recognition by touch remains intact (Efron, 1966-68). The effects of such lesions suggest that localized areas of the brain are sufficiently specific to resemble the functioning of modules.

Experiments with Light

Some surprising experiments by Land (1960 and 1983) indicate that light of a single wavelength can give rise to the perception of many colors. If the experiments are valid they further indicate the brain's creativity. According to Land, whose explanation of the phenomenon is very involved, the brain actually produces the colors out of the different *intensities* of light even without the benefit of the different wavelengths. This experiment lends experimental evidence that the brain *creates* color, as mentioned in an earlier chapter (as if further proof is needed since only light *waves*, not colors are present in the environment.)

In one of Land's experiments (1960, p. 88) two projectors are used to cast overlapping areas of white light on a screen. With no transparency in either projector, a red filter is held in front of one projector. This causes it to project a red beam while the other projector still casts a white beam. The result is a pink light on the screen. Then if black-and-white transparencies, filmed with the use of proper color filters, are placed in the projectors, the resulting image is not in shades of pink, as one would expect, but has a full array of color. If the red filter is removed, the image becomes black-and-white. If the filter is replaced, the picture, again, has an array of colors. The experiment indicates and it is now well accepted, that the eye or brain "sees" color not only as a result of the particular wavelengths which the eye receives but from the relative proportion of the wavelengths.

Modules Distinguished from Consciousness Cores

We should clarify the distinction between modules and the putative consciousness cores. Both would be accomplishments of nerve cells or relatively small groupings of cells in the brain (though not necessarily in the cerebral *cortex*.) We have also postulated that the determining elements of the consciousness cores might be precerebral, even in the periphery of the body. We conceive of the consciousness cores as originating the qualitative elements of consciousness involving such items as individual colors, sounds, emotions, and so forth, but the modules on the other hand would not originate the qualitative elements. Instead they would either filter out, or allow to pass through, the related nerve impulses.

Another difference is that the consciousness cores would be innate. The modules *might* be innate but there are also indications that they result from plasticity, that is, that they are arranged by experience, especially early in infancy. As mentioned above in the studies of kittens and mice, only commonly encountered features are segregated by modules. As to humans, a study shows that most Americans recognize vertical or horizontal lines more quickly than slanting lines, while members of a certain tribe of native Americans, presumably because of what they are accustomed to from infancy onward, recognize slanting lines more quickly.

Theoretically modules would also not be as diverse in regard to sense modalities as are consciousness cores, since different sense modalities could be filtered by the same modules. For instance, motion could be discriminated either visually or by proprioception, and in either case might be filtered through the same modules.

Summary

Nerve cells consist anatomically of a cell body with branches (fibers) called axons and dendrites. Axons carry cell impulses away from the cell body while dendrites carry them toward the cell body. Cellular junctions are called synapses. Each cell may have hundreds or thousands of fibers coming from or leading to other cells. Numerous different substances are secreted at the synapses of different types of cells by means of which one cell stimulates or inhibits the next cell in a series. The intercellular substances may be partly responsible for the various consciousness cores. Physiologically, association of the cores, implies nerve cell connections. Modules are nerve cells in a physical arrangement which transmits nerve impulses from incoming fibers which have a similar arrangement. Impulses which do not have a similar arrangement are blocked.

Chapter Fifteen

Preconscious Processes and Monitoring

Preconscious Processes

By the time that the reader has reached this point it should be clear that much of what goes on in the brain or mind is at a level which is beneath consciousness. The work of the modules discussed above would be one example. Until recent years many, if not most, writers on the subject of the mind, and of consciousness in particular, held the view that all that went on in the mind was conscious. The idea that they were not aware of what went on in their own minds simply seemed impossible and ridiculous. The conscious was synonymous with mind. With a very few notable exceptions, such was the general view prior to Freud. Even today many writers on the subject of consciousness are neither comfortable with nor accept the extensiveness of the subconscious workings of the mind. This, despite the fact that it is now taught in regular college psychology courses.

In this writing we are not using the term, preconscious, in the Freudian sense. Freudian use of the term refers to those items which can be made conscious by simple *voluntary* effort, for example, one's phone number. We are using "preconscious" as synonymous with "subconscious" in the sense in which non-Freudians are increasingly beginning to use "subconscious", that is, in reference to an item or neurophysiological process which is unconscious but is tending toward consciousness and may become conscious with or *without* volition. An example of "preconscious" would be a melody which spontaneously becomes conscious.

Incidentally, let us be clear about the term, nerve cell. A nerve cell can be located in the brain, where it may be called a brain cell, or in the spinal cord or in the periphery of the body. A nerve cell does not necessarily have to be part of a nerve proper such as is found in the arm or the leg. For example, the nerve cells in the spinal cord and brain are not within nerves. Nerves are composed of the fibers of a large number of nerve cells and the fibers extend for relatively long distances. Nerve cells initiate impulses which can correctly be called either nerve impulses or nerve cell impulses. In this regard it does not matter where the cells are located.

While we are discussing terminology, we will be explicit about the meanings of the term "unconscious" in addition to the comments made in Chapter Two. We are using it as synonymous with "subconscious", that is, simply beneath the conscious level and by no means are we limiting it to the popular notion of the "Freudian" sense of the word. The *popular notion* of the Freudian usage, which is much too narrow and dramatic, is that the unconscious includes only strong passions such as sex or hate.

Not only do the simpler, less intellectual, processes take place at an unconscious level but meanings may do so as well. People in mental health work are well acquainted with the fact that attitudes, emotions, meanings, and the like do not have to be conscious or even available to consciousness by means of volition. Even businesses regularly use the fact of unconscious meanings in merchandising. The box in which toothpaste is packaged is often white. Unconsciously, white means clean to many people. What we call "body language" is often unconscious but nevertheless can be quite meaningful to an observer. A person's way of sitting in a "relaxed" posture often conveys the message that he or she is at ease—a message which is often not consciously noticed by the observer but which may nevertheless be heeded. The background music in movies frequently has a similar character. One is too engrossed in the action to deliberately pay attention to the music. These are simple examples but they will suffice as other examples are commonplace.

To summarize our usage of the terms related to the unconscious vis-à-vis the conscious: "Subconscious" is equated with "unconscious." "Preconscious" means unconscious or subconscious but tending to become conscious either spontaneously or due to volition. On the surface it is as if there is a continuum between the unconscious and the conscious but the overt presentation depends upon dynamic influences which we will now discuss.

Monitoring

Having commented upon preconscious and unconscious processes, we are in a position to discuss monitoring. There must be constant "monitoring" of unconscious perceptual processes by "higher levels" while these processes move toward becoming fully processed consciousness. Evidently from early in the neural chains, the processes are facilitated or inhibited depending both on their interest value and on the strength or weakness of the stimuli. A very forceful initial stimulus, such as a loud noise, immediately arouses emotional interest and attention. An unexpected explosion would be a danger but an explosion heard while watching fireworks on the Fourth of July might be a delight. Either would be likely to reach the conscious level. All other preconscious impulses occurring at that moment would be terminated either by not being facilitated or even by being suppressed, that is, neurologically and unconsciously inhibited. We shall discuss below, the process of the selection of what is to be perceived and what is to be excluded from perception. For the selection to be accomplished, it is clear that the nerve processes would have to be monitored. The "higher levels" would have to control the monitoring and selection.

Interests and Anxieties

At this point a legitimate question may be asked. Have we made a serious backward slip? If processes are "monitored" from above, have we fallen back into the concept of a homunculus which does the monitoring? We will elaborate later upon this issue as we consider it to be of the utmost significance. For the moment, however, we will simply say that the monitoring is not influenced by a central observer in the sense of a separate entity with a quasi-mind of its own, but by experiences and their mostly unconscious attendant emotions, that is, by *the net effect of interests and anxieties.*

We use the terms, interests and anxieties, in a general sense. "Interests" provide a facilitative influence of the "higher levels" on incoming nerve cell impulses. The result of interests is that the impulses are allowed to pass on toward consciousness. By "anxieties" we mean to imply inhibiting influences. They would tend to keep stimuli from reaching consciousness. Perhaps "positive" and "negative" or "pleasurable" and "displeasurable" would be clearer in meaning than interests and anxieties but we prefer "interests and anxieties" because "positive" and "negative" strike us as being too vague. "Pleasurable" and "displeasurable" are too limited in that they are generally associated with consciousness. Yet, there are situations, of course, when anxiety is the particular reason for allowing an input into consciousness, such as when one is crossing a street and an automobile is bearing down on one. In such a situation the net result of the "experiences and their attendant emotions" would militate for the passage of the input to the level of becoming conscious.

The influences of interests and anxieties constitute a large measure of what psychoanalysts call functions of the Ego. Actually, we prefer to use "interests and anxieties" as these terms suggest limited and numerous processes at the neurophysiological level, while the term, Ego, with which we have no quarrel if it is properly understood, lends itself to being looked upon as a separate entity rather than a function. It suggests something more akin to a central observer or a homunculus—a mind within the mind. (This is the same fault which we find with some interpretations of consciousness, that it is a separate and functioning entity.) The term, ego, also tends to be anthropomorphic, a view which we believe we need to avoid whenever it is not too awkward linguistically to do so. We will have more to say about anthropomorphism later on as we believe the it can be unavoidable and even useful at times.

It will be explained further in a later chapter but for the moment let us be clear that interests and anxieties are present in the mind as a result of earlier experiences. They are present in memory—memory which may be either deeply unconscious or available to consciousness. Incoming stimuli are immediately tied to the interests and anxieties from which the stimuli receive appropriate emotional tone. The stimuli are then facilitated or inhibited at each step, from the input of the sense receptors all the way to consciousness. As we mentioned in an earlier chapter, nerve cells typically facilitate or inhibit the action of other nerve cells. An example of facilitation, which was mentioned earlier under the topic of emotion, is the tendency of food to taste and smell better if we are hungry. If we are alone in the house at night we hear the creaks and thumps which we would otherwise not notice.

Selectivity in Perception

The process of monitoring applies to what is clearly a selection process which takes place in perception. Everything in our visual field, for instance, does not register in our consciousness. We perceive only that to which we are attending and our attention can be directed from within ourselves or it can be attracted from without. In either case, early in the process of perception, the nerve cell impulses, which control the sensory inputs which are selected or those which are blocked from reaching consciousness, have to originate "higher up" in the brain. As discussed above under "monitoring", emotions, meanings, and the like are the factors which frequently determine which ascending impulses reach consciousness and which do not.

The thoroughgoing idealist might say that the mind has complete control over what reaches consciousness. By selecting what it wishes or what fits its hereditary disposition, the mind even determines what comprises reality for us. Instead of such strong idealism, we offer that the way in which items from the environment are perceived or interpreted depends to a great extent upon our past experience; but past experience is not the exclusive determinant of what reaches consciousness. The mind also registers experiences which have not been encountered previously.

Where the selection process actually takes place anatomically within the nervous system is not certain. As stated earlier the cellular modules can perform a function of screening out nerve impulses. The selection process, however, is much broader than that which is thought to be performed by the modules. The modules react to specific inputs such as size and motion but the process of selection involves all inputs including those from objects, memory, emotion, etc. The selection process in one respect is like consciousness in that the neurological processes which achieve it occur presumably in many areas in the brain, particularly those involved in memory.

Recall that there are some indications that selection, as determined by the action of higher centers, can even take shape in the peripheral receptors. Such was the case in the example of the tennis player mentioned earlier in whom the process, of selecting which items from his visual fields would become conscious, extended as far peripherally as his retinas. The cellular mechanisms by which impulses are facilitated or inhibited have already been described elsewhere.

Dreams

Dreams and hallucinations are given consideration in very few writings about consciousness apparently both because they are little understood and because they do not fit well into the usual definitions of the topic—dreams occur during sleep and many writers do not consider them as representing consciousness. Also hallucinations are "abnormal" and are therefore excluded. In our view, however, both phenomena are instances of consciousness and we have little problem fitting them into our theory. Both dreams and hallucinations of various sorts (including the psychotic, hypnogogic, and hysterical) (hypnogogic = while falling asleep) are interesting and revealing in themselves as phenomena involving consciousness. While they are influenced by physical conditions, such as drugs, for example, they are also indicative of the psychological and dynamic nature of mental functions.

The process of selection is important in dreams as well as in the waking state. In the mental state of sleep the peripheral receptor organs are largely shut down or ignored. The shutting down is often, but not exclusively, outside the control of the higher centers as indicated by the fact that sleep occurs so regularly. It is also indicated by the circumstance that a person can stay awake for only a limited time regardless of the strength of the wish to do so. The outside stimuli are then shut out despite the state of the person's higher centers. As is well known, during normal sleep the shut down is not complete. A loud noise or the cry of a mother's baby will get through the system. The shift in the source of inputs is the determining difference between the dreaming state and the waking state. The contacts with external reality are now gone or greatly diminished. Instead of originating to a considerable extent from external sources, the inputs to consciousness well up mostly from memory. The dynamic character of consciousness still continues but the selection process is now guided more exclusively from the internal areas alone rather than by concerns with inputs from the external sense receptors or with reality. With the inputs from the outside largely shut off, the mind elaborates contexts around the inputs from the inside, this being the only source available.

According to Freud (1953) the inputs are largely from emotional residues, which Freud termed as "wishes" which have not had time to be dissipated. Freud termed the residues as wishes, not only in the sense of conscious desires, but also in the sense of an emotional propensity or an unconscious urge. The emotional residues may be associated with current situations or with their past connections. The inputs also stem from bodily stimuli which occur during sleep. The wish is often to avoid recognition of the sources of the physical stimuli in order to defer awakening which implies changing position, etc. Freud described going to bed thirsty and consequently dreaming of drinking water (Brill, 1938). If the dreamer is physically uncomfortable, such as from an uncomfortable bodily position, he is apt to dream of some uncomfortable situation which he is unable to correct, until the real discomfort becomes sufficiently intense to awaken him.

The "manifest content" of the dream is frequently distorted, or consists of a superficially more or less chaotic collection of images, with the result that the dream's underlying sources are unrecognizable to the dreamer. According to Freud, one reason for this distortion is that the dreamer is protected by the ego (by interests and anxieties) from conscious recognition of the unacceptable underlying sources. Another reason for chaotic dreams must be that the minimal reality checking gives free vent to the various mental forces and elements which are "unresolved" and are therefore active and moving toward the level of consciousness.

One would seem justified in assuming that the deeper the sleep, the more the disparate internal factors would influence the course of the dream and that the dream would be more chaotic. Yet, often the factors which influence the course of the dream are such that the dream develops a more consistent manifest theme and becomes less incoherent. This is possibly due to a more tranquil state of mind with a lessened need to express "wilder", conflicting elements. However, the opposite is also often the case. Apparently under the influence of strong emotion, very disturbing dreams can be coherent. The mind, that is, the ego, or "higher centers" is obviously capable of organizing coherent themes without the involvement of conscious volition. As is commonly experienced many dreams seem to the dreamer to be quite coherent even though after awakening they prove to be very unrealistic.

The psychoanalytic reason given for the tendency to forget dreams is that the underlying motivation for the dream is unacceptable to the conscious mind. We have no doubt that this is true in many cases. Other factors being equal, however, the more coherent dreams are the ones which are more apt to be remembered. This is partly because their continuity is recognizable. The theme is understandable to the awake rational mind. Without understandability there is little handle by which to remember the dream. Incoherent dreams, or rather, the fragments of which they consist, can usually be remembered for only a few seconds or a few minutes after awakening. The exception, of course, is the fragment which is quite pleasing or quite frightening.

Freud (1938, p. 516) and others have considered it likely that dreams are in progress throughout sleep. This is brought into question by electroencephalographic (brain wave) evidence of so-called REM sleep. "REM" is an acronym used in reference to rapid eye movements during sleep which are thought to accompany dreams. Apparently the eyes move in response to visual images. Without describing the electroencephalographic details let us say that we suspect that actually dreams occur all during sleep but, as mentioned above, they are not sufficiently coherent, thematic or emotion laden to be remembered and reported. It fits our theory of brain activity more nicely if dreaming does continue throughout sleep as we do not have to make additional assumptions. However the theory is not impaired if this is not the case.

Hallucinations

In the phenomena of hallucinations as well as in dreams, we are inclined to take a thoroughly naturalistic approach. For the most part, we consider the same basic brain mechanisms to be at work whether the person is awake or asleep, or whether the perceptions are "normal" or abnormal. Hallucinations are very similar to dreams in that they consist of perceptions without the benefit of external stimulations. In hallucinations the external receptor organs are not shut down but they are relatively ignored. The emotional needs of the person, the interests or anxieties, are sufficiently strong to dominate the selection process.

The question arises in the case of hallucinations, as to what could be the source of the imaginary perceptions, particularly those resulting from alcohol or drugs. They are apt to seem to us as quite bizarre and to have relatively little in common with reality. Actually, hallucinations are hardly more bizarre, and very often less so, than dreams. The source of the imagery in both cases has to be memory. True the memory units can be combined in very odd ways, but they are memory units nevertheless. Even a dream such as flapping ones arms and flying, are from memory. The dreamer has never flown in such a manner but she has seen birds flying, and substitutions are common in dreams. According to Freud, the distortions serve a similar function for the hallucinator as for the dreamer. The function expresses the emotional needs while concealing them from the person herself. In that way she does not have to squarely face the emotions or "wishes" to which her mind is giving expression. Again, as in dreams, hallucinations are apparently the mind's way of integrating elements which are *released* and are given access to consciousness but are distorted with the result that their underlying origins are often not recognizable. Apparently the interests and anxieties of the individual result in blocking from consciousness the promptings of the unconscious origins while allowing substituted, that is, related expressions to become overt.

Summary

In this writing "preconscious" is used in reference to items or neurophysiological processes which are unconscious but may become conscious with or without volition. We also use "subconscious" as synonymous with "unconscious." "Higher" mental centers influence perceptual processes by means of facilitation and inhibition of nerve cell impulses. This is done "automatically." Facilitation is produced by "interests" while inhibition results from "anxieties." This means that there are negative and positive reactions which have the effect of a process of selectivity in perception. The selectivity applies in dreams and hallucinations as well as in ordinary perception.

Chapter Sixteen

Identity Theory

New Concept of Consciousness Needed

In attempting to cope with the frustration of trying to explain consciousness, it has been tempting to both scientists and philosophers to believe that an entirely new approach is required. For many years it has been known that nerve impulses are electrochemical in nature. This is a physical process and indeed on the surface it has seemed impossible that a physical process could produce what are supposedly and "clearly" non-physical phenomena such as abstract ideas, feelings, volitions, and consciousness.

Mysticism is one way of attempting to cope with the seeming impossibility of explaining consciousness. Those people, known as dualists, who consider the mind and the brain to be two separate and distinct entities, regard the mind as resulting from something non-physical, something metaphysical, perhaps the soul. Even if one is not a dualist, it is tempting to feel that somehow the vast numbers of neurons in the brain, with their enormously greater number of interconnections, are capable of producing consciousness by virtue of networks and subnetworks of interactions. This does not seem at all likely, however. One could hardly imagine that vast numbers of telephones, no matter how they are interconnected, could produce consciousness. We are prone to imbue computers with more magic than telephones but computers, too, lack something which is present in the brain. People working in the field of artificial intelligence are creating "intelligent" machines. The networks of such machines involve considerably more than simple connections like those in telephones. But the "intelligence", as useful and complicated as it is, is something short of consciousness, short of an epistemic system, which actually understands, senses, and feels. As we stressed in a previous chapter, *the machines lack what we regard as the elementary ingredients of consciousness, the qualitative cores.* Something possessing the nature of such cores would be an absolutely necessary component of consciousness. Eventually machines may have consciousness cores but at this time they are far from reaching that degree of sophistication.

The view that computers could produce consciousness would seem reasonable if one held the belief that perceptions are created entirely by the manipulation of nerve cell impulses since such impulses are conventionally understood as functioning much like electrical impulses. Computers process electrical impulses extremely well but the manipulation of the impulses does not include the element of consciousness. To believe that computers, at the present time, can produce consciousness without consciousness cores would necessitate the further belief that consciousness and external reality are devoid of many genuine qualilties. Consciousness produced by computers would be an illusion. There are some who might question whether or not all consciousness is an illusion but the conclusion that this is not the case results from the additional very real fact that perceptions are engendered originally from energies which stem from objects. Objects emit or reflect light energy; they produce sound waves, and so forth. It is not as if the brain invents perceptions without inputs from the environment.

Consciousness is Experiencing

Preliminary to describing our manner of considering the identity theory, there is another concept which is needed. It is vital to our theory of consciousness. This is the concept that *consciousness is experiencing*. We have postulated that consciousness is composed of consciousness cores singly or in combination and that consciousness cores are the units of all experience. We consider consciousness to be experience and only experience.

The explanation of many processes is assisted by the use of analogy. But a unique problem in using this method is presented by the fact that consciousness is experience. No analogy is revealing in the case of consciousness because consciousness occupies the most fundamental position in our experience. There are no more basic experiences and there are no analogies involving consciousness except those involving consciousness itself.

Nevertheless we should keep the concept of consciousness as clean neurologically and as sharply delineated as possible. It should be limited to consciousness alone. In the individual, prior to the development of a consciousness content there is recursive processing of sensory stimuli. After consciousness has occurred, the related impulses are transmitted to brain cells involving further processes which are not an integral part of the consciousness. These are processes such as introspection, motor action, possibly memory, and so on. An impulse which constitutes consciousness is unlikely to be something different at the same time. It is true that the fibers leading away from nerve cells (axons) do branch and an impulse follows the branches and becomes a number of impulses which traverse the various branches simultaneously. Nevertheless, even though more than one set of neurons becomes involved, we need to conceptually regard consciousness as a single process. Otherwise its boundaries overlap various other psychological concepts and our thinking about consciousness becomes hopelessly unclear. (One might question how an impulse can become many impulses without losing power. The energy for the impulse is not supplied from the cell body. This is analogous to the action of a firecracker fuse. The fuse is lit by a match and then travels down the length of the fuse without receiving further heat from the match. The heat for the fuse is supplied by the burning powder all along the path. However, to be exact, according to Pribram (1999), impulses do diminish slightly in amplitude and speed as they progress from thicker to thinner branches of an axon.)

Identity Theory—Nerve Cell Activity Experienced as Consciousness

The theory that we wish to discuss at this point is not entirely new. We are referring to what is known as the identity theory. In its usual form the theory simply states that there is an identity between the mind and the brain. This means that the mind is a function of the brain; that it is not an entity separate in any way from the nervous system, contrary to the way it was so lastingly promulgated by Descartes.

We will present the identity theory at this time for the sake of background information and to indicate the direction in which we are proceeding. But prior to our discussion of the theory we wish to be clear that, according to our view, the term, "identity", applies only to the end stage of the process by which sensory inputs become consciousness. For the theory to seem to be more than an unsupported statement we hold that there is an extensive, though very rapid, processing which takes place between the reception of sensory stimuli and their becoming consciousness. Without a description of the processing there is a large causal gap in the explanation. After our description of the theory we will offer several concepts which are needed in filling the gap and which considerably support the theory's credibility.

An estimate of the status of the identity theory of consciousness can be obtained from the following quotation from Lockwood (1989, p. 71):

> There are various different versions of materialism, of varying degrees of sophistication and plausibility. But the simplest to state, albeit ... far from simple to defend, is what goes by the name of the *identity theory*. According to the identity theory mental states and processes, both conscious and unconscious, just *are* states and processes in the brain. Hobbes' remark [Thomas Hobbes, 1588-1679]...that 'sense...can be nothing else than a motion in some of the internal parts of the sentient' shows him clearly to have been an advocate of the identity theory. And its twentieth century adherents have included Bertrand Russell (1927, 1949), Herbert Feigl (1967),

J. J. C. Smart (1959, 1963, pp. 88-105) and David Armstrong (1968).

A number of others could be added to the above list of names. In fact the identity theory has become fairly popular. However, the adherents of the identity theory do not go beyond the bare bones descriptions stated in the above quotation. This is no doubt partly because it is "far from simple to defend" as stated by Crick. Yet a simple statement is by no means proof and is not convincing. Philosophers have conceived the notion of the identity theory intuitively but have been unable to support it. Merely stating the concept is insufficient. Nevertheless a statement is all that has been available.

We wish to apply the theory specifically to consciousness and to support it, fleshing it out considerably. First we will state the theory, which is the basic theme of this book, in various ways in order to convey the central concept. The theory at present is so unelaborated that giving it more depth is fairly tantamount to inventing a new theory. As the reader will see, our version involves some radical departures from what is generally believed about consciousness. Our discussion in this chapter will not complete our discussion of the theory. Further support will be left for later chapters.

In relation to consciousness, identity means that relevant nerve cell activities in the brain are identical with consciousness. To state it differently, *the nerve cells or their impulses simply are consciousness.* This statement is meant to be taken altogether literally. The neural processes constitute both the neurological and the psychological. It is at this level that the historical gap exists between mind and body. But the gap exists only in our hitherto way of considering the matter. It does not exist in actuality.

Another method of approaching the identity theory is to consider the inside and outside perspectives of consciousness. Recall (from chapter eight) that by the "inside perspective" we refer to the experiencing of consciousness; by the "outside perspective" we mean the observation of consciousness as in the observation of the consciousness of other people. In regard to nerve cells or their impulses, which we presume are the neurological substrate of consciousness, *that which is appreciated from the outside perspective as nerve cell impulses is appreciated from the "inside perspective" as consciousness.* We need to be clear about the perspective particularly to elucidate the idea that nerve cells or impulses *are* consciousness. It is the "inside perspective" which is consciousness in the form of light, sound, pain, etc.

We can also describe the identity of consciousness in terms of the first and third person. The identity of consciousness with nerve cells involves considering the cells from the first person perspective. From this perspective the cells and their activity are consciousness. This perspective consists of the senses as "I" am aware of them—as light and sound etc. This is not easy to imagine; yet it must be so.

The first person perspective of nerve cells is the same as the "inside perspective." We should not confuse the first person perspective or the inside perspective with the inside view or structure of nerve cells. The inside structure involves literally the physical inside of a cell as it can be seen through a microscope. One can see the intracellular features such as the nucleus, etc. This is viewing the inside structures from the third person perspective.

An explanation of consciousness is the center of the ancient mind-body problem but philosophers and scientists alike have historically had no generally accepted way of resolving the problem. The problem has been considered to be the "mind-body enigma" which has gathered dust on the shelf. Lockwood (1989, p. 2) expresses an interesting reaction and we think not without considerable justification:

> Perhaps I should make it clear that 'no-nonsense' materialism, as I understand it, is characterized not so much by what it asserts, namely the identity of conscious states and processes with certain physiological states and processes, but by an accompanying failure to appreciate that there is anything philosophically problematic about such an identification. I am not saying that the identification is necessarily mistaken. But it is clear that there are some exceedingly formidable philosophical obstacles that will have somehow to be overcome if such an identification is to be made to work. Hobbes, for one, seems blithely unaware of these obstacles, or of the philosophical problems that the identification leaves unresolved.

We suspect that the appearance of the "blithe unawareness" of the problem has not been so much unawareness as simply the utter inability to know where or how to solve the problem. Actually there can be much doubt that the problem *can* be resolved philosophically. It may be that what is needed is empirical evidence. There is now some evidence which indicates the way. Nevertheless the evidence from neurology and physics, as we have indicated previously, still runs afoul of what is an almost insuperable barrier to scientific research. The barrier is that consciousness is unable to examine itself. Practitioners of meditation attempt to experience pure consciousness but their best efforts have been unable to examine the mechanisms by which it functions.

The descriptions of the identity theory, which simply state that the mind, including consciousness, is a product of brain activity, no doubt sound as if they are arbitrary or as if they beg the question of how to explain consciousness. The statements therefore not only need much elaboration but require a considerable adjustment in our usual way of regarding the subject. The ensuing explanations may sound polemic or even dogmatic and many if not most readers will have difficulty accepting them. This is another reason for which we will attempt to state the matter in different ways and in different contexts. Further, we have discussed much of this before. We shall now draw together a number of the concepts and reinforce them in the present context.

We believe that the problem is mainly not that the statements are complicated and therefore difficult to comprehend but rather that they require a markedly non-customary point of view or mind set which is not easy to acquire and is equally difficult to keep in mind. They are like our earlier statements about light and sound as being only in the mind. Those statements, like the identity theory, are counterintuitive—not in accord with our customary surface oriented way of regarding consciousness. Even after understanding them it is very easy to fall back into the usual way of thinking and into the usual terminology. The customary terminology has a strong tendency to draw one back into the "older", conventional mode of thinking. As we analyze the problem, in addition to the concept's being non-customary, there are deep reasons for the difficulty of understanding and being comfortable with the identity theory. There is a huge chasm between accepting that the brain produces consciousness and accepting that brain activity *is* consciousness. There has not been any even plausible way to cross the chasm. We feel that we can now start to bridge the gap.

To be exact, there is a difference between an explanation of the concept of the identity theory and an explanation of consciousness. An explanation of the identity need only illustrate how consciousness can conceivably be identical with nerve cell activity. That explanation alone becomes a very difficult task if one attempts to extend the concept beyond the general statement and to reduce it to concrete particulars. However, by explaining consciousness in neurological terms, since we are asserting that consciousness is identical with neurological mechanisms, we are at the same time explaining the supportive background of the concept of the identity theory. The more we make progress in our explanation of consciousness, the more plausible the identity theory becomes and the more it appears to be correct.

To adequately explain the identity of consciousness with nerve cells or impulses more than one concept is necessary. Two of these concepts, which we have already discussed, are that consciousness is multiple and that it is composed of qualitative cores. We have also discussed some ancillary concepts but we have yet to discuss other concepts, both major and minor.

To more concretely explain our view of the identity theory, let us return to some of the salient points and apply them to items which we discussed under the topic of the consciousness cores. Remember that *light is not in the environment.* Only electromagnetic waves are there. *Light is only in the brain. It is a form of consciousness.* To conceive of it as such one must not reify light. It is the brain's way of "interpreting" nerve impulses of a particular variety. Stating the matter more accurately, it is the *experiencing* of nerve cells or cell impulses. There is even a possibility that specific nerve cells or substances within particular nerve cells give rise to or *are* individual sensations. In other words, particular molecules may form the basis of the consciousness cores of the sensations. *Consciousness is not separate from the nerve impulses. In the case of light the impulses constitute the particular type of consciousness which to us is light.* To state it differently, *the nerve cells or impulses actually are light.* As far as we know, *light is nothing else.* There is nothing else that light can be. How, one might ask, could it be anything else? The only way the brain "knows" or has any connection with light is as nerve cells or their activity. This statement holds, regardless of the theory one might entertain, as long as one agrees that the brain or nervous system somehow results in consciousness.

To understand the prior paragraph, we must not forget that there is a clear distinction between light energy and perceived light. Light energy is electromagnetic vibration in the environment but perceived light results from nerve cell impulses and exists only in the mind. It is subjective. The experiencing of light is initiated from outside the body where objects are located. We therefore typically think of light as also being outside. Pain and hunger seem to be different because they are initiated from the inside the body and do not depend upon external stimuli. It is less of a departure from our customary thinking to regard nerve impulses as being what we call pain or hunger than it is to regard impulses as being what we call light. Therefore there may be those who would argue that the difference between light and pain is truly significant. This "habit of thinking" interferes with one's understanding of the concept we are attempting to expound. In both cases it is important to stress that consciousness has to result from nerve impulses. Electromagnetic vibrations in the environment are not consciousness. The vibrations first have to be transformed into nerve cell impulses. It is the cellular impulses which are or become light.

The principle described for light is the same for the perception of nerve cell impulses of sound, touch, taste, or smell. We also regard mental phenomena which are internal, such as ideas, emotions, memories, dreams, and hallucinations, to be perceptions produced within the brain by nerve impulses. The impulses are the materials of which consciousness is composed. They, in turn, may either be consciousness cores or may be made up of them.

None of this should sound entirely incredible if one begins with the idea that the mind, including consciousness, is a product of the nervous system, mainly the brain. At the basic level, consciousness must consist of the experiencing of nerve cells or their activity. There is nothing else in the nervous system for consciousness to be except cells which provide "support" structurally or metabolically and do not produce impulses.

As we have stressed before, it is very doubtful that there is consciousness in the sense of a single entity, that there is one consciousness. It is not a separate perceiving entity. Instead, we consider it to be a rapid sequence of single events which give the impression of being a single entity. Again, we are dealing with a "category" change, a change in our way of understanding the matter, a conceptual switch. Another "conceptual switch" is that consciousness does not *have* contents. It consists of the contents. To use the notion of an idea for an analogy, just as we often use the term, content of consciousness, we could similarly refer to the content of an idea. In the same manner that the content of an idea *is* the idea, the content of consciousness *is* consciousness. The two expressions, "content of consciousness" and "consciousness", have the same meaning.

We might emphasize that, being on the "inside" of the nerve impulses, one becomes aware of *consciousness cores* or combinations of them. The nerve cell impulses comprise the consciousness cores. It is in the consideration of the consciousness cores that identity of the "physical" with the "mental" pertains; the cores are at the same time both physical and mental. One does not have to convert or transduce the consciousness cores into consciousness. Their potential to become consciousness is present from birth or within a few years afterward. They are elements of consciousness and with the proper processing they become full blown consciousness.

We have never seen the cores from the outside perspective and *quite possibly never will*. It is from the third person perspective that they have an outside perspective and have an appearance as nerve cells; but from that perspective they have no subjective quality. We do not feel the other person's sensations. To know consciousness cores is to do so from the inside perspective, to experience them. From the outside they are merely nerve cell impulses, molecules, microtubules, or some other such substrate. The difference between being inside and outside consciousness is like the difference between hearing the music and reading the score. One includes the particular quality, the consciousness of the sound, but the other does not.

(If there is validity to the quantum theories of consciousness, it is at the level of the consciousness cores that the theories would apply. However, for the present time, and for a considerable period in the future, quantum phenomena can be related to consciousness only from the outside perspective. It is still not possible, therefore, to know that they *are* consciousness.)

Abstract Concepts Test Identity Theory. (The Mental Develops from the Physical)

The identity theory, is particularly tested by the consideration of abstractions. Abstractions even more that physical objects, tend to pose a problem to the identity theory. By definition, abstractions are not physical. Earlier in this chapter a section was titled, Nerve Cell Impulses Experienced as Consciousness." This is a statement of the identity theory. Yet nerve cell impulses are physical while consciousness is mental. How can something which is not physical *be* something which is physical? This sounds like a direct contradiction. However, it is actually the same question as raised by the mind-body problem. How can the body, which is physical, be the cause of the mind which (it has been supposed) is non-physical? The identity theory states that the mind is a function of the brain, that the mind and the brain are one; yet it does so in the face of the fact that the two concepts seem to be totally incompatible, contradictory in principle, and therefore impossible to resolve.

We again find ourselves in the throes of the ancient problem. However, the identity theory explains the seeming contradiction. The answer is found in a person's individual development. We have indicated that, beginning in earliest infancy, *the mental develops from the physical,* that is, the nerve cells or, more specifically, nerve cells and their impulses begin to become a mind. *By combining the sensory inputs (visual, auditory, etc.,) which we receive from internal and external sources, with inputs from emotions, we construct our mental world.* The construction includes all of the abstractions and meanings which we acquire. They are elaborated from infancy onward in the same way that perceptions of objects, are elaborated—from qualitative cores and their becoming associated (connected). This point is deserving of strong emphasis. It is a necessary component of the identity theory if the theory is to be extended sufficiently to be applied to an understanding of how consciousness develops. (We shall discuss the process by which cores are linked in a later section.)

In order for the idea that the mental develops from the physical to be credible, it seems necessary to have explanations and concrete illustrations of the process by which the transition occurs. Recall that experience is in the first person but illustrations of consciousness, as we have explained, can be given only from the third person perspective as outside observers. Further, since the process develops over time, we have to begin the

132

explanation at the beginning of the process. It becomes almost impossible to trace if we attempt to take an example from later in life. We cannot jump in at the middle or at the end as that would create an explanatory gap. It would be like trying to explain carbohydrates or potatoes by talking about the subatomic composition of carbon atoms.

Webster's Dictionary defines "abstract" as "thought of apart from any particular instances or material objects; not concrete." Abstractions are examples of both consciousness and of meanings. If words are heard or read, they enter consciousness and they also convey meaning. In this chapter we are primarily concerned with consciousness but we will describe the relationship to meaning in a later chapter.

Let us describe how the abstract concept of "motherhood" probably develops. We have to make some assumptions because we cannot experience what the infant experiences. Assume that the infant begins its mental development by experiencing pain from the usual spank on the buttocks. (The exact order and intensities of the early stimuli are irrelevant; it is the principle which interests us.) After the initial spank which we shall assume stirs the infant into consciousness, there is touch (being held), sound (being spoken to), and light (the light within the room), and so forth. Visual objects begin to become distinct and to be associated with sound. Early on, the infant associates feeding with the relief of hunger. Still later it associates the bottle or the breast with such relief. Later yet these are associated with a person and with the word "mother." Once the concept of mother is understood, it is but a short step to learning that other children have mothers and the abstract concept of "motherhood" has then been acquired.

We can clearly make the claim that the child has then merged the physical with the mental, the physical with the abstract. "Motherhood" has different meanings to different people, but the meanings are all based on experience. The abstractions, being ultimately based on experiences, result from *solid contacts with external reality.* The abstractions then, in the final analysis, are not abstract. They are developed from real experiences in relation to concrete objects.

Let us use one more example of the development of an abstraction—this time the development of the concept of "circularity." In an early grade in school the teacher says to the students, "All right, boys and girls, each of you draw a circle on your writing pad." After saying the words the teacher draws a circle on the blackboard. The students thereby both see a circle and hear the term, connecting the two in memory. After seeing other circles and circular objects over a period of time, the generalization to the abstraction of "circularity" is an easy step.

Taking into account the rapidity with which the mind works, specifically the speed with which abstract concepts are understood and utilized, their constructions have to be such that to recall them from memory requires no more time than to recall a single item. In order to think of the concept, ten, we do not have to start from the beginning and combine ten ones. Evidently we somehow bridge across the top of the construction and do not have to reconstruct all of the stages below the top. In a later chapter a method of accomplishing the bridging is offered.

Abstractions Based on Contact with Reality—Additional Illustrations

Our theory for explaining consciousness now can use additional reinforcement in order to make it more credible. Further examples in which the mental arises from the physical are needed, two of which come to mind. Both are examples familiar to many people in which abstractions in the form of words are learned from concrete contexts, or as we have mentioned previously, from "solid contacts with reality." Both examples are deliberately taken from early in the learning process so as not to begin at the middle of the process.

The first is from a Tarzan movie. Tarzan had just met Jane and they began their acquaintance by learning each other's names. Tarzan uttered the words which became famous, "Tarzan...Jane." While saying this he pointed first to himself and then to Jane. He then repeated the activity. The meaning of his actions was clear to the viewer of the movie, just as it was to Jane, that his name was Tarzan and hers was Jane.

Notice that the learning of the names was accomplished by association with actions: he pointed to himself and to Jane while saying their names. He repeated the process, so that there was little chance for misunderstanding his meaning.

A second example, also taken from a movie and also occurring at the beginning of a learning process, is from a film in which Cornell Wilde and a little African native girl were in the jungle. The little girl, who was wise in the ways of survival, found and killed a small animal which was then roasted and eaten by the two of them. While eating, the girl smiled broadly and said, "Sah-**voo**-dee, sah-**voo**-dee!" Her meaning was immediately quite clear to Cornell Wilde who repeated, "sah-**voo**-dee", also while eating and with a large smile and much emphasis. The meaning of the word was "good!" and this is readily understood by the viewer of the movie. Note that the meaning was acquired by the actor and by the viewer from context, specifically from actions and sounds, that is, from "solid contact with reality." No book of translations was used or needed.

Words are probably the best and most common example of abstractions. As with other abstractions, they are based on experience, on contact with reality. Words are used within contexts and it is the contexts which imply the experience.

Nothing, such as a homunculus, is needed to perceive the nerve impulses of consciousness. Nor are the nerve impulses appreciated by a *central organ* of consciousness. They *are* consciousness. They may have to be screened, selected, combined or otherwise processed to become full blown consciousness as we know it but the elements are present in the nerve cell impulses. There are those who would still challenge this by asking, "But isn't someone needed to appreciate the consciousness, someone who becomes aware of the contents?" If we are correct in regarding consciousness as being a matter of *identity* then the question itself is problematical. It presupposes a central perceiver. It slips back into the traditional thinking of a Cartesian theater and an audience. The answer to the question is: "The contents of consciousness *are* consciousness. No homunculus is needed to appreciate them."

However, we have still not finished with the matter. One might still ask, "If no central observer is needed, where does the self fit in? Is the consciousness content not appreciated by the self? After all isn't the self the same as the person who is conscious?" These are basically the same questions as the ones in the previous paragraph but they reflect a very commonly held opinion. In the next chapter we will discuss the role of the self.

Summary

Identity of some aspect of nervous system activity with consciousness means that the two are actually one and the same. Consciousness is postulated to be the "inside perspective" of nerve cells or nerve cell impulses. Because they are non-material, abstractions particularly test the identity theory which is materialistic. In a basic sense, concepts and so-called abstractions are not abstract since they originate in solid contacts with reality.

Chapter Seventeen

The Self

Self as a Concept

Before answering the questions from the previous chapter we need some background about the self. The Journal of Consciousness Studies relatively recently devoted an entire issue to the problem of the self. The "Editor's Introduction" by Shaun Gallagher and Jonathan Shear (1997) presented an overview:

> There is a long history of inquiry about human nature and the nature of the self. It stretches from the ancient tradition of Socratic self-knowledge in the context of ethical life to contemporary discussions of brain function in cognitive science... Briefly stated, the problem involves finding criteria that can account for the unity of the self in conscious experience over time. Locke's solution— that consciousness maintains its identity over time only so far as memory extends to encompass past experience—almost immediately produced philosophical controversies that have not abated to this day. If the self is not a soul, not a Cartesian substance, if its psychological continuity is tenuous, then why do we still believe that we have a certain identity over time? Thus the variety of responses to the problem of the self includes assertions that there is no self, that the idea is a logical, psychological, or grammatical fiction; that the sense of self is properly understood and defined in terms of brain processes; that it is merely a constructed sociological locus; that it is the centre of personal and public narratives; or that it belongs in an ineffable category all its own. Among these responses there is no consensus about how to approach the problems of self, much less what the appropriate resolution might be. In short, the modern philosophers have rendered both our commonsensical and our philosophical notions of self utterly problematic.

Strawson (1997, p. 405), in his keynote article in the same issue of the Journal of Consciousness Studies, cites several opening quotations which include one from Hume (1739): "The soul, so far as we can conceive it is nothing but a system or train of different perceptions." In addition there is a quotation from Dennett (1991): "A self...is...an abstraction..."; and one from Farrell (1996): "My body is an object all right, but my self jolly well is not!" In our own opinion, the self is definitely not a physical entity such as a chair nor does it have a particular location in the brain.

In his presentation of his "approach to the problem of the self", Strawson (p. 408) mentions:

> What, then, is the ordinary, human sense of the self, in so far as we can generalize about it? I propose that it is (at least) the sense that people have of themselves as being, specifically, a mental presence: a mental someone: a single mental thing that is a conscious subject of experience, that has a certain character or personality, and that is in some sense distinct from all its particular experiences, thoughts, and so on, and indeed from all other things.

While he seems to favor the self as being a "mental thing", he also gives weight to the self as a physical thing "in some robust sense" (neurons functioning as an entity or unit) and as a perceiving agent.

Before continuing with our answer to the questions from the previous chapter, we will make the presupposition that the conscious self has legitimacy only as a concept, as an ideational content of the mind. *In our view a person's self, insofar as he or she is conscious of it, is simply the person's concept of himself or herself at any particular moment.* In daily operation there are many selves often heavily colored by current experience. This view is largely in agreement with the opinion expressed by Strawson (p. 424) that: "many mental selves exist, one at a time and one after another..." The concept that there is one self seems to be partly an extrapolation of the fact that there is one body. Some aspects of one's concept of one's self are relatively permanent. For example, one may have high or low self-esteem. However, the self-concept changes depending upon one's current sense of accomplishment or failure, righteousness or guiltiness, etc. This is considering the self from the individual's own perspective. We can also consider the idea of someone else's self, or selves in general, but this is likely to be done only by theorists of philosophy. (Psychotherapists generally consider one's self-esteem but not the self per se.) Ordinarily we would consider someone else's personality but not his or her self. Regarding the conscious self as a concept lessens the quandary about it. It appears to be the realistic way to regard the conscious self and also offers a unifying view which accommodates the great variation in theories. In our own view the "problem of the self" results from the circumstance that important aspects of the self are unconscious but we will withhold detailed discussion of them until we have discussed the mechanism of consciousness in a later chapter.

Self as Perceiver of Consciousness Contents

In the previous chapter we raised the question as to whether or not the self is the perceiver of the contents of consciousness. That it is such a percipient has been a common understanding since ancient times. Such a view has to comprise an intuitive judgment rather than an empirical observation. If we accept the identity theory as valid, we may now consider the answer to the question to be that *we no longer need to regard the self as a perceiver.* Consciousness does not need a separate entity to make its contents complete.

Furthermore, if the conscious self is regarded as merely a concept rather than an independent or functioning entity, it would have no capacity to shoulder any activity at all. The idea of a perceiver harks back once again to the feeling that a homunculus must be needed. In relation to an entity which becomes aware of perceptions, there is little or no difference between the self and a homunculus. If the self is considered to be the perceiver of consciousness, then an entity, or a mechanism, is still needed by which the self perceives. Both the perceiving self and the central observer, like the homunculus, are the beginning of a reduction to the absurd.

Even if one views the self as the perceiver of consciousness, the view does not provide a satisfactory explanation of consciousness. To state that the self perceives consciousness offers little more than that the person perceives consciousness. How the psychological mechanism for the completion of consciousness is accomplished has been partly discussed under the topics of monitoring and selection of consciousness contents. We will explain the matter further under the topic of memory hierarchies but for the moment let us simply state that the completion depends heavily upon memory of past experience. It does not depend upon a self which is in effect a consciousness belonging to a second mind.

Probably the strongest reason why no additional entity such as a self is needed for consciousness is that the contents *are* consciousness without having to be appreciated by a second consciousness. For contents to be appreciated *means* that they become consciousness, that the contents themselves are consciousness. They do not need to be appreciated further. We recognize that such statements appear arbitrary but we believe that they will no longer seem so after we have completed our explanation in the remainder of this book. Also, it is the further explanation which should prevent our view from appearing to be "explaining consciousness away"— as Searle (1997) remarked about the "multiple drafts" theory expounded in Dennett's *Consciousness Explained* (1981).

Immediately following a content of consciousness one may still have a conscious memory of the content and assume, since the content was present, that a self must also have been present. We agree with this impression, but in a limited sense and not in the sense of an entity which observes the contents of consciousness. In agreement with Locke's solution to the problem of the self (mentioned in the quotation above from Gallagher), we hold that when we speak of our selves we are actually referring to a *memory*. A simple example may help: If we make a statement that we like the taste of a certain food, we may not be actively experiencing the liking of the food at that moment. The words may be spoken from memory of having liked the food. *It is clear that the concept of the self often stems from one's memory of consciousness contents.*

It is not difficult to understand how there has been much confusion about the meaning of the self. It would appear that a major part of the confusion has been due to the fact that, even in the not too distant past, theorists who were interested in explaining consciousness were unaware of the unconscious. Recall that in the days of John Locke, the lack of an understanding of the unconscious, made it difficult to even consider *memory* of something, which was not conscious at the time. It was thought that consciousness was synonymous with the mind.

The Self and Memory

The importance of memory in connection with the self, needs further elaboration. Underwood, Paterson, and Chapman (1997) consider the self to be,

> ...inseparable from the phenomenon of consciousness... If we are conscious of our mental events, and in particular of our perceptions and memories, then it is inevitable that we will be conscious of our own personal involvement in those perceptions and experiences. That is to say, our memories of events will include ourselves as a participant in those events.

It should be borne in mind that only if a memory which contributes to a sense of self is "activated" or retrieved is it conscious. Otherwise memory is a vast store which is unconscious. Without memories, consciousness alone could not develop a concept of self (or of any other concept) or of being an individual to whom experiences occurred. A person could only experience. One could not remember the experience and therefore could not think of "I" or of a self which had the experience. Awarenesses would come and go without a trace or a connection. This is perhaps what happens in many lower animals, the frog for instance. The consciousness of memories ties awarenesses together and maintains the concept of a self. Even after lapses in consciousness, as in anesthesia and possibly in sleep, it is memory which allows for re-establishment of the *apparent* continuity of consciousness and the concept of self. *Because we recall having had experiences yesterday and a year ago we correctly conclude that we exist continuously and it is that knowledge which results in the development of the concept of self.*

Revision of Terminology

Having discussed the concept that the self is not a perceiver of consciousness contents, it is desirable to use language which is more appropriate than the traditional terminology for the concepts being presented. It is preferable to use the phraseology that an item "becomes *consciousness*", rather than the prior terminology that an item "becomes *conscious.*" Even though, at first, such phraseology sounds odd, our reasons for the change are several: If an item becomes "conscious" there is a theoretical need for a consciousness to observe the item and thereby complete the process of perception; if not a consciousness then a different additional perceiving element is required such as a homunculus or central observer, . But *if an item becomes consciousness, we can understand that nothing further is needed to complete the process;* consciousness has already occurred. (Let the reader not make the mistake of thinking that we are simply toying with language.) This concept incorporates a radical change from conventional thinking but we consider it to be of paramount importance. The need for a homunculus has been a constant stumbling block in conventional theories for a century or two if not considerably longer.

A further reason for the change in terminology is in accord with the identity theory which, as we have previously asserted, we consider to be correct. The point of the identity theory is that *nerve cells or their activities are consciousness.* No activity beyond the nerve cell action is needed for consciousness to be complete.

Our reasoning may leave the reader with an impression of our having explained consciousness away, that our explanation does not result in consciousness. But in our view of the "multiplicity of consciousness", each consciousness content is its own instance of consciousness. At the level of the nerve cell, there is identity of the involved cells with consciousness. There is no need for an all encompassing perceiver. Each item becomes consciousness for an instant and there is then a further action or reaction and a further consciousness.

In our view we need to discard the notion of consciousness as an over-all perceiving entity. This is not psychologically easy to accomplish. We believe the attempt to do so runs counter to a deeply ingrained conception of ourselves as human beings. To eliminate an over-all consciousness portends a very serious implication. It implies it is not "we" who are conscious but it is our nerve cells. If there is no conscious entity, then there is a strong sense of loss. There is no "we" (or I) which is the entity. Stating the matter even more dramatically, it implies "we", our mental selves, in a limited sense do not exist. Let us quickly reassure the reader, however, we are not taking the idealist position that all is imaginary. People fully experience consciousness but it is simply not a single entity. We experience separate contents which occur without a noticeable interval thereby affording *the illusion of consciousness as an entity*. This view will be expounded further in a subsequent chapter.

Summary
The self is regarded as a concept on the part of an individual and awareness of a self is regarded as a memory of experience. The self is not regarded as an existing entity and, like the homunculus, it is not needed as a perceiver of consciousness contents. (Further, it is ruled out as such by a *reductio ad absurdum*). According to our "multiplicity" concept, consciousness is also not viewed as an entity. Each consciousness content is an instance of consciousness in a sequence of contents sufficiently rapid to furnish the impression of being an uninterrupted entity.

Chapter Eighteen

Hierarchies

We have elaborated (Brooks, 1994) upon the concept that memory is hierarchical and it now appears that the central idea is the generally accepted view. It is our contention that not only is memory hierarchical but also that hierarchical memory formations are heavily involved in the process of perception. We will use the terms, memory hierarchy and perceptual hierarchy, interchangeably.

Hebb (1980, p.46) made a statement which is supportive of the concept of hierarchical development:

> "I propose that the human capacity for recognizing patterns…is possible only as the result of intensive and prolonged visual training that goes on from the moment of birth, during every moment that the eyes are open, with an increase in skill over a period of 12 to 16 years at least."

Hebb also commented about perceptual organization and mentioned that experience plays a large part in perception (p. 111).

Locke (1975, p. 106) mentioned in answer to his own rhetorical question as to the source of ideas or meanings,

> "Whence [come]…all the materials of Reason and Knowledge? To this I answer, in one word, From *Experience*: In that, all our Knowledge is founded;…"

He applied this statement all inclusively, to external objects as well as to our knowledge of the "internal Operations of our Minds,…" There is a clear implication of a process of building up over time as knowledge is certainly not acquired all at once. If a hierarchy is to develop there is a requirement for some perceptions to result in memory.

Hierarchical development of memory is strongly indicated by the way a child's perceptual abilities and understanding start quite slowly and accelerate rapidly. Each new item of knowledge does not have to be learned from the very beginning of the subject but is built on previously acquired knowledge. An example of this is the way a child learns the meaning of words and is able to use them. The first words are acquired one at a time and roughly one word every day or so, beginning often with "ma ma" or "da da." The rate of learning increases gradually at first but accelerates until very soon we are amazed at the size of the child's vocabulary. As words are learned, the words and their meanings assist in the acquisition of new words. This makes it clear that new acquisitions are built with additions to or changes in prior accumulations. The fact that the process builds at an increasing rate suggests that the hierarchy branches in a widening manner. Once a child learns the meaning of the word, "No", it applies in innumerable situations. Concrete terms lead to abstractions, and singular terms lead to plurals, and so forth. A most important example of the hierarchical structure of memory is the manner in which the learning of the skill of reading branches into many areas of learning.

The role of hierarchical development of memory and the role of memory in perception is an essential element for the concept of consciousness promulgated in this book. It would appear that many efforts to explain consciousness have foundered due to the lack of such a concept. Consciousness has usually been treated as if it is present in its fully developed form at birth or not long afterward. In the adult it is generally treated as if perceptions have to be accomplished by the brain entirely from the present impingements upon the senses. This applies particularly in regard to external objects. Yet "ideas" are also inputs to consciousness and no doubt also develop over time.

All of the components of a consciousness content are not present at the time that the related sensory stimuli are received. Only the incoming impulses are current and the perception which results is formed to a large extent from levels of the memory hierarchy. *The levels of the hierarchy are developed over time through the acquisition of experience from birth onward.* The development starts with the qualitative cores—exteroceptive, somatic, and emotional—as well as with the capacity for memory which allows for the linking of cores. Simple experiences which occur closely enough together in time or in meaning are related to each other. The process of association continues to build throughout life as the individual has experiences and retains impressions of them. There then have to be mechanisms which keep the hierarchy from becoming too large and unwieldy. As experiences accumulate the non-essential meanings, that is, the associations which are not consistent, become inactive. We have already presented the concept of synecdoche and we shall discuss the use of primarily the uppermost levels of the memory hierarchy in a later chapter.

The foregoing discussion of perceptual hierarchies indicates that they can be arbitrarily divided into two temporal groups, those which develop from birth onward, to which we will refer as "vertical," and those which develop in adulthood, to which we will refer to as "horizontal." The difference between these two groups is only a relative one. Both would involve new experience with the stimulation of sensory inputs and their integration and storage in memory. The distinction, in neurological and psychological terms, is that the concepts acquired later in life are likely to be built upon much more highly developed memories than the concepts acquired earlier in life.

We not only conceive of memory as developing horizontally and vertically in a neurological sense but also psychologically in relation to associations and categories of meanings. We may think of memory as being composed of an overall hierarchy or of any number of subhierarchies. For example, in the infant the knowledge of foods begins with liquids and progresses to include solids. The liquids later include not only milk but juices etc., while the solids proceed to include different fruits, and so on. We should also point out that the acquisition would hardly be acquired in as logical a sequence as we have just stated. New perceptions become subhierarchies in memory and are retained "on top" of previously acquired hierarchies. Objects have usually been treated in writings about consciousness as if they are perceived "all at once", as whole concepts, instead of their having had a hierarchical development. There can be little doubt that concepts, let us say horses, for example, have simple beginnings but expand greatly as knowledge and experiences are accumulated.

We also wish to be clear about what we mean by a hierarchy "level." In the hierarchy described in the previous paragraph, each new bit of knowledge about horses would add to a new level of the "horse" hierarchy. "Levels" could also be referred to as a hierarchy "item" or "memory item."

There is a further point which should be added. We wish to emphasize that each level or item is connected to (associated with) many other levels horizontally, vertically, diagonally, and in three dimensions, so to speak. For example, a horse connects with motion, riding, travel, fields, socialization, etc., etc.

Random Access

In relation to physiology, until now we have mainly been using the metaphor of simple nerve cell impulses. A simple impulse arrangement has nerve cells connected one after another in a straight succession. Such connections make hierarchical development of memory possible but the situation is seldom if ever that uncomplicated. Aside from the fact that impulses occur in volleys, there are loops which extend back to the levels of recent or remote times and connect with impulses of the earlier levels. Numerous horizontal and vertical connections at each level of development result in the formation of extremely complex networks. The networks allow for connections to be established between current experiences and the memories of earlier experiences. In relation to the complexity of the connections, the term "network" adds to the concept of "hierarchy." "Hierarchical network" may be a better term than simply "hierarchy" as it adds to the concept of complexity. However, we will continue with the term "hierarchy" for the sake of brevity and because it seems to lend itself better to the concept of development over time and to the inclusion of "levels" in the terminology.

At each level of development, the memory item is available to recall. This availability at all levels of the hierarchy is what is meant by random access. Current inputs may find connections in recent memory or may signal the calling up of remote events. The access is both vertical as well as horizontal.

Emotion and Hierarchical Development

We need to call special attention to the fact that emotions undergo hierarchical development. The common view of emotion is that it is purely qualitative. We are "happy"; we are "sad"; we are "angry", etc. These terms do not include the ideational or cognitive connections of the feelings. Such connections would involve memory and would also be hierarchical. Only in the newborn infant, or in very early childhood, can the emotions conceivably exist without context. Such emotions would be included among "qualitative" or "consciousness cores." Exceptions might be the consciousness cores of emotions for which there is an inborn capacity but which possibly do not develop for a period of time, perhaps even years. (They might apply to sexual and other sensations.) Not enough is known about primary emotions or emotional development in general to indicate their temporal origins.

Summary

New sensory inputs are combined with memory hierarchies to form current perceptions. A new perception becomes the latest level in the hierarchy. It may be an addition to the earlier level or an amendment. In either case it becomes available to add to the development of the next related perception. Memory hierarchies are developed over the years and at each level are subject to recall, that is, to random access. Emotions with their connections to experiences also have hierarchical development.

Chapter Nineteen

Memory

In an earlier chapter we discussed the importance of memory in relation to the self. In the chapter previous to this one we later discussed its role in the formation of hierarchies. There are further points which should be presented about memory in connection with consciousness. The importance of many aspects of memory in relation to consciousness and to psychological functions of all sorts can hardly be overemphasized. Yet when memory is discussed in the literature relating to consciousness, even though its importance to concept formation is recognized, memory is often mentioned in a negative connection—that nature had to limit memory lest the mind be overloaded (Tye, 1995).

Consciousness and Memory

Let us say we taste something, a strawberry. For a moment, possibly only for a fleeting instant, there is a taste. (We suspect that what seems like a more prolonged taste may actually be a number of experiences.) After that there is only memory. Or let us say we hear a brief sound, a click. A second later we know that we heard the sound and we could recognize it if we heard it again, but we no longer hear the sound itself. When we try to examine the sound, we can only examine the memory of it. We know the sound was loud or soft, high or low in pitch, and had a certain quality but we cannot remember the sound with the degree of vividness with which we heard it in the first instance.

A memory may be enhanced by our degree of sophistication about sound. We may recognize that a particular musical note is a "C", or that it is a quarter note, etc. This directs attention to certain aspects of the memory and may increase its accuracy. Intellectual details about the sound, however, do not bring back the sound in its original brightness. Our examination of the memory of the sound can be fairly accurate but it is not examining the original consciousness. The longer the time interval between the hearing of the sound and the examination of it, the fainter the memory becomes. Under normal circumstances, it fades even though we wish to retain it.

A seeming exception to the idea that memory of a conscious event is less intense than the original experience, is found in dreams. Making the fairly safe assumption that dreams derive basically from memory (where else could they normally originate except in some instances when they result from an uncomfortable body position, etc.), an explanation of the intensity of many dreams is that dreams are a collection of components taken from various experiences and that the sense of vividness and the strong emotions are drawn from experiences which often are not part of the manifest content of the dream. For instance, we may have seen a friendly dog during the day, but dream of the same dog as being huge and terrifying. The frightening emotion in the dream could, for example, be an element from an experience in which one's boss made a remark which threatened one's job. Such displacements were described at length by Freud (1938, p. 246).

Hallucinations are also exceptions to the idea that memory is less vivid than the original experience. Hallucinations, like dreams, can also be extremely intense and frightening. Strictly speaking, one would suspect that it is not the hallucination which is frightening. It is more likely to be the reverse; the fear is the stimulus for the production of the hallucination. This is typically true of the terrifying hallucinations associated with the withdrawal from prolonged alcoholism, a condition known as delirium tremens. The explanation for this seeming exception is the same as in the case of dreams. Hallucinations, like dreams, derive basically from memory and the emotion accompanying them is a displacement from experiences which often are not manifested in the hallucination or dream itself.

Little is known about the neurophysiology of memory. One theory of memory involves reverberating circuits: An item is laid down in the form of nerve impulses. A nerve cell (or volley of nerve impulses), stimulates another, which in turn stimulates still another, and so on until the impulses return to the original cells and in this manner keep going indefinitely. In another theory memory items are laid down in proteins or DNA within nerve cells. In a third theory the connections between nerve cells, known as the synapses, are altered with the result that the circuits are permanently preserved. Quantum effects associated with microtubules within nerve cells are also suspected.

Gleitman's textbook of psychology (1981, b) lends some support to the idea of the closeness of memory and consciousness:

> We usually think of memory in terms of a past that is reckoned in hours, days, or years. But memory actually comes into play as soon as the stimulus is registered on the senses. An example is a telephone number we look up and retain just long enough to complete the dialing; here the interval between acquisition and retrieval is a matter of mere seconds. Similarly, to understand speech one must still remember the beginning of a sentence by the time one hears its end. Clearly, we use memory to reach back both into the remote and the quite immediate past.

147

Gleitman (1981, c) also states,

> The distinction between short-term and long-term memory appears to fit the way in which we consciously experience our remembered past. The remote past is experienced as gone and done with. The movie seen last night, the dinner enjoyed an hour ago, are in the past tense; they are remembered but not perceived. This is not so for events that happened just a few seconds ago. We hear a melody and seem to perceive much or all of it in the present, even though the first chord has already ebbed away by the time the last note of the musical phrase reaches our ears. This distinction based on conscious experience was described ninety years ago by America's first psychologist, William James:
>
>> An object which is recollected, is one which has been absent from consciousness altogether, and now revives anew. It is brought back, recalled, fished up, so to speak, from a reservoir in which, with countless other objects, it lay buried and lost from view. But an object of primary memory is not thus brought back; it never was lost; its date was never cut off in consciousness from that of the immediately present moment. In fact it comes to us as belonging to the rearward portion of the present space of time, and not to the genuine past (James, 1890, p. 646-47).

It is usually assumed that there are neurophysiological differences which account for the different duration times in short and long term memory but this has not been proven. We suspect that all memory is produced by the same neurophysiological mechanism and that the time span for the retention of short and long term memory is spread over a continuum. We further suspect that both types are registered by the same process but longer retention is due to additional factors. Three such factors are commonly observed: (1) Revisiting, or repetition, undoubtedly makes for reinforcement of memory with longer retention. Teachers are aware that the more often a subject is presented the better it is retained by students. (2) Emotional content and (3) context in general also influence the duration of memory items. We remember being bitten by a dog much longer than we remember seeing a dog chase a squirrel. (We have theorized that a new hierarchical level is established each time a memory is revisited.) Our theory eliminates the need for separate neurophysiological explanations for the registration of short and long term memory. Both are registered by the same process but longer retention is due to additional factors.

We wish to call attention at this time to a similarity between memory and consciousness. Superficially, at least, registrations in both memory and consciousness seem to occur quickly and both seem to occur at the same time. We feel that this is more than coincidence. *Perception (consciousness) and memory may even be part of the same intra- or intercellular processes.* Such would be all the more likely if consciousness is within neurons as is suggested by the identity theory. In a later chapter we will offer that memory and consciousness are indeed part of the same neurophysiological process.

There is a question as to whether or not *all* perceptions result in memory. This was suggested by Freud. There may be some degree of memory in connection with all items which enter consciousness, even if the memory is only of the briefest sort or if the item is of little or no importance to us. We remember for a few seconds even very minor items—minor at the time that they occur—for instance, the location of a pencil we had put down a moment earlier. We can often aid another person who has lost a train of thought by furnishing a reminder of the idea. It is also true that minimal perceptions can fail to become consciousness until a few seconds after the sensory inputs occur, as indicated when someone says, "I heard the sound but I wasn't paying attention."

The possibility that perception involves the establishment of memory is suggested by an experience reported by a woman who had been in an elevator together with several people. The people included a man whom she did not know, who had no importance to her whatsoever, and to whom she paid no noticeable attention. Yet that night he appeared in a dream! Upon awakening, it took a while for her to remember where she had seen him. Such experiences are not uncommon to people who are interested in dreams.

Perceptual Patterns and Memory

Hebb (1980, pp. 13-15) and others have stressed the importance of patterns in perception. A neurologist, W. R. Brain (1951), some of whose ideas are similar to those expressed in our writing, stated, "There is evidence, too, that patterns play an integral part in our recognition of objects, in our understanding of words and sentences and in our comprehension of ideas."

We think of neural patterns in a narrow sense as having a feature of repetition (as in a plaid cloth) and in a broader sense as not being repetitious but simply being an arrangement of nerve cells or impulses (as in the memory of an object or idea). In either case the patterns must be present in the form of memory hierarchies. (In this writing, when we mention hierarchies, that is, in the plural form, we usually are referring to subhierarchies.) It is the memory hierarchy which is the underlying neurological/psychological structure. As indicated by the identity theory, patterns are the neural substrates of objects of perception.

However, patterns should not be looked upon as if they are simply faithfully copied nerve cell reflections of the spatial and temporal aspects of objects. Patterns also have meanings. The meanings depend upon context or associated relationships which will be discussed further in the penultimate section of chapter twenty-five. It has been already considered that it is quite doubtful that patterns of light or sound energy emanating from *whole* objects remain intact throughout the perceptual process and become consciousness as a pattern of the whole object. What we have already said about objects in general also applies to patterns in connection with synecdoche, parallel processing, monitoring and selection . Brain's mention of the idea "...that patterns play an integral part in our recognition of objects...", implies that memory is heavily involved in the perceptual process.

Searching of Memory

Let us say that one sees an object which is made of metal. The registered stimulus patterns emanating originally from the object are unconsciously *compared with patterns in memory.* If the patterns match sufficiently they reach consciousness as features of a particular automobile. If they do not match sufficiently they might match the pattern of a non-specific automobile and reach consciousness as that meaning. If the latter comparison is still not sufficient to resemble an established pattern, the incoming patterns can be perceived merely as metal with wheels, as an object of art, or even as an unrecognized object.

For fear of oversimplifying the matter of perception, we should add that the success of the patterns in becoming consciousness depends not only on what they match as to sensory content but also on what they match as to their emotional contexts, to the interests of the individual, etc. (The concept of contexts would seem to be fairly similar in principle to Bruner's (1973) concept of categories, the "category" being a classification grouping.)

Considering the rapidity with which the brain works, a method of searching for patterns in memory must be used in speaking. During speech, words must be obtained from memory, an action which is accomplished either voluntarily or unconsciously. In either case memory has to be searched and the desired words retrieved. For example, many people pause or interject the expression, "uh", while speaking as they consciously or unconsciously search for the proper word. Whether an activity involves recognition of objects, comprehension of ideas, or thinking in general, a requirement is that patterns in memory be found and be made consciously available. Ordinarily such actions happen extremely quickly and certainly require some method of very detailed cross indexing of meanings as well as random access to the meanings within memory.

Boolean Search Strategy

Probably the mechanism which contributes the most to efficiency in searching "memory" in a library or particularly in searching for information in a computer is called a Boolean search strategy. Categories are searched according to subject headings and then according to subtopics under the headings. The process continues, becoming progressively narrower until finally the particularly desired topic is located. For example, if one wishes to find information specifically about chocolate candy, one might start with the topic of substances. Then, under the topic of substances one chooses the topic of food. Next under the topic of food, one selects candy, and then, finally, chocolate. Such a method is undoubtedly much simpler than that used by the brain. The brain seems to accomplish its very rapid searches on the basis of associations and thoroughly random access. It often seems to reach directly or almost directly to the desired item rather than progressing through a laborious Boolean type of search.

We consider memory and memory hierarchies to be of such overarching importance for the understanding of the workings of the mind in perception and in general that we offer another example: We glance at a small, black object sitting on a shelf. The image of the object occupies only small areas of our retinas. The nerve cell impulses from the retinas travel inward where monitoring, matching, and selection occur. The matching involves a search of memory hierarchies resulting in a match only for a small, black object. There is then a further selection of the retinal impulses which results in a further match of the object. This time, interest in the impulses is narrowed from the entire retina to the object alone. The process of refinement may take several iterations until the object is matched as being a pair of binoculars. The impulses then proceed to become consciousness. The exact order of the iterations between retinal registrations, monitoring, selection, matching and consciousness are not altogether material to our description of the process. Our purpose is to present the concept of a recursive process which is complex but nevertheless takes place very quickly. The rapidity with which patterns become meanings determines the time which is needed for perception.

Sensory Impulses and Memory

Common sense and so-called folk psychology tell us that memory is something which happens only after consciousness has been reached, that we can remember something only after we have been aware of it in the first place. As counterintuitive as it may seem, sensory impulses do not necessarily have to be registered consciously to be retained in memory. Sensory psychologists (Merikle, 1998) have convincingly demonstrated what is called unconscious perception or "subliminal perception." (Incidentally, according to Lockwood (1989, p. 170-1), a major difference between the terms, "sense-data" and "qualia" is that G. E. Moore (1942, 1953), the originator in 1910 of "sense-data", believed that representations resulted from both conscious and unconscious perceptions and that there might be discriminations beyond our powers of awareness. The originator of "qualia", C. I. Lewis in 1929 (see 1956) believed that they resulted only from conscious perceptions and objected to the implication in "sense-data" that mental representations were indistinct. As for ourselves, we have some difficulty with both concepts particularly with regard to their being representations of entire perceptions or of whole objects, as discussed under mental representations in general and under "synecdoche.")

The ability of the blindsight patient to retain in memory, something of which he had never been conscious, is quite surprising and supports the idea that sensory inputs do not need to become conscious, at least not fully conscious, to be registered in memory. Nevertheless, as indicated by the blindsight patient's unconscious "knowledge" of the material which had been presented to him, the inputs evidently were not as completely processed as those which had attained consciousness. One explanation of the phenomenon may be that the patient had the item in storage but it was not retrievable. The *accessing* of items in memory, in order to make them conscious, is a process separate from the registration and storage. This is very evident when we cannot "think" of a person's name but are able to do so at a later time with little or no effort. Clearly, accessing items in memory and bringing them to consciousness is a process separate from simply retaining the items.

The explanation of blindsight may be something other than being unable to access the memory item. It suggests a process involving unconscious association. Unconscious association is at work in our theory of perception; a sensory input is unconsciously associated with a previously existing memory hierarchy level with the formation of a new level. A different phenomenon apparently involving unconscious association occurs in recollection. We recall an item from memory, which was recently conscious, more readily than an item which was not conscious for a longer period of time. For example, reviewing school material the day before a test makes recollection more likely on examination day. It is generally easier to recall the name of a person we have seen or thought about recently, than to recall the name of someone we have not seen for a long period of time.

Motor Memory

That *some* types of impulses are normally registered in memory before they reach consciousness or without reaching consciousness at all, is also clearly indicated by motor memory. By motor memory we refer to the memory involved in muscular activity such as in bicycling. We tend to overlook motor memory as being memory or to regard it as being a different type of memory. Since we have almost no knowledge of the neurophysiology of any sort of memory, we have no reason to regard the neurophysiology of motor memory as being of a fundamentally different type. One reason for regarding motor memory as being of a different sort is that movements and patterns of movements often develop without conscious or voluntary effort. A large part of a motor pattern, for example playing tennis or golf, is learned and remembered without the player's becoming aware of the motions utilized in the coordinated movements. Adding to the golfer's awareness of the movements is a large part of the work of the golf "pro." (The larger movements are often determined mainly by an *unconscious* attitude—for example, the "machismo" attempt to "kill" the ball.)

Even when we are aware of voluntary effort in producing movement, we are not aware of any mechanism by which our minds do so. We simply move our arms. We do not consciously think, "I am going to initiate the effort to move my arm now." The concept of "will", "volition", and "intentionality" are often invoked as an explanation for the movement but these terms are not given a neurophysiological explanation. In the next chapter we will offer some degree of explanation in connection with "higher centers."

Contrary to conventional thinking, the neurological mechanism for the retention of motor skills may be the same as for the memory of "intellectual" activity. The cerebral cortex is thought to be the locus of intellectual memory while the cerebellum, at the rear of the brain, is thought to be the locus of motor memory. Yet, at the intercellular or intracellular level the actual process of registration and retention might well be the same for all types of memory. We are aware of no theoretical principal which would preclude them from being the same.

The arrangement of neurons in the cerebellum as seen under the microscope is clearly different from the many arrangements of cells in the cerebrum. Nevertheless this may relate much more with coordination of muscle stimulation than with registration and retention of patterns. Muscle stimulation would occur at the end of the sequence of neuronal impulses while registration of patterns would occur earlier.

We tend to think that remembering is something that we do consciously, but overlook the remembering that our brains accomplish without our intellectual effort or volitional participation of any sort. Even the act of "memorizing" material such as a poem or a speech is accomplished almost as easily by simply reading it several times while understanding the overall material, as by attempting to directly commit it to memory by carefully attending to each sentence, word by word, and emphasizing isolated parts repeatedly to oneself.

The idea that material does not have to reach full consciousness to be registered in memory, suggests that memory is an automatic, built-in part of the process of perception. We will later develop this idea further in connection with the role of recognition in perception.

Perception from Within

Previous to this point in our writing we have concerned ourselves with the traditional attempt to explain perception of the outside world. Toward the more complete understanding of the mechanisms involved, we also wish to be explicit in regard to perception which occurs in the opposite direction, that is, from within memory into consciousness. It is obvious, if one considers the proper examples, that inputs to memory and to consciousness do not originate exclusively from the environment. We have stated, in agreement with the "English philosophers", that memory is a vast store of items which originate in the environment. We have also described the searching of memory in the process of perception. In our description memory is passive and is searched until a suitable item is found. We should also clearly state that memory may supply inputs without being called upon to do so in response to external stimulation. The most immediate examples are those from dreams and hallucinations. In such cases the inputs are generally stimulated from "areas" within memory itself. While the roots lie in the outside world, it would not be incorrect to regard many conscious expressions to have originated, now "free floating", so to speak, from within. There is apparently a pressure for expression. At the level of neurophysiology, it would be consistent with our theorizing to consider this "pressure" to result from the discharge of neuronal impulses and the competition of those impulses in reaching the level of consciousness. The "spontaneous" singing or whistling of a tune is not an uncommon example. Much more common is the manner in which thoughts and promptings appear in consciousness seemingly "out of nowhere." One continuously reviews episodes from past experience or considers plans for future actions which obviously are based on the past. More important yet is the effect of unconscious memories and emotions upon attitudes and behavior. Such promptings, even though they are usually not perceived, are fully cogent in their influence.

Summary

Memory is clearly of great importance in all sorts of mental functions. There may be some degree of memory in connection with all perceptions. Little is known about the neurophysiology of memory. There is no doubt that there is some amount of unconscious perception. In perception the input stimuli are matched against patterns in memory. The brain apparently searches for patterns in memory using random access and does so extremely rapidly. Memory may be passive, as when it is searched, or active, as when impulses originate within memory itself.

Chapter Twenty

"Higher Centers"

In an earlier chapter we discussed dreams. We stated that during sleep the inputs to consciousness from outside the body were largely shut off and that the inputs which were present were mainly from the inside. We also stated that the selection process which was applied to these inputs was controlled in part by the "higher centers." As to what is meant by "higher centers", we can now be considerably more specific.

If we make the assumption that memory is blank at birth, an assumption which cannot be too incorrect, then anything which is more or less permanently in the mind and is not inborn, is within what we call memory. Any personality traits, desires, fears, ambitions, habits, volitions, etc., which are not strictly current, are from stored sources, or to put it differently, from memory. (Some of these terms obviously overlap and we are not attempting to be exact in their use.) We will now present the concept that it is memory which constitutes the "higher centers." As memory is hierarchical, it is the memory hierarchy which best fills the requirements for being the psychological structure which constitutes the "higher centers." The memory hierarchy can also be considered to be the control center of the mind.

In fact the memory hierarchies are the only designated psychological faculties with such an overarching scope and capability. They meet the main requirements of being sufficiently complex and of functioning from an "inside" position in regard to the neurological-psychological identity. They are a major component of the mental organization. Furthermore they are in a position to pass on information for further use. By further use, we include the recursive registration in memory itself as well as participation in reactions to perceptions either by motor action or by ideational activity.

The memory hierarchies constitute the "higher centers" not by virtue of being a mind within the mind—which would be like a homunculus. They differ greatly from a homunculus in that they are not a hypothetical center for consciousness. They neither have a mind of their own with which to "appreciate" the contents of consciousness, nor are they an audience in a Cartesian theater. On the other hand they do have great executive power over much that transpires. The control which they exercise is not by a mysterious or magical capacity. They do so by virtue of nerve cell facilitations (stimulations) and inhibitions. These are exercised mindlessly in a sense. That which is anxiety producing is typically automatically evaded. That which is pleasurable is automatically facilitated. The net result is actually a "trade off", an algebraic sum, so to speak, of negatives and positives. It should be emphasized that the "trade off" is the result of all of one's experiences, values, and beliefs.

We would also like to use the term, ego, as suitably equivalent to the "higher centers" or memory hierarchies. Ego, as we have mentioned in connection with dreams, in its original psychoanalytic usage, meant the part of the mind which was the integrating element between the id drives and the superego restrictions. It thus was conceptualized as having mind controlling functions and in this sense is equivalent to the "higher centers" or memory hierarchies. Of course, it has also now become a non-technical popular expression often equivalent with self-esteem.

At this point let us interject a clear distinction between the mind and the brain. The brain involves more than just neurons. The brain includes support cells called astrocytes, and other cells which are not nerve cells. It also includes the coverings of the brain, the blood vessels, and so on. The mind, on the other hand, is defined by Webster's dictionary as "that which thinks, perceives, feels..." It is the psychological part of the mind-brain complex, a part of the functioning of the brain.

In the first paragraph of this chapter we mentioned that the higher centers control the production of dreams. The components of dreams, coming from inside the mind, from areas of memory, cannot be shut out entirely as can the external stimuli. It is as if they are already inside the door. They therefore have to be managed by the higher centers. The centers cope with them by giving them context—it either constructs a dream around them or fits them into a dream. Further, the meanings are those which, by and large, are harmonious with the centers and are psychologically compatible with the condition of sleep. When a dream becomes too threatening it is no longer compatible with sleep and the dreamer awakens. As stated in the earlier chapter, in sleep there is much less "reality checking" or influence by the environment than occurs in the waking state.

Linking of Consciousness Cores

We have said that meanings arise from qualitative cores and the linking of cores. Just what is meant by "linking"? How is it accomplished neurophysiologically? The latter question is an extremely important one which remains to be worked out but the "cell assembly" approach of Hebb (1980) seems to be a good start in that direction. Hebb's approach involves a detailing of theoretical connections between nerve cells which could apply in perception, particularly in the visual mode. The connections are quite interesting as indications of the way the physiology could work. At the simplest level these connections involve the facilitating and inhibiting effect of cells upon other cells as well as upon circular or "feed back" arrangements. Another physiological linking mechanism is that the outputs of the nerve cells are added together. This is accomplished when the impulses of more than one cell impinge upon the same cell so that the effects of the separate impulses are combined and then proceed as one impulse. This process is known as "summation." (See illustration No.9.) The summated impulse is not known to be different chemically from the individual impulses which add their effects to form the summation, however, the summated impulse would carry a more advanced order of "information."

Illustration No. 9

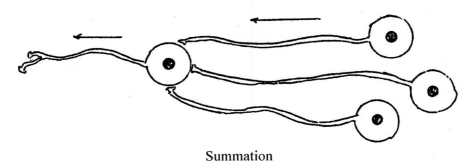

Summation

Very complex arrangements, including what are called "networks", have also been devised by researchers working in the field of "artificial intelligence." The networks consist of cell assemblies which are more complicated than those of Hebb but, as we understand them, they are based on the same principles.

At the psychological level, the linking of cores would be similar to the "associations" of Locke. Two consciousness events which occur in close succession are related or associated—they become connected. Subsequent to having become associated, the occurrence of either of the events brings the other event toward consciousness. If we see a face, it tends to bring to mind the name with which it is "associated." Since, in the newborn infant, the memory is a clean or almost clean slate, the infant's experiences would consist of its raw qualitative cores. These become associated one to the other, and let us not forget that they include emotion, particularly pleasure and pain (displeasure).

At this point we will delve deeper into the hypothetical. Even though there are problems with the following construction, some such system must take place: As hierarchical development occurs through experience, the associated elements would become *more and more elaborate.* Hierarchy formation must have a neurological substrate. It has been suggested that the DNA in the nuclei of cells is long enough to be considered as a suitable recording medium for memory. Nevertheless, even though DNA can be very long, there must be some limits on the amount of compounding that can take place in one lifetime. As we mentioned earlier, we will offer a suggestion in later pages as to how hierarchical development may be accomplished.

It is worth emphasizing, as we have done before, that consciousness is constituted of combinations of consciousness cores. This carries the implication that the memories of consciousness contents are combined with new perceptions to become new, further developed contents. The items are all composed of qualitative cores which are associated. The associated cores constitute consciousness contents in the infant and become the foundations for the consciousness contents in the adult. "Shorthand", including synecdoche and extracting the consistently associated, would be used in the formation of new contents, new combinations.

In support of the concept of consciousness cores and their being associated, we again refer to John Locke. In his writing that all ideas come from "SENSATION or REFLECTION" (1975, p. 106), "SENSATION" can be interpreted as corresponding with consciousness cores. He was writing about the development, including the early development, of the mind. His "REFLECTION" requires that current items have a conscious connection to items in memory.

Relation of Association to Logic and Experience

It is interesting that for items to become associated in the hierarchies of memory they do not necessarily need to be logically connected or related to survival value; they merely need to be related meaningfully or temporally in experience. Pavlov's experiments with the conditioned responses of dogs illustrate this. The sound of a bell becomes associated with food and results in salivating because the bell and the presentation of food occur at the same time, not because there is any logical connection between bells and food.

Not only is it true that for items to become associated they do not necessarily need to be logically related or related as to meaning but that the process can, in fact, work in the opposite direction, that is, what we come to view as logical is often that which has become associated. We formerly considered it to be completely logical that because of gravity, "Everything which goes up, *must* come down." We considered it to be eminently logical because the two conditions were always associated and we took into consideration no reason why it would not be so. It was also considered to be logical rather than egocentric that the sun should travel around the earth. Many religious and social traditions, the origins of which are lost in antiquity, are considered to be logical because they have long been associated in practice. The reasons given to explain the logic of such traditions depend largely upon which "authority" is asked about it.

Events which have considerable emotional value to an individual can become associated very quickly. The way events which are fairly neutral emotionally become associated is not by being *occasionally* connected however. We have said that what is associated is that which has a *consistent* relationship in one's experience. As was stated by Locke, logic is ultimately based on experience rather than on reason alone. Locke's approach was a naturalistic one, not mystical. Logic, after all, as we have indicated in connection with abstraction, has to develop in a natural manner.

The opposite view, that logic and abstraction would not be based on experience, is suggestive of the ancient concept (since Plato) of *a priori* knowledge, a dubious concept at best. Obviously the concept of *a priori* knowledge filled a need in the theory of knowledge. It has evolved over the course of history, and its meaning is not altogether definite, but it has been defined since Kant as knowledge existing in the mind prior to and independent of experience. We prefer to interpret the term as being knowledge which is inborn and is triggered into becoming conscious by observation. The concept of *a priori* knowledge developed long before any theory resembling the hierarchical development of knowledge was available. In ancient times, if other sources of knowledge were not known, it would not be unreasonable for knowledge to be thought to originate from some innate source. If one does not take hierarchical development into account, (or some sort of development of concepts over time) the larger part of a perception would, indeed, appear to be derived from within the mind by some form of inherited knowledge or by a magical process.

Summary

It is offered that memory hierarchies constitute the "higher centers" of the mind, that is, the control centers which correspond roughly to the "ego." The control centers function not by being a mind within the mind but by automatically facilitating or inhibiting nerve cell impulses according to whether or not the impulses further interests or anxieties.

Perceptions arise from consciousness cores and the linking of the cores. The linking is accomplished physiologically by summation of cell impulses. Associations are based not necessarily on logic but on experience. Knowledge is thus acquired through experience. We consider the concept of *a priori* knowledge to be fallacious.

Chapter Twenty-one

Representations

Partial Resolution of the Question of Representations

We have not yet given a definite answer to the question as to whether or not a representation is necessary for perception. Representationalists have reasoned that in order to see an object there has to be some way of internalizing the image of the object. (This would be the quale or sense-datum). An internal representation of the object has to be formed. How would this be possible? Our answer will be covered in this and the next two chapters. If, in the process of seeing an object, a representation is formed in the mind of the perceiver, then there needs to be some way in which the representation becomes consciousness without the services of a homunculus.

It seem reasonable that there needs to be a way for the mind to have within it some sort of representation of objects not only for the perception of external objects, but also when we recall something from memory. When we bring out of memory an item we wish to "picture", we then experience the memory. How else can we "picture" something; how else can we recognize an external object when we see it? For instance, if we are looking for something, how will we know we have found it if there is nothing in our minds with which to compare? There needs to be something in the mind to be recognized as having been found in the environment.

Perception is Largely Recognition

We agree with the concept that there are representations but let us quickly add, that *contrary to the usual understanding of a representation, most of a representation is not of the external object.* To make this statement intelligible, consider the nerve impulses which result in perception. There is the impingement of light waves or sound waves or other form of energy onto the peripheral receptors. As discussed in an earlier chapter, the sensory input, particularly in the case of light energy, is extremely scanty as compared with the total possible inputs from the whole object. After the stimulation of the peripheral receptors and after intercurrent processing, *the sensory impulses are matched or compared with items in memory.* The items in memory have developed as levels of the hierarchy from the time of the child's first vague perceptions of light, sound, and the warmth of its mother, etc., to the present day concepts and knowledge in general. *It is the item in memory, or the synecdoche of the item, which is most of the representation.* When the comparison is sufficient, the related impulses are combined and progress to the stage of consciousness. If the comparison is not sufficient, that is, an adequate match is not present, the object is not recognized. The impulses do not form an understandable item. Also, there may be only a vague perception or, sometimes none at all—the object may register on the receptors but still be simply "overlooked." The latter happens often in the proofreading of a manuscript. A few pages earlier, the typist had typed "we" but meant to type "were." After proofreading the sentence more than once, she still had not perceived the error. Her mind simply filled in the meaning of the missing letters. Fortunately someone else's perception did not miss the error. The person recognized that the erroneous letters did not match the "image" of the word in her mind.

Another simple illustration, which is perhaps better, is the familiar type of picture puzzle in which the viewer attempts to find objects which are present in the picture but requires scrutinizing the picture in order to perceive them. There may be lions and tigers in the picture but they are not "seen." The picture as perceived by the viewer is that of an uncomplicated, peaceful landscape.

It becomes apparent that *by far the greater part of perception is actually recognition.* Whatever is perceived, that which becomes consciousness, is perceived in terms of the past. For example, if a cave man, who is familiar with spear throwing, sees a bolt of lightning, he perceives a spear being thrown by a god. William James made the observation that, "The *preperception...*is half of the perception of the looked for thing." (1890, p.442). A similar statement, first published in 1900, was made by Freud (1948). Speaking of the function which we call attention, he wrote, "Its activity meets the sense impressions half-way instead of awaiting their appearance."

Another way of understanding the matter is in relation to the memory hierarchies. The internal aspect of a perception is present in the memory hierarchies. It is the memory hierarchies which are searched for a match to the incoming stimuli. This process occurs in connection with any perception and therefore examples abound. It becomes quite clear that the perceiver furnishes most of the information involved in a perception when we consider what happens in many ordinary conversations: If a person is talking and has to pause to grope for a word, the listener will often supply the sought for word. The word is supplied by the listener without the specific input from the speaker. Only the context is provided by the speaker. This is enough for the listener's memory hierarchies to be searched which then results in finding the desired word.

It is the current input, together with connections to earlier levels, that becomes the current memory item, the latest level of the memory hierarchy.

The recalling of memory levels may either be initiated voluntarily or unconsciously. In either case the subsequent process is the same. The recalled item may be abbreviated due to "shorthand." It also has new components added from present experience. The new components may be either an addition to an earlier memory or may be a correction or refinement. The new memory trace is a new hierarchy level which is then available as a new memory item when recalled in relation to future perceptions.

Relation of Representations to Synecdoche and Qualia

In the final analysis regarding representations, we can say that in a sense there is seldom, if ever, a complete representation. *What we perceive as a representation is only partial and relatively limited at that.* In the first place, as has been mentioned in earlier pages, it would be impossible to perceive all the aspects of any object. The aspects, for example, of an object of vision are virtually unlimited.

As we reviewed above, the principal reason we are interested in representations as being only relatively complete is that what we perceive as a representation stems in large part from one's memory hierarchies. The degree to which the representation arises from memory depends upon the object under observation. For instance, if the object is an abstract noun such as "America", then the representation is mainly from within memory. The representation in this case would be called a meaning, and the meaning would depend to a large extent upon the listener. In other cases of words, the meanings of which are composed of relatively few memory components, the representation is closer to the actual extrinsic aspects of the represented object. However, at this point we should be reminded again that the external aspects are limitless and, as propounded by Kant, objects as they are "in themselves" are "unknowable."

The relationship of qualia to representations now becomes clearer. *There actually are no qualia* if by qualia we mean internalizations of whole objects or anything approaching complete representations. As we have explained above, relatively little of an object is currently internalized. Therefore no quale is formed. There is, of course, a perception but the perception is largely from within. In our view the term, perception, is more suitable than "qualia" and if "qualia" is to be retained, and perhaps it should since it is so widely used, then its meaning should include the contribution of the memory hierarchy.

Representations—Recursive Comparisons

To definitively answer the question about representations, we agree with the critics of classic representationalism that the representations are not an image in the sense of an exact likeness of the object. According to Bruner's statement (1973, p. 10), "We have long since given up simulacral theories of representation." Because perception is largely recognition, what are regarded as representations of current perceptions are usually much closer to being representations of past objects. Let us emphasize that a representation is a combination of the sensory inputs of the object and the pattern from the memory hierarchy. *Apparently because the memory component is unconscious, a perceiver regards the combination as being the object.* Furthermore the combination becomes consciousness without being perceived by a central observer or homunculus-like entity. *The combination becomes consciousness by virtue of the identity of consciousness with nerve cells and their impulses.*

Some further points are also needed to complete the answer. Not only are the past inputs to memory developed hierarchically but there is another process of development. This time the development is in the incoming impulses which arise from the external object. It may be an oversimplification to say that the impulses are simply compared with hierarchies in memory and are then allowed to become consciousness when a sufficient match is attained. The process may be more involved than simply trying a number of keys in a lock until one is found which fits and turns the lock. Perception would involve a creative development in a two way process. There must be a recursive comparison between the incoming material and the memory hierarchies with a progressive development of the resulting material. When a point is reached at which the combined arrangement is satisfactorily complete it is allowed to become consciousness. Also a new memory hierarchy is established. (This topic was introduced under the heading of "Selectivity in Perception" in chapter fifteen.) Anglin in his introduction to Bruner (1973, p. xxii) made the following statement:

> Construction [perception] usually involves a recursive process in which the first step is an inferential leap from sense data to a tentative hypothesis achieved by relating incoming information to an internally stored model of the world based upon past experience. The second step is essentially a confirmation check in which the tentative hypothesis is tested against further sense data. In the face of a match the hypothesis is maintained; in the face of a mismatch the hypothesis is altered in a way that acknowledges the discrepant evidence.

We are in accord with Anglin's statement but we prefer to be more specific. In our formulation the "internally stored model of the world" is "altered" by the formation of a *new memory hierarchy.* Consciousness cores are added, subtracted, rearranged, or there is a combination of these alterations. As neuroscientist McCullough (1947) mentioned in a somewhat different context, "If you end on a success, you begin on a success. If you end on a failure, you begin on a failure." His statement can be applied to the recursive process of comparing the sensory inputs with the levels of the memory hierarchy. The accuracy and completeness of a perception depends in large measure on previous observation.

We would also add that even if the inputs initially match the item in memory, there is probably still a new item established which is the same as the old item. At the psychological level of speaking this means that the item in memory is "refreshed" and is all the more readily accessible for future use. The process of perception as described above sounds as if it would be too involved and therefore too time consuming to be the mechanism which is actually used by the brain. But do not overlook the fact that the brain operates extremely rapidly and also uses methods of "shorthand."

At this point we will temporarily discontinue the discussion of representations but will describe them more completely after we have discussed meanings in a later chapter.

Summary

Some sort of representation of objects certainly seems to be required for perception. However, perception is largely recognition. Sensory inputs are recursively matched against and alter items in memory. It is the item in memory, or the synecdoche of the item, which is most of the representation. New perceptions become new memory hierarchies and are used in future perceptions.

Chapter Twenty-two

Additional Aspects of Consciousness

Consciousness Is in the Present

In accord with our discussion of the identity theory we have stated that nerve cell impulses *are* consciousness and that no central observer, homunculus or ego is required to register the event. We have also stated that consciousness is experience and only experience. The view that consciousness is experience follows logically from the concept of the consciousness core. The consciousness cores are "within" or constitute consciousness. They are experiences, and consciousness, which is composed of them, is experience. The view that consciousness is experience is forced upon us if we are to be consistent with the concept that qualitative elements, the consciousness cores, form the basis of consciousness.

There is another point which needs to be made fully explicit. Not only is consciousness experience, but *the experience is in the present.* To correctly describe it, one should use the present tense. It is not actually inaccurate to state, as we did above that "consciousness is experience" but it would be more accurate and more informative to state that "consciousness is experienc*ing.*" We have consciousness only at the present time: "I think this" or "I am that", etc. We never have the experiencing of consciousness in the past. We have recall of past events but the recollection, too, is at the present time.

That consciousness is experiencing is important in relation to the identity theory as well as in the ongoing attempt to specify the nerve cells or components of nerve cells which are consciousness. The identity theory states that nerve cell impulses *are* consciousness contents, not that they were so in the past or will be in the future. Whether the impulses which constitute a single content occur in a tenth of a second or a thousandth of a second, the elements which produce consciousness do so only at the present time and are experienced accordingly.

Consciousness Components May Already Be Before Us

In the attempt to further develop a concept of consciousness it is important to first reemphasize that we cannot appreciate our own consciousness from the "outside" perspective. Our perspective is only from the "inside." A paradoxical implication of the concept, that consciousness is experience and can be known directly only from the "inside", is the idea that science may already be aware of and regularly observes the physical substrate items of which consciousness is constituted. In this statement we refer to nerve cell impulses, interneuronal substances, intraneuronal molecules, networks, quantum effects, or whatever the substrate items might be. The important entities may already be well known but without their significance for consciousness being recognized or proven. Since we cannot appreciate such entities from the "inside", we cannot correlate them with consciousness. When we examine these items we do not experience the consciousness that they produce. Therefore we do not realize that these are the items which *are* the consciousness contents.

This is the unique problem which we have previously mentioned in connection with animals and children. There is no way that we can view anyone's consciousness as an "it" (from the third person perspective) and at the same time know it as an experience (from the first person perspective). Either we are "inside" consciousness or we are "outside" it. Either we are experiencing it as in the case of our own consciousness or we are observing it as in the case of someone else's consciousness. The nerve cells or impulses which are consciousness have an entirely different quality when viewed from each of the two different perspectives. To be more exact, we should say that the impulses have none of the qualities of consciousness when viewed from the "outside." To fully understand how consciousness is produced we need to concomitantly experience it and, at the *very same time*, to observe the mechanism by which it happens. The processes take place so rapidly that if they are not viewed at the same time we can not be sure that we are observing the correct process. We need to correlate the neural processes with the experiencing of them and, further, the correlations will have to be repeated consistently for a number of times. Correlating such evanescent activity in the third person perspective, for instance as a pattern on an oscilloscope, with first person consciousness content will not be an easy research endeavor.

It is for this reason that we have been unable to demonstrate causes of consciousness even if we already know them. We have been unable to connect the observed phenomena with consciousness. Hameroff, Penrose (1996) and others point within nerve cells to certain fairly recently discovered structures called microtubules. These structures can be seen with the electron microscope. Even the chemical composition and arrangement of the molecules within the structures has been worked out. Proceeding with that knowledge, the authors jump over a gap in the causal chain. They postulate that quantum phenomena within the microtubules produce consciousness. Even if they are correct there is no way to prove their theory. Crick and Koch's view is that the 40 Hz (40 cycles per second) rhythm coordinated between nerve cells, may be the answer to the puzzle of consciousness. As Crick has recently said, there is no way of proving that it is causative. This is in agreement with our own thinking. Even if we could produce artificial nerve fibers which genuinely contain consciousness, we could not become aware of the consciousness. We could not experience it. To us it would be like someone else's consciousness.

Nevertheless, we wish to emphasize in regard to consciousness *as being nerve cells or impulses*, that there is apparently nothing else for consciousness to be. (We are referring to nerve cell impulses as inclusive of the effects of microtubules, 40Hz rhythm, and so forth.) This becomes obvious and altogether unavoidable if we have a naturalistic point of view. It is believed that the nervous system produces consciousness and that the nervous system functions by means of nerve cell activity. As long as this is considered to be correct, we are required to think that consciousness is the same as neuronal activity. The reason consciousness does not *seem* to be nerve cells or their impulses may be that we are accustomed to considering objects only from the third person perspective—as outside of ourselves. But we can know consciousness only from the first person perspective. We have never been outside our nerve cells. We only know our own impulses as the inside of consciousness. We are like the fish which is able to experience the world only through the water in which it swims. We have never been outside our own world. We can be told about the other person's world, but we are also on the outside of that. And even if we could get into the other person's world, it would not look basically different from our own. We would still be inside a world, inside consciousness. Our only personal experience with consciousness is consciousness itself.

Crick (1994) has sought what he calls "consciousness neurons" in the brain. As we understand his concept of consciousness neurons, our concept is somewhat different. We, too, suspect that there are consciousness neurons in the sensory system, as we have said earlier without giving them a specific name. However, we believe that the initial elements of consciousness may be present at the beginning or throughout the chain of sensory neurons. This is speculative and a fairly radical departure from the usual thinking, but there are indications to this effect. The beginnings of the sensory chains are in the skin, the eyes, the nose, the stomach, etc. We regard the sensory neurons as possibly being the basis of the putative qualitative cores.

Researchers who are looking for consciousness at a location where it arises or where "it all comes together", would seem destined to be severely hampered, if not completely thwarted, in their attempts to find nerve cells which are responsible for consciousness. To be sure that the cells are those they are seeking, they would have to observe them from the "inside perspective", which, of course, they cannot do. There is the further consideration that consciousness is almost certainly hierarchical which means that it would not be present *as we know it* in any one cell or group of cells. *We are considering consciousness (perception) as having been developed both from memory and from current sensory input in a recursive process of comparison.* These points were discussed more fully under the earlier section entitled "Perception is Mainly Recognition" and will be touched upon again a few paragraphs below.

Are each of the consciousness cores, which we have hypothesized, a tiny Cartesian theater with an implied homunculus to be aware of the core? Not as we conceive of it. The consciousness cores, in accordance with our version of the identity theory, each contain the elements of consciousness. If consciousness cores are *"within"* the neurons of the sensory system, are an intrinsic part of them, the need is removed for locating the sensory neurons (or any neurons) where their activity is transformed into consciousness. Instead, we have postulated (in the section under the heading of "Dynamicity of Consciousness") that the consciousness cores are "within" the system wherever consciousness is present. The cores become consciousness when they are selected over the multitude of other sensory stimuli which are impinging upon the sense receptors at all times. There might still be a "coming together" as when the color and shape of an object are perceived. However, as explained under the concept of synecdoche, such a coming together might be more apparent than real in as much as the perception of one or more sensory modalities might provide the illusion of a "coming together." We have already discussed both the mechanism by which impulses are selected for facilitation into becoming consciousness by "interests and anxieties." We have also mentioned the memory hierarchies as the selecting body.

The progression of Dennett's (1991) approach toward an explanation of consciousness is basically from the psychological level downward to the neurological substrate, a direction opposite to that of Crick whose approach is primarily from the neurological level upward. Dennett presents a considerable amount of neurophysiology, but the effect is to support his basic view of consciousness, that there are "multiple drafts", a reference to the various drafts or revisions which may be made in the writing of a letter or a book—the sensory inputs undergo multiple drafts in the brain. He presents an eloquent view of what we refer to as the dynamicity of brain processes. His answer to "when does it all come together?", however, is a very direct, "Never." The accusation by Searle (1992a) that Dennett explains consciousness "away", rather than explains it, is understandable.

Redefinition of "Sensory"

Upon reading the passage immediately above, the reader may notice that we use the term, sensory, in a way which is not the customary one. We referred to it in chapter three but we will do so again as we consider it to be important to our concept of consciousness. The conventional usage of the word applies to nerve cell fibers which carry sensory impulses, mainly of the so-called five senses, upward *toward the cerebral cortex.* This definition of "sensory" is based on anatomy and on the concept that consciousness arises entirely in the cerebral cortex. In distinction, we generally prefer to use the term in a broader functional rather than anatomical sense. The two meanings do not coincide in some contexts. In our broader sense, anything which is preconscious, or is an "input to consciousness", is sensory. Emotions, memories, and "ideas" would be included in this category. Another point is that the customary usage of the term becomes unclear in the cortical and subcortical structures where the neural processes are recursive. Recursive impulses can be traveling *either toward or away from* the cortex, or in a loop extending from and back to the cortex, but in any case can still be involved in progress *toward becoming consciousness* and in that sense they are sensory.

Nerve Cells, Impulses, and Identity

It is perhaps somewhat overdue that we explicitly describe our view of *nerve cells* and *nerve cell impulses* in relation to perceptual physiology. The two terms are, of course, very closely related and we, as well as other authors, tend to use the terms interchangeably. Crick, for example, uses both concepts when he writes of the 40 Hz rhythm of *impulses* and also writes of "consciousness neurons." Until now we have tried to use both terms in order to keep our theorizing broadly based but we should now point out the significance of a distinction between the two. It is not known whether the nerve cell impulses or the cells alone, apart from their impulses, are the principle elements as sources of consciousness. The impulses, of course, are activity of the cells and as far as nervous system processing is concerned, it is somewhat like "splitting hairs" to make a distinction between the two. Nevertheless, we feel that there is considerable attractiveness in the concept that the impulses merely produce changes which enable the *cells* to become consciousness by switching the cells "on."

Theorists who consider microtubules or other structures within nerve cells to be the source of consciousness are looking within cells while those who regard networks of cells as the important neurophysiology are concentrating their attention on impulses, specifically their strength, timing and arrangements. If computers are considered to be capable of having consciousness, the relative importance of impulses would be increased since computers do not have cells, and computer chips are basically merely mechanisms for switching impulses. It appears to be quite unlikely that impulses alone contain the final elements of consciousness. However, it is also conceivable that cells are merely switching mechanisms for impulses. No doubt both impulses and cells participate in consciousness since cells produce impulses which in turn stimulate other cells, but one or the other may culminate as consciousness. According to our view of the identity theory, it appears to be probable that cells, rather than impulses or intercellular molecules, have identity with consciousness at the cerebral end of the series. The impulses *stimulate* the cells but it is the cells (inclusive of microtubules or other subcellular structures) which are the final elements of consciousness. The light bulb at the end of the electric wire is the operative component.

We have previously discussed the possibility that *initial* elements of consciousness, whether they are simply sensory impulses or specific molecules, may originate in the periphery of the body. While we have no empirical reason for thinking so, it nevertheless seems more likely that consciousness, may be physically inside cells. This arrangement suggests that consciousness may reside in cells located at the ends of sensory chains in the brain in areas which are specific for individual sensory modalities. Such an arrangement would be consistent with the situation in the remainder of the body where impulses stimulate muscle cells or secretory cells, etc., but it is the cells which carry out the action. Of course, both ends of the sensory chain might contain original elements.

To be more succinct, the elements which become consciousness by virtue of identity include one or more of four possibilities. They are either (1) in the brain within only the final cells in the sensory series. (2) In cells both in the brain and in those in the sensory chain along the way to the brain. (3) In cellular impulses. (4) In intercellular substances—molecules which are extruded at synapses in the stimulation of cells. We cannot be more specific at this time; even the concept of identity is still theoretical. Like links in a chain, until the level of consciousness is reached, all of these are necessary. (We should also point out for the sake of completeness that cellular impulses are literally both within and outside nerve cells, involving electrically charged portions of atoms called ions. The ions regularly traverse in and out of the cell walls in a wave which progresses along a fiber and constitutes the electrical impulse.)

If cells in a sensory series prior to the final consciousness contain earlier elements such as molecules, which are passed from one cell to the next all the way to the "final" cells, then the impulses, the intermediate cells, and the final cells all contain the consciousness elements. Such an arrangement would not require that the individual molecules be passed from the periphery all the way to the brain. It would only require that molecules, similar to the ones which enter a cell at one end, be extruded from the cell at the other end. Also, let us be clear that by "consciousness elements" we do not mean full or "final" consciousness. The prior elements, if indeed there are such, do not become a part of "final consciousness" until they reach the appropriate cells in the brain.

In the remainder of this book we will refer only to nerve cells as the site of identity with consciousness but the reader should understand that we do so with some reservation. In a subsequent chapter we will discuss the close relationship of memory with consciousness.

Summary

Consciousness is experience and is always in the present. Its neurological substrate may actually be known but neither proven nor recognized as such. To correlate nerve cells or neurological processes with consciousness in an isolated manner and on a sufficiently fine scale is virtually impossible at this time because consciousness is only in the first person and the processes are perceived only in the third person.

"Sensory" is redefined as any nerve cell impulses which are inputs to consciousness. This involves not only inputs from the senses but emotions, memories, and "ideas" as well.

In one's thinking about the primary elements of consciousness, it would be well to explicitly distinguish between nerve cell impulses, nerve cells, and the components of each. The primary elements of consciousness may be present within cells which are either located in the cerebral cortex, the remainder of the body, or both.

Chapter Twenty-three

Attention and Automaticity

Attention

Attention clearly plays a central role in the mechanism by which sensory inputs become consciousness. A typical definition characterizes attention as the act of directing one's mind, or of mental concentration, onto something of interest. This directing of one's mind determines for the most part which objects will be brought into consciousness. Under the section heading of "Perception is Largely Recognition" in chapter twenty-one, we quoted James (1890, p. 442) and Freud (1948) in statements made prior to the turn of the last century, in which both expressed the idea that attention meets sensory inputs "half-way." We will expand upon these statements, applying the concepts we have previously developed about the memory hierarchy and consciousness.

Freud (1938b) writing in 1900 considered attention to be a matter of the shifting of energy from cognitive functions to sensory functions, that is, from thinking to perceiving. In relation to consciousness, he stated "The act of becoming conscious depends upon a definite psychic function—attention—being brought to bear." Bleuler (1924), a Swiss psychiatrist who introduced the term, schizophrenia, wrote of two types of attention, the "active" and the "passive" type. The two types, which are descriptive at the behavioral level, became the conventional manner of regarding attention. We will designate his view as the "Bleuler model" and will employ the model's usefulness for illustrating the attention mechanism.

Very briefly, in the passive form of attention the stimulus is unexpected. For instance, a sudden loud noise imposes itself upon our sense receptors. We then immediately make a dodging movement or glance toward the sound. The movement is often characterized as a "reflex" because of it appears to be "automatic."

In contrast to passive attention, the active form of attention is the general counterpart of questions such as "What was that I heard?" or "What was that I thought?" We may define "active" attention as *the seeking of information.* There is the deliberate turning of our vision in the direction of a noise. One hears a bird call but the call is not alarming enough to result in an immediate startle reaction. Instead the initial stimulus simply fails to find a sufficiently satisfying match in the memory hierarchies. The sound is recognized as a bird call but the song is unfamiliar. According to the Bleuler model, one then *volitionally* looks for the source of the input.

173

We are in agreement with the above view of passive and active attention but only as it is descriptive on the surface, that is, on the behavioral level, observable both to ourselves and to others. We would like to examine the attention mechanism at a deeper level, at the neurocellular level. Let us begin our description with the mechanism of so-called "passive" attention.

In the case of a sudden loud noise, as mentioned above, a stimulus reaches the ears and sensory impulses proceed to the brain. A search of the memory hierarchies is conducted but the individual is not prepared for the sound, and a match with a particular level of the memory hierarchy is not likely to be sufficiently complete for the sound to be immediately recognized. The impulses from the initial stimulus then reach other relevant levels of the memory hierarchy.

We can now generalize that *the control of the sensory mechanism stems from the memory hierarchy.* The hierarchy, in recursive activity and largely under the influence of the emotional configuration, prepares appropriate areas of itself and the sensory mechanisms for the reception of stimuli. (Recall that the levels of the memory hierarchy have associated emotional elements. We have previously described the emotional components in general as interests and anxieties. In the case of a sudden loud noise the emotion is very likely to be closer to anxiety than to interest.) The action of the memory hierarchy is adjusted during execution. The category within the hierarchy which most closely aligns with the sound, is selected and readied to receive impulses from the appropriate sensory organs; the ears are "attuned"; the head may be turned in the proper direction; the eyes may be pointed in the direction of the sound. One receives further stimulation from the sound and gains information about its meaning. (We should be clear about the "attuning" of the ears. It is more likely that the "attuning" involves an adjustment within the memory hierarchy itself rather than in an alteration in the receptor mechanisms of the ears.)

Is there any empirical observation which substantiates that the initial stimulus is matched against and combined with a level of the memory hierarchy? The involvement of the memory hierarchy and the matching process is indicated by the behavioral action which results. For example, if a helicopter unexpectedly flies rather low over one's head, the lowering of the head is a selective reaction stemming from memory. If the unexpected noise does not have some meaning of danger, rather than lower one's head, one might rotate the head upward. Or, in crossing a mine field, in the event of an explosion, one might jump forward rather than drop one's body to the ground. In the adult the exact form of the reaction depends upon a preexisting available pattern. The selection of the reaction pattern is often accomplished at an unconscious level by the memory hierarchy. In contrast to the selection of a reaction, the startle reaction of the newborn infant

("Moro reflex") is clearly inborn and is not selective. The infant, which is lying on its back, suddenly jerks its arms and legs upward. The reaction is the same regardless of whether there is a sudden loud sound or whether one jars the table upon which the infant is lying.

We wish to make it clear that even though the memory hierarchy initiates muscular action, we are not anthropomorphizing the hierarchy. We are not attributing to it the powers of an independent "mind." It reacts not from its own volition but in automatic response to the sensory input which it receives, a response which is heavily influenced by the associated emotions.

Muscle action may be minimal. In the act of listening to a sound there may be little or no overt muscular movement. Nevertheless, the listening apparently involves a readying of appropriate memory hierarchy levels for the reception of impulses. The same may apply in the anticipation of a mild touch to the skin. A reaction different from muscular action, is a reaction within the so-called autonomic nervous system. This would involve perspiring, a change in respiration or heart rate, or other mostly unconscious activity. *The characteristic elements of the attention mechanisms, whether of the "passive" or the "active" type, are the activity of the memory hierarchies and the recursive matching process.*

Let us not become confused between the process of attention and that of consciousness. The mechanism of consciousness, to be described in the next chapter, employs the same process but carries it a step further.

The above description is, of course, a simplification of the actual situation. There is a continuum in the activity between the "active" and the "passive" form of attention. There are degrees of startle reaction as well as degrees of the "seeking of information." Also, some processes of perception may involve very little of the attention mechanism; one's interests are elsewhere at the time and the perception is therefore minimal.

In our consideration, without the application of a matching process, a stimulus does not progress toward becoming consciousness and theoretically does not reach the level of perception. This applies whether the stimulus is from within the "mind" or from external sources. There must be comparisons made with patterns of the memory hierarchy. Without comparisons, items which are perceived in the visual field, for example, are not recognized as being items. Instead they are treated similarly to abstract paintings which have meanings as paintings but not as specific objects within the paintings. Any sensory input which becomes consciousness has been matched against patterns of memory hierarchy. *We consider the matching process to invariably be a part of the process of perception.* There may be an exception in the case of the infant, where the early sensory impulses would theoretically have no memory behind them and would initially register stimuli only in terms of their qualities.

The matching process undoubtedly results from an inborn mechanism. It is present in human beings and appears to be present in many lower animals. In the case of the lower animals the capability to discriminate food from non-food strongly suggests a comparison between a stimulus and an item of memory. For example, a cat or dog smells or tastes its food before eating it.

Can we answer the question as to whether or not attention is necessary for perception? The answer probably depends upon one's exact understanding of attention and consciousness. At the minimal level of each of them, there would be a fine line to draw between "no attention" and "very little attention." For instance, in subliminal stimulation, is there any attention? By definition, there is no consciousness of the subliminal item. In our view, there would apparently be slight attention or the item would not be retained in memory. Another situation which tests our understanding is "blind-sight" in which an item enters the "mind" (more specifically, the memory), but is not available to become consciousness. Attention to the item is necessarily present in order for the item to be registered in memory but the attention (the matching process) is subconscious. Except possibly for quite unusual circumstances, some degree of attention is required for perception.

Now let us return to the matter of whether attention should be considered "active" or "passive." For it to be considered "active" means that the activity must be *initiated* by the mind or more specifically by the memory hierarchies. At the level of overt behavior, in contrast to the neurocellular level, the concept of attention bears considerable resemblance to being active. We speak of "paying attention" or of "giving attention." It is difficult to think of attention as being completely passive. Further, at the cellular level there is activity in the attempt to find a match between the impulses, which result from the initial stimulus, and the memory hierarchy levels.

Yet, at the neurocellular level it becomes very reasonable that there is only one type of attention, the passive type. Even the activity which we have included under the "active" category is also passive at the neuronal level. The matching process occurs in response to stimulation and is *automatic*. As a result we regard it from a technical standpoint as passive. It is carried out under the control of the memory hierarchies but, the memory hierarchies in turn react under the determining influence of interests and anxieties. Recall, too, that interests and anxieties result from past experiences of pleasure and displeasure, from gratifications and discomforts. The attention can be regarded as active only if one views the memory hierarchies as being capable of initiating activity entirely on their own prerogative, as if they have a mind of their own. At the neurophysiological level to regard the process as active is to view it as if the memory hierarchies initiate the seeking of a match, a concept which implies anthropomorphism. The memory hierarchies merely *react*. In the final analysis, we regard attention which appears to be "active" at the behavioral level of description, as actually passive at the physiological level. The attention behavior is not initiated by the memory hierarchies.

Automaticity

We need to further address the matter of automaticity. If there is no "central observer" to initiate the activity involved in reaction to a stimulus, there is a clear implication that an individual's reactions are automatic. A "central observer" functions as if it is a mind within the mind and perceives the contents of consciousness. The idea that reactions are automatic is, of course, quite unconventional but we wish to present our reasons for believing that it is correct.

Reactions are the result of past experiences. When stimuli are received the match which is found within the hierarchies is the closest that is available and similarly the reaction is the most suitable that can be obtained. The reaction is managed by cellular activities which are established by previous activity. *It is the automaticity of the reaction which we wish to distinguish from volitional action of an imaginary homunculus or a putative "central observer."* Contrary to a "central observer", the functioning of the cellular activity described in the memory hierarchies results, as we have indicated, from the facilitations and inhibitions associated with interests and anxieties.

The fact of automaticity, however, does not mean that there is depersonalization, that there is no sense of self. People still have a sense of self (which we consider to be quite normal but illusional) which is relatively permanent. They still feel that they are individuals with a mind and a will.

For an explanation of the apparent difference between automaticity and control by the self, we again turn to the memory hierarchies. Memory is responsible for the sense of continuity which is present day in and day out. There is consistency in interests and anxieties. They are permanent unless amended by experience. If I like baseball today, I still like it tomorrow. If I am afraid of driving an automobile today, I am still afraid of it tomorrow. If I know how to perform my work today, I know how to handle it tomorrow. Not only my likes, dislikes and skills but my emotional associations and behavior in general have a large degree of consistency. This is even true of my appearance in the mirror. All of these are present in memory and by and large remain the same. In sum there is no loss of the sense of being a person, of having a self, or of comfort in using the pronoun, "I."

177

Aside from the theoretical justification for the concept of automaticity, the evidence for it is very commonplace if one is receptive to such an interpretation. For example, memories are often recalled without voluntary effort. A name that one could not recall a moment ago suddenly appears in consciousness considerably later than the attempted recollection. Even without a voluntary effort, one becomes aware of a melody, a particular verbal expression, or a noticeable thought. In fact, the persistence in consciousness of contents such as melodies, images or experiences, which involve a high level of emotion, can be difficult to remove from one's thinking. The "flashbacks" of combat veterans can be particularly disturbing. Dreams are examples of automaticity common to everyone and the fact of hallucinations is well established.

Freedom of Will

It seems there is now no avoiding the contentious problem of the freedom of will. If the memory hierarchies automatically determine our actions, how can we explain freedom of will? We must state that we regard freedom of will, like the unitary self, as only apparent. To a determinist, someone who believes in natural causes, free will must be illusory if our minds and our brains function as the result of cells which, in the final analysis, do not have their own brains and are composed of inanimate molecules.

Our resolution of the problem of the freedom of will is simply that the interests and anxieties in our memory hierarchies determine our actions. We feel as if *we* determine the actions because they result from *our* interests and anxieties and not simply by chance. In a very real sense, since the actions result from *our* interests and anxieties then, *even though the actions are automatic, they are our actions, compatible with our feelings, our morals, and our values at the time of the action* (at the instant even if not in the long term). Yet, the actions are instigated not by our selves but by our memory hierarchies.

Volition

Volition is the "output" side of the activity of the memory hierarchies. If I choose to raise my hand, I do so because something prompts my doing it. I may do so in order to test my feeling of having free will or for some other reason. But, regardless, there is always some desire or need which leads to the action. The action is not initiated in a vacuum. There is always a prior cause to any action. Indeed, at the cellular level, the action is a reaction. It does not happen simply because of will.

Do we have a choice in the action which we select? Our actions are selected on the basis of our interests and anxieties and are within the armamentarium and constraints of actions available to us. We might "will" to flap our arms and attempt to fly, but we do not do so because we know in advance that we simply do not have the capacity to fly. We might "will" to eat less in order to lose weight but fail repeatedly because of contrary desires and unconscious promptings.

In chapter four under the section entitled "Preperceptual Processes" we described Libet's experiment in which electrical activity in the brain occurred prior to a person's consciousness of an intention to move a finger. The experiment strongly supports our contention that we may regard our actions as being instigated not by our selves but by our brains. Yet, as we mentioned above, in a larger sense the "choices" of our actions and their timing are our own since our actions are determined by the net effect of the interests and anxieties which are included within the scope of our memory hierarchies.

Our concepts of both the absence of free will and of consciousness, have relevance to the "mind-body problem" and offer the solution that the mind and the body are the same, they are not separate. Our concept of the absence of free will offers a solution since the motor actions of the body are determined by the memory hierarchies. Also, consciousness, rather than being produced in some mysterious manner by the "mind", is in the final analysis identical with the body, that is, with nerve cells and their activity.

Curiosity

There is an ancillary point in connection with our theory of memory hierarchies and attention. The theory readily fits an explanation of curiosity. *Curiosity* is defined as a desire to know or understand, which manifests itself in questions such as "What produced the sound?" Curiosity is physiologically a form of attention but occupies its own niche in the description of behavior.

We consider curiosity to be a reflection of the manner in which the memory hierarchies function in the human and in many species of the animal kingdom in general. Any sensory input is applied to the process of matching against memory hierarchies. *The hierarchies (or ego) respond to an emotional need to have more input about a stimulus insufficiently understood.* This gives rise to "attention" with the facilitation of sensory impulses to proceed through the process of monitoring, matching, and screening. Those inputs which are selected over all other stimuli at the instant under consideration stimulate the cells which finally are consciousness. It is quite apparent that curiosity would have great advantages in the process of evolution. For instance when an object is noticed but is not recognized, human beings as well as lower animals need further information in order to know whether the object bodes well or ill.

(There are also possible disadvantages as in the case of the proverbial cat which "curiosity killed", or children who attempt to taste or explore almost anything which they can put into their mouths.)

Summary

We regard the mechanism of attention as an inborn part of the sensory process which leads to consciousness. The memory hierarchy levels, acting under the automatic influence of previous experiences with their associated emotions, accomplish the directing of the muscles and the "attuning" of the sensory organs. The hierarchy operates with the use of recursive matching of sensory inputs to hierarchy levels. The sources of stimuli include those which are from outside the body as well as from emotions and from separate levels within the memory hierarchies themselves.

Conventional descriptions include "active" and "passive" attention but at the neuronal level attention is a reaction to conscious or unconscious stimulation and thus is passive in the final analysis. The activity of the memory hierarchies in perception and in volition is automatic as determined by the net effect of one's "interests and anxieties." The process is fully determined but remains within the scope of one's feelings and values and within one's armamentarium of behavioral reactions. The behavioral reactions are within the constraints of our knowledge of reality. To state the matter more pointedly, we do not have free will but our actions are nevertheless "our" actions.

Curiosity is a form of attention which is present fairly generally in the animal kingdom and results from an inborn process stemming from the memory hierarchies. The hierarchies assign attention to sensory inputs from which further information is desired.

Chapter Twenty-four

Becoming Consciousness

The Crux of Becoming Consciousness

At this point, we shall coordinate some aspects of our theory of consciousness, utilizing most of the concepts which we have previously developed. We have presented the idea of the qualitative core and that perception involves a recursive interplay between the incoming sensory elements and the hierarchies in memory. The two elements combine to form a new perception as well as a new hierarchical level or pattern in memory. We have also said that consciousness is experience and only experience and that to have *knowledge* of our own consciousness in addition to the bare experience, *requires conscious memory of the event.* Without the conscious memory of an experience we can react but cannot be aware that we have had the experience. The latter statement becomes important in the discussion to follow. The initial experience and the memory of the experience are actually two separate instances of consciousness.

We can now put together, mostly from previously mentioned constructions, the schema by which an item becomes consciousness. As with the attention mechanism described in the preceding chapter, the process involves a sensory input and memory hierarchies. It is a process, which is often or possibly always recursive, in which the inputs from the sensory organs are matched against and combined with memory hierarchy patterns. *The combination of sensory inputs with memory hierarchy patterns then becomes consciousness by virtue of identity.* *The nerve cells when considered from the "inside" perspective are experienced by an individual as consciousness.* The neuronal activities simply *are* consciousness. Recall that we regard consciousness as being a series of events rather than a single experiencing entity. Recall, too, that we may refer to the inside perspective as the "first person" perspective in contradistinction to the "outside" or third person perspective.

We wish to make it clear and to acknowledge that we have provided no proof that identity is involved. Yet in a general sense, as we have stated before, if it is nervous system activity which results in consciousness, then at some level of neurophysiology nervous system activity must be identical with consciousness. To believe otherwise one must reach beyond natural mechanisms.

It should be made clear that there is memory of the consciousness content and that the content becomes a *new level of the memory hierarchy.*

(Recall that memory hierarchy levels are unconscious or preconscious until they reach the surface and become consciousness.) The origin of a new level of memory hierarchy can be diagrammed as follows:

Sensory impulse + memory hierarchy level—> consciousness—> new memory hierarchy level

Having become a part of the memory hierarchy, a new perception helps in the controlling influence which the memory hierarchies have over the selection of subsequent incoming sensory patterns and over the reactions to them. Whether the reactions result from stimuli which come from the within the body (which includes the memory hierarchies themselves) or from without, a reaction is automatic and its specific form depends upon the past experiences of the individual. (As discussed in the previous chapter, this indicates determinism and has negative implications for the existence of free will.)

There are additional points to be mentioned in relation to the concept that a level of memory hierarchy is composed of a combination of a new input and a previous hierarchy level. The relative proportion of the two varies depending upon the nature of the sensory material involved. A new experience, such as a very severe pain, may have a relatively small proportion of previous memory hierarchy within it. At the other end of the continuum, the consciousness of a mathematical concept or of a word such as "family" has a relatively large proportion of the memory hierarchy level (the previously existing understanding) while the proportion of the immediate sensory component is relatively small.

The sensory input and the previously existing memory level both consist essentially of qualitative cores which have become associated. It should be emphasized that the qualitative cores comprise the preconscious memory levels as well as the stage of consciousness. The whole process, from the stimulation of receptor organs to the stage of consciousness, functions extremely quickly—in a matter of fractions of a second.

The reader may still be strongly inclined to ask, "But who becomes aware of the consciousness? Who sees the object; who feels the pain or senses the pleasure? If it is not the central observer, or the memory hierarchies or the ego, is it no one? Can it be true that no one is needed to become aware of the consciousness content; that the nerve cells *are* consciousness?"

The matter is complicated by the basis of the question. The basis is such that it is impossible to give a fully satisfactory answer because the question stems from a presumption which is incorrect. The presumption is that the answer is from "outside" the nerve cells, from the third person perspective. To answer "Who sees the object?" from the third person perspective is to state that some agency of the mind does so. *"It* sees the object." The agency might be a homunculus, a central observer, the ego, the memory hierarchies, or any other agency of the mind one might consider. *Any* such answer has the same problem that we have described with the homunculus. A second agency is needed to do the seeing for the first agency; and thus begins a reduction to the absurd.

We need to understand that the question has to seek an answer which is from an "inside" perspective. It is not even correct to call this the "first person perspective" in a literal sense. If the answer to the question is "I see the object", "I" in that context should be understood as merely an intellectual construction and not a faculty of the mind, not an entity. Further, to state that the self sees the content is also incorrect. The self is merely a content of consciousness and, like "I", does not exist as an entity. Any attempts at full explanations of "Who sees the object", without the understanding that one needs an "inside" perspective of nerve cell impulses and that "I" is merely a concept, fails to reach the mark. To be specific, explanations in terms of third person perspectives such as nerve cells, nerve cell impulses, intercellular transmitters, microtubules with quantum effects, 40 cycle per second coordinated rhythms, nerve cell networks, etc., are hollow. Even if one or more of these "explanations" actually entails the correct physiology, it still fails badly. One's perspective must be from a location "inside the nerve cells"; one must think of the nerve cell impulses *not as impulses* but as *consciousness contents.* One must have in mind the first person perspective. One must be cognizant of the smell, of the color, or of the thought. Such is the "inside" nature of the cells. According to the concept of identity, we must remember that there are two entirely different ways of regarding the nerve cells. From the "inside" perspective the impulses or the cells which they stimulate are consciousness cores. They simply are what we call light, or sound and consciousness contents in general. *They are what light is and has always been.* No matter how complex, the contents are composed of consciousness cores. Recall that they are the basic sensory elements of consciousness.

In view of our model of the mechanism of consciousness, we believe we can understand why Dennett answered the question, "when does it all come together?" as consciousness with "Never!" (See Searle, 1992.) As we understand it, Dennett did not include identity as part of the explanation of consciousness. In our own model, *without the identity of consciousness with nerve cells or impulses, consciousness would not occur.* The sensory impulses combined with the hierarchy level would simply be a new hierarchy level (a new "draft" in Dennett's conception) without consciousness. Without postulating identity, none of Dennett's "drafts" become consciousness.

Let us emphasize again that *in accord with the identity theory* the neurons or their activities simply are consciousness. An agency of consciousness does not have a separate existence. To become consciousness the impulses of the combined input and hierarchical level simply have to be facilitated and allowed to surface. They are then the only impulses which are uninhibitedly present. *They are consciousness.* At the same time as the occurrence of the consciousness, the myriad of other nerve cell impulses which are sensory from all over the body are either not facilitated or are neuronally blocked (inhibited). They do not reach the stage of consciousness. After the consciousness contents reach the surface, the consciousness does not have to be sensed by some other faculty. The process merely continues: the new consciousness content becomes a new level of the memory hierarchy. There is also a reaction which may be one of ideation or motor activity.

We have previously described consciousness as not being unitary and as consisting of consciousness cores. We have also described the consciousness cores as being sensory in nature. It now becomes clearer that *there is no such thing as consciousness as a single entity.* There are only sensory impulses which are preconscious and become consciousness. It is these elements which are touch, pain, internal sensations, memory inputs, emotion, "ideas", and so on.

Consciousness, *as an entity*, is a collective term. In this regard it is similar to terms such as neighborhood, crowd, and wealth. The terms are abstractions or concepts which are composed in the final analysis of concretes, that is, of particulars. Neighborhoods, for instance, consist of houses. It is the houses that are real and exist as things. Crowds are composed of individual people and wealth consists, in the final analysis, of dollars. It is the latter items that are existents, not abstractions. It is in this sense that there is no consciousness as a single entity. There is no entity which receives all sensory impulses and renders them sentient.

This model of the mechanism of consciousness may seem to some theorists as if consciousness does not actually occur. It may seem as if the nerve cells or cellular activities, which we postulate simply *are* consciousness, are not consciousness at all. The problem, according to such skepticism, may concern the absence of an entity which accomplishes the function of awareness. Again, let us state that a brain which is capable of creating sensations such as pain can, by virtue of the same principle, create consciousness. We regard consciousness as sensations which *are* consciousness and do not need to be perceived by a separate entity; the sensations are consciousness in themselves. They are followed by reactions involving further consciousness contents as determined by interests and anxieties.

It appears that throughout history, like the Man of La Mancha, we have been "chasing windmills." We have been trying to explain consciousness as a single entity but it does not exist as such. Each of the combinations of consciousness cores which reaches the finish line becomes its own example of consciousness. And, again, it does so by virtue of identity. *The nerve cells or impulses, from the inside perspective, have the quality of consciousness.* They do not need to be appreciated by a superior entity.

The *Reductio* in Relation to an Observer

In the preceding section we mentioned that "I" is merely a concept and is not a perceiving entity. For "I" to be an observer of consciousness, a major problem immediately presents itself. Even though the "I" is not explicit, its implication still has the problem of the *reductio*. (If I feel the pain, how do I do so? Who or what feels the pain for the "I"?)

The same problem occurs when we rely at the neural level on processes such as nerve cell networks, coordinated rhythms of nerve cells, quantum effects, etc. Conceptually any of these are observing entities or phenomena and as such they require further entities or phenomena to become aware of the awareness. The concept of identity avoids the serious problem of the *reductio.*

Where does the implicit "I" fit into our scheme? We have previously explained that perceptions are comprised in good measure from the memory hierarchies. In our discussion of the mechanism of "Attention" and the "Crux of Becoming Consciousness" we stated that perceptions result from sensory inputs which are matched with levels of the memory hierarchy. There is a combination of the two with the formation of a new level which becomes consciousness. If I see a pebble on the ground, it may be fairly neutral emotionally, but it still has a meaning *in relation to me.* *The meanings result from the circumstance that the memory hierarchy levels derive from past experiences.* The memory hierarchies not only contribute to the consciousness of the stimulus but do so in relation to past experiences *which make the meaning personal.* The conventional interpretation of the perception is that it is seen by me, that is, by my self. Perceptions have importance in relation to the self but the self is not there as a separate observer. A person's experiences become part of perception and help to shape them but the "I" or the self is not present as an entity.

Are we now contradicting ourselves? If perceptions are always "in relation to me" it may seem as if we regard the self to be present. But there is a distinction between one's self and something which is in "relation to me." As we have previously discussed, "I" and the self are concepts which are the consciousness content occasionally for brief moments when there happens to be a specific introspective awareness of the concepts. At other times "I" and the concept of self are not consciously present. They are merely available as the implications of background memory hierarchies. As mentioned above, the memory hierarchy levels are from one's past experience but the present consciousness is constituted from both past experiences and from current sensory inputs. Only a relevant hierarchy level is included in current perception.

Origin of the Self

Perhaps we need to elaborate upon the origin of the self in order to more fully explain how we can conceive of it as being so tidily removed as a single functioning element which is the observer of consciousness. Our description of the mechanism of becoming consciousness may give the impression that we have performed a sleight of hand maneuver in which the self simply evaporates or is absent during the perceptual process.

In our view the self originates, as does any other concept, in the memory hierarchies. The hierarchies develop from the time of birth or thereabouts. The first sensory impulses have no previously formed memory hierarchy. They are merely isolated impulses. Reactions to them can perhaps be best considered to be a type of reflexive reaction. It is after the sensory impulses become associated that they become a significant memory hierarchy. Gradually, as the memory hierarchy develops, the infant becomes a person with a "mentality." On the behavioral surface, the change occurs imperceptibly. The early infant overtly seems to exhibit mentality in some ways but not in others. It cries when it becomes hungry or uncomfortable but how much of this is "mindless" or "reflex" and how much is genuinely or fully "mental" is open to question. It soon "learns" to anticipate the nipple. Then, or not long afterward, its actions appear to be based on experience rather than simply on "reflex." But between such actions it again falls asleep and into a state of semiconsciousness or unconsciousness.

When experiences begin to be retained in memory something which gave pleasure yesterday is remembered and tends to be sought today. Something which gave pain yesterday is avoided today. The permanence of memory provides the basis for considering oneself to be a person or an "I" or a self. A person exists mentally by virtue of having had experiences. Memory of the experiences mean to one that she is an individual with a mind and body and that she is alive. Both have continuity in relation to time.

As we have previously stated, however, we regard the conscious self to be merely a concept. William James (1890, p. 334) gives a good description which is apropos:

Each of us when he awakens says, Here's the same old self again, just as he says, Here's the same old bed, the same old room, the same old world.

The sense of our own personal identity [the self], then, is exactly like any one of our other perceptions of sameness among phenomena. It is a conclusion grounded either on a resemblance in a fundamental respect, or on the continuity before the mind [memory] of the phenomena compared.

The Real Self

It now becomes apparent that the reasons for the vagueness of the self are first, that *the sense of self stems mainly from the memory hierarchies.* Furthermore, the hierarchies are apt to be unconscious; they are the unconscious *background* of perceptions. Specifically, it is the elements of the hierarchy which give one the sense of self and which relate the hierarchy to the individual. If one sees an object, one regards the object itself as the entire perception. Instead of recognizing the contribution of the hierarchies to one's perceptions, individuals psychologically "project" the entire perception as if it stems solely from the perceived object. That the elements are unconscious offers an explanation of why the self is so intangible, why it is so difficult to "put one's finger on it." An individual feels that there must be a self involved in perceptions but this has to be an intellectual conclusion as there is no consciousness of the self per se. We regard the so-called "conscious sense of self" to be a conscious intellectualization based on perceptions of the moment and on memory of past perceptions.

We have stated that perceptions are "in relation to me." It is that "me" which is the self or "I." The impermanence of the self helps to confirm that it is merely a concept. While it tends to have a degree of permanence, the mood of the moment may change it considerably. One's "self" may be a source of pride or of shame, a sense of competence or incompetence depending upon the current situation.

Memory and Consciousness May Be In Same Neurons

The large involvement of memory in perception indicates that memory and consciousness are indeed very closely related functionally. It is conventionally thought that memory and consciousness occupy different areas of the brain or involve different neurons but the separation is not clear cut. It has simply been an assumption. For us, this raises the question as to whether or not the functions are actually *located in the same nerve cells or processes.*

187

There is a suggestion that consciousness and memory are very closely interlocked in our explanation of John Locke's "primary sensations" such as the perception of size, shape, and motion. Our explanation involved "directionality" in which perception resulted from two or more observations. In explaining the perception of motion we stated, "...memory would be involved in the perception...since the perception of the changing of direction would require remembering the beginning position and its comparison with a later position." The memory of the two observations in any of the "primary sensations" would usually not reach consciousness. Similarly, in noticing the size of an object, we usually simply become aware of the size, without paying attention to the location of the opposite edges or to the distance between them. The implication is that the location of the edge which is the first to be registered is held in memory until the opposite edge is registered. The two observations then become consciousness simply as size rather than as locations of edges. The arrangement provides a strong suggestion that memory and consciousness may not be as separate as is generally thought. There is also a suggestion involving meaning since the observations of the two edges are perceived as size, that is, they "mean" size to us. (We will have considerably more to say about meaning in the next chapter.)

"Consciousness neurons" (Crick 1994), if there are such, may be utilized for both consciousness and memory. Admittedly this is speculative but there would seem to be no reason why this might not be the case. Memory has been most commonly postulated as somehow resulting from changes in the interconnections between cells (synapses) which occur when nerve impulses pass through. If consciousness develops among the same cells as memory, both anatomically and functionally, then such an arrangement would certainly be highly efficient in terms of time and space. And evolution has been very proficient at settling into such efficiencies.

Consciousness as the Surface of Memory

If consciousness and memory are located in the same cells then the elaborating patterns of the memory hierarchy and the consciousness contents of a single perception could both develop simultaneously. There is even a further possibility which is contrary to conventional thinking but which we believe has much appeal: *Consciousness may simply be the final stage of the memory process.* In other words, a content of consciousness may simply be a level of memory hierarchy which reaches the finish line. The memory pattern, which is acceptable to the larger body of hierarchies, becomes the final pattern and then is consciousness simply by virtue of the inhibition of rival impulses. The impulses proceed until they are allowed to reach the point at which they are uncontested and stand alone in stimulating the "final" cells. The impulses are allowed to proceed because they are the loudest or the brightest, so to speak. More to the point, they are the uppermost in interest. Upon stimulating the "final" cells, it is as if the wraps are simply removed from the cells which are the particular consciousness. (In accordance with our previously developed theory, the *elements* of consciousness may be present in the impulses both before and when they are allowed to proceed to stimulate the "final" neurons.) Memory hierarchy levels which do not reach the surface to become consciousness at a particular moment are those which are inhibited and remain available to possibly become consciousness at a future time.

In the above paragraphs we have been pointing out how consciousness and memory seem to be very closely related. Actually we have come to the impression that the two are essentially not different at all in structure; that *consciousness is simply memory which is allowed to surface.* This has resemblance to a pod of whales which are busily swimming below the surface but one at a time they rise through the surface and become visible. All along, as we have developed our theory, we have held the view that only one, or a very few items, were allowed to become consciousness at the same instant.

Actually, within our theory, it becomes simply a matter of how we wish to look upon the impulse (impulse volley) which outdistances its rivals. We may look upon it either as being a combination of a hierarchical memory level with a new sensory input or as consciousness. We suggest that at the cellular level the two are the same. The sensory input is given its shape or meaning by the memory level with which it is combined. Once the combination becomes consciousness it is also the latest level of the memory hierarchies. Its facilitation into becoming consciousness is due to its having greater interest than rival inputs.

Let us be clear that the sensory-memory combination has a different structure from the memory hierarchies in general in that the sensory content of the combination contains the latest input. This makes it a new memory "item" or a new "consciousness content." Further, let us be clear in stating that consciousness and memory have the same structure but the difference between them is that consciousness is experience in the present but conscious memory, even though it is experience in the present, can be consciousness or memory of a past experience. Consciousness of a past experience involves consciousness of a memory hierarchy level without significant input from current sensation.

Of course, this view of the relationship between consciousness and the memory hierarchies does not fully explain consciousness. We still need the identity of the impulses with consciousness. We also wish to point out that an individual memory item is generally looked upon as being composed of a relatively limited number of brain cells (or synapses) and that if a sensory-memory level reaches the stage of consciousness then the consciousness content is also composed of a limited number of brain cells. This militates rather strongly toward our conception of consciousness as being multiple rather than a single, separate entity which would probably require a relatively large number of cells and likely constitute a substantial part of the cerebral cortex.

Introspection

Introspection is the turning of attention inward with the result that one becomes conscious of one's own thoughts or feelings, that is, of one's own consciousness contents. Armstrong (1993) and other theorists believe that introspection is necessary for consciousness to occur; that it is an invariable part of consciousness. This is not the usual view and we are largely in disagreement with it. Our discussion of the mechanism, which we believe to be involved, will make clear our reasons for disagreeing as well as sharpen our understanding of introspection.

In our view there is a distinct difference between the initial consciousness content and the introspected content. Introspection is a second step which follows the initial consciousness and is actually a memory of the initial consciousness. It is consciousness of the initial consciousness. (This is reminiscent of the "awareness of awareness" which was mentioned in the introduction to this book and which, in the case of introspection, we regard as being correct as far as it goes.)

The extent of the difference between the initial consciousness content and the introspected content depends heavily upon the amount of time which elapses between the two events. With new experiences intervening between them, an act of introspection can occur a fraction of a second, minutes, days or years after the initial consciousness. What is introspected is actually a memory and over time the memory component may suffer a lessened degree of vividness, modification due to biases, confusion with other memories, or other alterations.

If the time difference between an initial perception and its introspection is extremely short, then the two consciousness contents are indistinguishable to the individual undergoing the experiences. Such a case is illustrated in the following quotation: "I hear the bell." Not only are the hearing itself (the initial consciousness) and the introspection of the initial consciousness content indistinguishable to the individual but the time difference between the two is imperceptible. Similarly, in the quotation, "I remember the incident", the time difference, between the act of remembering and the verbalization about the act, is imperceptible. It seems to the individual to be only one consciousness event. But if the time difference is extensive, then the two memory hierarchy levels can be quite different depending upon the intercurrent experiences. It is well known that time often modifies memory. Details may either be altered or lost altogether. We can therefore say, even though the two memory levels may appear to be the same, that the underlying neurophysiology requires that they are likely to be different.

That introspection is actually a memory, accounts for the fact that two people observing the same stimulus, the performance of a crime for example, may report greatly different experiences. As is well known, a source of discrepancy is present in their reports of the crime due to differences in their memories of their initial perceptions. The sooner the reports are given, the less variation there is likely to be. A less well recognized source of discrepancy is that even the initial perceptions are genuinely different due to differences in the preexisting memory hierarchies which form the background of the perceptions. This applies even when the reports are taken immediately after the witnessing of the crime. Emotional biases and previous experiences, that is, memory hierarchies, may distort initial perceptions quite markedly.

Those who would argue that introspection is a necessary part of consciousness are, according to our scheme, applying their thinking to the case in which there is no appreciable time difference between the initial consciousness and the introspection. We feel that this is only a special case of introspection. On the other hand, we acknowledge that introspection could theoretically be a part of any consciousness event and that it is virtually impossible to ascertain this by introspection itself or by empirical methods. Examples will give some indication of the situation: If I am engrossed in speaking and have a mild itch on my face, I scratch the spot "without thinking", that is, without introspection. If I touch a hot stove, I immediately withdraw my hand. I do not progress through the thought process, "That burns, I will therefore withdraw my hand." It is highly questionable that there is introspection in either of the two situations. However, both of these examples may be atypical, the first because the reaction was performed "without thinking" and the second, because the reaction could possibly be considered to be a "reflex." Whether or not the more usual consciousness content, such as seeing an object or hearing a sound, involves introspection is an unsettled issue. Yet it is in keeping with out theory of consciousness and introspection, that much more often than we usually take into account, we merely react to consciousness contents and do so without introspection, certainly without significant introspection. Our reactions for the most part occur with little or no examination or dwelling upon the stimulus. As mentioned earlier, introspection involves "awareness of the awareness." We regard the second awareness to be typically present only occasionally and, when it occurs, it does so as a memory. According to our theory, the conscious memory of the stimulus, that is, introspection, is not the same as the initial consciousness.

Another point is importantly relevant to the question as to whether or not introspection is necessary for consciousness. To regard introspection as necessary seems to raise the same problem that we had with the homunculus. If introspection is necessary for consciousness, would not a second introspection be needed to become conscious of the first introspection and so on? Our theory supports the view that consciousness and introspection are different. Introspection involves a second consciousness content but both contents are consciousness by virtue of identity and no homunculus is needed. The cells *are* consciousness.

That introspection of consciousness is consciousness of a memory allows for the appearance of degrees of consciousness. Such has been indicated many times in both professional and non-professional literature. People are often described as being semiconscious, half asleep, not paying attention, and so forth. But to regard consciousness as occurring in degrees puts a burden on our theory. Individual neurons either discharge or they do not. In this sense they are digital and one might think that consciousness should occur either in full force or not at all. However, digital elements can result in imperceptible degrees of change at the observed level. For example, music reproduced digitally need have no noticeable gaps between notes even when notes slide from one note to the next (portamento). Similarly, there need be no noticeable grain in digitally produced pictures.

The neurophysiological explanation for the degrees of consciousness would depend upon the extensiveness of the matching process between a stimulus and the memory hierarchies, that is, on the amount of attention which is given to the stimulus. Stimuli which are of little interest and are minimally matched (or not matched at all) would result in little or no awareness. The initial stimulus can remain practically unconscious. We do not notice "background" sounds or sensations. Yet they are often available to become consciousness if attention is applied retrospectively. This implies that consciousness and memory go "hand in hand", that there was some degree of consciousness of the "background" sounds.

Higher Centers and Memory

A question in regard to our explanation of consciousness, the answer to which we have touched upon before, is "How do the memory hierarchies act as the 'higher centers' and accomplish the directing of attention as well as the monitoring and selecting of material which is to become consciousness?" Neuronally this is done as the net result of the facilitations and inhibitions which take place. The facilitations and inhibitions are the same functions we would assign to a homunculus if there were one. Instead we might assign the monitoring and selecting which are involved, to the ego. And this would not be incorrect. But, again, it is somewhat vague and anthropomorphic. To be more specific, *the facilitations and inhibitions stem from the hierarchical memories of past experiences.* The memories all carry emotional associations and it is the emotions which provide weight and direction. This happens automatically, without volition. The emotional components of the memories are in place and they exert their decisive influence. If something is unpleasant, it is generally inhibited (avoided); if it is pleasurable, it is generally facilitated. Even when inputs to the memory hierarchy stem from different areas of the hierarchy itself there is a prior emotional influence which is automatic and influences the direction of activity.

Other Theories of the Arrival of Consciousness

Crick (1994), in the scientific tradition, stresses that the best way to find the explanation of consciousness is to start from solid ground and to work one's way up. He begins from the base of empirical neurophysiology, particularly the neurophysiology of vision because that is the area of perception about which the most is known. While he thoroughly disavows any value in seeking a homunculus, in discussing Dennett's book (1991), Crick states that Dennett is probably right, there is no single place in the brain where consciousness resides but "it is possible that there are distributed Cartesian theaters" (Crick, 1994, p. 282). Despite his stated intent to do otherwise, this nevertheless seems to slip into the pursuit of Cartesian Theaters. It would seem that the objections that are raised against one Cartesian theater could just as validly be raised against many of them; there is no one to be the audience—the observer. Distributing the theaters simply means there are many little theaters and many little homunculi which comprise the audiences. Nevertheless, we notice that Crick's "distributed Cartesian theaters" and his suggestion of "consciousness neurons" implies a leaning toward a concept of multiplicity of consciousness which we have postulated and to which we give considerable weight.

Ranson's textbook of neuroanatomy (1943) refers to consciousness as a "synthesis" of sensations:

> It is known that the cerebral cortex is the organ within which occur at least the majority of those complex and highly variable correlations and integrations which have consciousness as their counterpart. A single object may appeal to many sense organs, and our perception of that object involves a synthesis of a corresponding number of sensations and their comparison with past experience. For example, when I meet a friend and grasp his hand in greeting,

my perception of him includes not only the image of his face but also the sound of his voice and the warm contact of his hand. Thus thermal, tactile, auditory, and visual sensations may be fused in the perception of a single object, and this involves an integration of the corresponding afferent impulses [sensory impulses] within the cerebral cortex.

It is not known how the various sensations are processed separately yet "all come together" to form a consciousness content. The question has been called the "binding problem." There is probably more than a single mechanism involved. We have touched upon Land's theory of how colors are blended. We have also mentioned the merging of sounds into chords and Locke's "primary qualities" (size, shape, motion, and solidity) in which two or more observations are merged as one distinct perception. We have also discussed the possibility that the different modalities, the consciousness cores, may remain separate but that we perceive the *illusion* that they terminate as being together. Another possibility is that synecdoches may be involved—one or a few consciousness cores may give the impression of an entire percept, particularly if they occur closely enough together in time. If needed, the perceiver can fill in any gaps in a percept, from further memory, and round out the inputs from "pictures" or impressions acquired earlier. And finally, we shall offer a further observation regarding the perception of objects in chapter twenty-six under the section heading of "Hierarchical Development of Objects."

We have described Dennett's view earlier: Instead of a "coming together", there are "multiple drafts" of consciousness in a continuing process. His theory does present a way of avoiding the need to explain who or what perceives the drafts but does so at the expense of *not* actually having the drafts perceived. One draft is formed after another but apparently none of them finally becomes consciousness.

Let us repeat (lest we, like Dennett, are accused of explaining consciousness away) that the nerve impulses which "reach the finish line" stimulate the cells *which are* consciousness. Nothing further needs to *happen* for the consciousness to be complete. No central faculty or higher center needs to become "aware" of the consciousness. It is consciousness by virtue of identity. The memory hierarchies may give it further attention or may become involved in something else.

Meditation

There are many researchers who attempt to explore consciousness by means of meditation. They attempt to find a state of "pure consciousness" and feel that they largely accomplish this objective. Regardless of whether or not the meditators reach a state of isolated consciousness, their accuracy in reporting and their attempts to be thoroughly objective are not in question. The Journal of Consciousness Studies devotes an issue to the topic of meditation (1998, vol. 5, No. 2). Here is a fairly typical description offered by Forman (1998):

> ...Teresa tells us that one reaches this [state of meditation] by gradually reducing thought and understanding, eventually becoming 'utterly dead' to things, encountering neither sensation, thought nor perceptions. One becomes as simple as possible. Eventually one stops thinking altogether, not able to 'think of any single thing ...arresting the use of her understanding... utterly dead to the things of the world'. And yet, she clearly implies, one remains awake.

There are numerous descriptions such as this one as well as analyses of them. Applying our theory of consciousness, it appears that the meditator is able to suspend, or to give himself or herself the impression of having suspended the process of matching sensory inputs against memory hierarchies. To fully suspend the process would mean that perception is not taking place. But our impression received from the clear statements of well respected mediators at a recent international conference on consciousness at Tucson, Arizona ("Tucson 2000") is that the meditator's exclusion of sensory inputs is selective rather than complete; that the meditator limits interest and most attention to the concept of "pure consciousness" rather than to more ordinary inputs. It is believed by some or many who are expert in the practice of meditation that a state of "pure consciousness" cannot be completely accomplished but that meditation may nevertheless have considerable value for revealing the subsurface workings of mental processes.

Summary

We have come to regard consciousness as a level of the memory hierarchy which is combined with a sensory input and which outdistances all competing impulses to reach the "finish line" where there is identity of the stimulated cells with consciousness. The content then becomes input for a new level of the memory hierarchy. Consciousness may simply be the latest or "surface" level of memory hierarchies.

We hold that there is no central observer of consciousness contents. The self, which is often intuitively regarded as such an observer, is considered to be a concept resulting from the memories of experiences. Consciousness contents and levels of the memory hierarchy, consist of combinations of consciousness cores.

Topics which are also related to consciousness but are little related to each other include introspection and meditation. We regard introspection as being a conscious memory of a previous consciousness content. Meditation is used as a method of attempting to exclude ordinary sensory inputs and thoughts from consciousness in the attempt to gain insight into consciousness in an isolated state.

Chapter Twenty-five

Consciousness and Meaning

Meaning

There is another conceptual shift to which we are now in a position to give attention—that *consciousness is a form of meaning.* This is perhaps not quite as fundamental as the conceptual shift stating that nerve cells or impulses *are* consciousness, but to become accustomed to it is probably just as difficult. It is nevertheless important for the understanding of both meaning and consciousness.

The understanding of meaning relates directly to the acquisition of knowledge. How we know, the subject of epistemology, has perplexed philosophers as long if not longer than the pursuit of an explanation of consciousness. Both subjects have been completely unfathomable. The conventional definitions of meanings and consciousness are, of course, quite different. Meaning applies to ideas and their understanding while consciousness applies to awareness. We can immediately recognize that there is a relationship, however. Meanings, in order to be understood, must be conscious and it is very doubtful that anything that is conscious is without meaning. *It is our contention that consciousness and meaning are fundamentally the same,* that the difference is a matter of customary thinking and semantics. Let us now attempt to justify our contention and to familiarize the reader with our thinking.

Meanings Are Hierarchical

One way to indicate that the two functions are equivalent would be to describe their detailed neurophysiology as being the same. There is considerable suggestion in the entire hypothetical development in the previous chapters that the two result from the same neurophysiological mechanism. The same process which applies for consciousness also applies to that which we call meanings. Like consciousness, meanings develop hierarchically. Mathematics affords obvious examples: A knowledge of arithmetic is required for algebra and a knowledge of algebra is required for trigonometry and so forth. Both consciousness and meanings result from sensory inputs which are matched against and combined with memory hierarchies with the creation of new hierarchy levels. Both are creations of the mind or of the "understanding" as phrased by Locke. The new hierarchies become both consciousness and meaning by virtue of identity with nerve cells.

197

It is not unusual to consider meanings to have developed hierarchically but consciousness is generally considered to result only from current input. For example, the meaning of the word, government, requires considerable understanding which in turn is acquired over a period of time and through experience. A child of five would hardly understand it at all. We do not conventionally think of consciousness on the other hand as having developed over time. We see a house and regard the entire process of the perception as having taken place at the moment. Yet the perception requires previous experience. We would not recognize it as a house if we had never before seen one. Our manner of considering meanings to have developed hierarchically but not so in the case of consciousness is not correct. Both consciousness and meaning have developed over time. Both have a history.

Objects as Meanings

The most difficulty in understanding consciousness as actually being meaning, is encountered when we try to regard consciousness of *objects*. Objects are thought of as being physical, entirely different from ideas and meanings. Yet, to perceive an object, if only as being an object, is to perceive a meaning.

The fact that the consciousness or perceived features of objects are looked upon as being *outside the body*, tends to set objects apart from meanings. Since meanings are generally regarded as being within the mind, it requires quite an adjustment of one's thinking to regard the perception of objects as being meanings. Our placement of objects and meanings in different categories probably stems in large measure from the fact that all of our lives we have considered our concept of objects to be entirely *outside of ourselves*, thereby mistaking their electromagnetic emanations ("light") etc., for the items themselves. As discussed in an early chapter, we generally consider sensory qualities, such as colors and sounds, to be at the sources of their stimulation in the environment instead of in the mind; we are completely unaware of the fact that the perception of the stimulations is within ourselves. Meanings have lost their external connections only in the way the situation superficially seems to us. The meanings of words, particularly nouns, such as house, dog, and tree clearly depend upon having seen them. Meanings are also acquired directly from appearances—a person's dress or bodily position. Similarly the meanings of actions—walking, running, writing—depend upon both performing them and seeing them performed. Statements derive their meanings from experiences to which the statements relate. In an earlier chapter we described the manner in which abstractions—meanings—are based on experience.

Another reason for the seemingly *internal* nature of meanings is probably due to the fact that the emotional connections of "meanings" are often greater than the emotional connections of "objects." The emotional value of "mother" is greater than that of a rock or a tree. However, as previously explained, the emotions are consciousness cores which, even though they are within us, have developed hierarchically in association with inputs from *outside* objects.

Consideration of Multiplicity

One question in the case of consciousness does not arise in regard to meanings. This is the question of whether consciousness is a single entity or is multiple. There is simply no similar question in regard to meanings because meanings have always been regarded as consisting of multiple, that is, separate contents. So far as we know, no one has ever suggested that meaning is a single entity in the way that consciousness has been regarded as being an entity which observes sensory inputs. Meanings consist of ideas and these have not been considered collectively to be unitary. Similarly to meanings, as we have discussed under the heading of "Multiplicity of Consciousness", we believe consciousness could hardly be a single, persistent entity.

(We must make a distinction between meanings themselves and the process by which the brain develops meanings. We consider the process to be single while meanings themselves are multiple. There would be little reason for considering that there is more than one process by which meanings are obtained. The process has historically hardly been considered at all because it has been viewed as so unfathomable that relatively little effort has been applied to it even in the field of artificial intelligence.)

Further Considerations of Equivalence

An objection might be raised to the idea that consciousness and meaning are the same on the basis that a single object can have more than one meaning. Examples abound: Let us use the spoken word as an example of an object. A single word can have different meanings. "Light" can mean light in weight or refer to the perception of a form of energy. Optical illusions present only one pattern on the retina but are perceived as different objects. However, the explanation in these cases is no different from the perception of an object which has only one meaning. In both cases the perception is given its meaning by a creation of the brain, that is, using Locke's term, perceptions are given meaning by the "Understanding." A rock, which we see, enters the brain, so to speak, by means of light energy and nerve cell impulses. The impulses find a match in the memory hierarchies and the consciousness (or the meaning) result accordingly. The brain registers the impulse pattern of a rock and the "image" produced by the pattern is the meaning of the pattern.

Unconscious Meanings

Let us now further relate the neurophysiology of meaning to that of consciousness. Meanings can be stored in memory where they are unconscious until they proceed farther and become consciousness. Your own name and telephone number will suffice as simple examples. However, the fact that meanings can be unconscious does not put a gulf between meanings and consciousness. Obviously consciousness has to be in a conscious form and we generally think of it as being at the end of a neurophysiological process; but before the end is reached, the items which are to become consciousness are still unconscious. Such items are referred to as "preconscious." Here, too, there are terms which can be substituted for each other. The earlier, unconscious processes could be regarded as "premeaning" as easily as they can be regarded as "preconscious." At a more advanced stage in the sequence of processes, they could be considered to be "meaning" as easily as "consciousness." The term "premeaning" implies that the meaning sooner or later becomes conscious. The relationship between the *preconscious* items and *consciousness contents* is parallel to that between unconscious and conscious *meanings*. In fact, as we view it, there is more than a parallel. The memory hierarchies which are unconscious meanings are also preconscious. They can become conscious meanings or simply consciousness. *Consciousness can be regarded simply as meaning which is conscious.*

However, we need to limit the statement that consciousness and meaning are the same but only from the standpoint of the common usage of the terms. In the area of the preconscious or the premeaning there is an important exception to the statement. The statement is actually based on a point of view which somewhat favors consciousness. Many meanings ("pre-meanings") never become consciousness and in practice there are strong factors which prevent their doing so. Nevertheless, this does not change the psychological concept that the two are the same. We have in mind the deeply unconscious levels of the memory hierarchy which form the foundation for all later levels and have shaped the individual's perception and personality. They may have been conscious in early childhood but they are not available to become consciousness in the adult. They may be unavailable because of repression, as indicated by Freud, or because the adult categories of meanings are so different from the early ones, that there are no available bridging associations and therefore no accessibility. In either case the foundational levels are simply not available to become consciousness but this does not change the process from the description we have given and does not indicate a physiological difference between meaning an consciousness. There are also experiences in the adult which never become consciousness but which are registered subconsciously and pass unnoticed. Among these are the so-called subliminal stimuli.

Meaning, Consciousness, and Synecdoche

In the chapter on synecdoche, in writing about the perception of objects, we mentioned that "One merely has the *impression* of a conscious whole object." In a single glimpse, at most only a few aspects of objects are actually observed. The same applies for concepts and items of memory. Where one has the impression of having consciously in mind an entire concept or a complete memory, one often finds there was only an inkling present. Observation of a part gives the impression of a whole. In the same way, the mechanism of synecdoche "makes the perception [consciousness] of objects similar to the perception of concepts and memories. All three are interpretations." (From Chap. 12, third page)

Having discussed meanings, we can appreciate that interpretations are meanings and that synecdoche is a form of meaning. Furthermore, since meaning and consciousness are basically the same, it is clear that synecdoche is a form of consciousness. This is both logical and is common experience. For instance, as in the example of synecdoche presented originally in which "wheels" *represented* an automobile, we now understand that "wheels" also has the *meaning* of automobile and the synecdoche can be viewed as an instance of consciousness or of meaning.

While "synecdoche is a form of consciousness", we would not fully equate synecdoche with consciousness. In synecdoche the part has the meaning of a larger whole but this is not always the case with consciousness. Simple sensations such as pains, odors, colors or touches are consciousness but they do not seem to represent larger wholes. Even though a pain would be perceived as a pain in a particular location in the body or as having been caused by a particular event, the meaning of the pain as such is still limited to the sensation. Similarly, a color would be an aspect of something, but if one's interest is in the color as a topic in itself, then the color is not part of a larger whole. One might take issue with this interpretation of simple sensations on the ground that one cannot form a perception that is in total isolation. The sensory input involved in the perception joins memory hierarchies which are the background for the perception and are a part of it. We wish to be clear that we have not changed our concept that perception results in large measure from memory and only in part from sensory input. We still maintain that perception rests on two feet. Nevertheless, synecdoche is a matter of meaning to an individual perceiver. There are memory hierarchy levels which shape the perception of objects but, of course, only those levels which pertain to the objects are utilized and these levels are apt to be personal to a considerable extent.

Semantic Considerations

It is no doubt more than coincidence that the word, perceive, is used for both meanings and consciousness. We speak of perceiving meanings and we also use the term, perception, in connection with consciousness. *That they are both perceptual processes, according to our explanation of perception, is a fundamental reason for considering them to be the same.* Remember that sensory inputs may stem from the mind (memory, emotion, "thoughts") or from the outside environment. Inputs not only become consciousness but also become meanings. Whether the inputs originate in the environment, leading to what we call consciousness, or in the brain, leading to what we call meanings, is not a significant difference. We regard the difference in the application of the terms "meaning" and "consciousness" to be a matter of superficial descriptive language which depends on a lack of consideration of the underlying mechanisms.

Sensory inputs are given their essential characters of both meaning and consciousness by the memory hierarchies. In both cases the mind "reads" something into the sensory inputs it receives. When we see a rock, the light energy which we receive has the meaning to us of "rock." We understand the light vibrations emanating from a tree as having the meaning of "tree." Correspondingly, we understand the sounds of a spoken sentence as being its meaning. In all such cases the brain creates something which is entirely new, a meaning, a content of consciousness. It will be become clearer as we further discuss the hierarchical aspects of meaning, that the psychological and neurological mechanisms underlying meaning and consciousness appear to be the same,

As words, "consciousness" and "meaning" have very different imports and uses. However, illustrating that in a basic sense they are the same, the word "meaning" could have been substituted in a number of sentences in the preceding chapters for the word "consciousness" with little or no ambiguity. There have been a number of examples in this book, some better than others. The next paragraph is a quotation from chapter twenty and the paragraph which follows the first is altered only in that the word "meaning" is substituted for "consciousness." Notice that the substitution is made without altering the import of the sentences.

It is worth emphasizing…that *consciousness* is constituted of combinations of consciousness cores. Also there is the implication that the *consciousness* contents themselves are combined with new perceptions to become new, further developed contents. The items are all based, however, on qualitative cores which are associated and retained in memory. The associated cores constitute *consciousness* contents in the infant and become the foundations for the *consciousness* contents in the adult.

It is worth emphasizing...that *meanings* are constituted of combinations of consciousness cores. Also there is the implication that the *meaning* contents themselves are combined with new perceptions to become new, further developed contents. The items are all based, however, on qualitative cores which are associated and retained in memory. The associated cores constitute *meaning* contents in the infant and become the foundations for the *meaning* contents in the adult.

In comparing the two paragraphs we arrive at the conclusion that *consciousness and meaning are equivalent.* If X can always be substituted for Y then X and Y must be the same.

In chapter twenty-three under the section entitled "Attention" we included a paragraph which we will restate in order to illustrate that *stimuli* can be described as producing either consciousness or meaning. This is but one more illustration that consciousness and meaning are the same. In discussing the startle reaction of newborn infants to a sudden loud noise, we stated:

The reaction is the same regardless of what constitutes the stimulus. In the adult, however, the specific reaction is somewhat selective, indicating that the reaction to the meaning [consciousness] of the initial stimulus is determined at least in part by previous experience, that is, by the memory hierarchies.

In the pages subsequent to this one, we will sometimes include the word "consciousness" in parentheses after the word "meaning" to indicate their equivalence. In this manner we hope to not only indicate the equivalence but to accustom the reader to it, thereby making it seem less strange and more acceptable. It is the customary uses which make the two terms seem so different from each other.

The question arises, are we only indulging in semantics to say that consciousness is a form of meaning? Are we merely redefining "meaning" to include consciousness? Hardly so. We regard the equating of the two as a reasonable and realistic appraisal of the situation. Fairly good evidence is supplied by the substitutions of one word with the other without changing the idea of the sentence.

Again, the distinction between the two terms appears to be conceptual rather than physiological. We are accustomed to using the term, meaning, when referring to something ideational and the term, consciousness, when referring to something physical. The difference between the terms, meaning and consciousness, simply depends upon the context in which the terms are used.

If we analyze the "adverbial" theories of Ducasse (1942) and of Chrisholm (1957) correctly, they were devised as attempts to avoid the concept of sense-data which is a form of representation. But the theories are compatible with the view that *meaning is basically perception* (consciousness). The authors, instead of writing "perceiving an object to be red", typically write "the object is perceived redly." They use adverbs instead of adjectives. The meaning of a word is the manner in which one interprets it. If one perceives the object as being redly, if such use of adverbs becomes one's customary use of words, then the perception of the color of the object is appropriately described as "redly." The consciousness of the color and the meaning, then, are the same. And, of course, the same reasoning applies to the perceiving of happiness, pain, or sexual sensation, etc. Admittedly, both the adverbial theory and the use of it to support the idea that consciousness and meaning are the same sounds more sophistical than one would like.

We may now summarize the equivalence of meaning and consciousness. The several relationships of consciousness we have presented throughout this writing also apply to meaning:

- Meanings consist of consciousness cores.
- They develop hierarchically.
- Meanings are retained in the form of memory hierarchies.
- Identity with nerve cells applies in the case of meanings as it does in consciousness.
- Perception of meanings involves matching of inputs against memory hierarchies.
- Synecdoche is used in meanings.
- Monitoring and selection of inputs for meanings is controlled by interests and anxieties.
- The self is a meaning, a concept.
- Abstractions are meanings.
- Meanings are subject to random access.
- Meanings are multiple.
- Both meanings and consciousness have unconscious preceding forms.

Experiencing the Latest Hierarchical Level as Meaning

Before proceeding with the present section, let us remind the reader of several concepts which have been presented previously. In chapter twenty-one, under the section entitled "Perception is Largely Recognition", we discussed the concept that it *"is the item in memory, or the synecdoche of the item, which is most of the representation."* In chapter sixteen we discussed our concept of identity—that nerve cell or nerve cell activity is experienced as consciousness. It is directly experienced as consciousness without an additional step involving the services of a central observer. In chapter twenty-four we stated, "It should be made clear that there is memory of the consciousness content and that the content becomes a *new level of the memory hierarchy*." In the present chapter, we offered the equivalence of consciousness and meaning. With these concepts as background, we shall now elaborate upon the relationship of the latest level of the memory hierarchy and meaning.

It is counterintuitive to think that the latest hierarchy could be a complete meaning. How could it be complete when it lacks the earlier meanings upon which the latest meaning is developed? One might think there would be no foundation beneath it. The answer which can be suggested is that meanings are derived from experiences and *the associations are largely horizontal, across the upper levels of relatively current hierarchies, rather than backward in time.* This is a key theoretical consideration. The meanings are largely independent of the remote past. The latest hierarchical level is the latest meaning and, we may emphasize, often satisfies one's understanding as a complete meaning. If the meaning derived from the horizontal levels is insufficient then vertical levels are consulted.

We should repeat that the process of memory hierarchy development in the adult is the same as in the infant. One might think that the hierarchies would be more complex in the adult simply because, in the adult, meanings are more advanced and more highly developed than those in the infant. The difference would be that in the adult the hierarchy would have many more horizontal and vertical connections supporting the later levels.

This raises a question as to how hierarchies can develop throughout life without becoming too large and unwieldy to be useful. It would seem that if meanings are hierarchical, later meanings would have to include earlier meanings upon which they are built. In forming perceptions the supporting meanings would have to be retraced in order to find matches and there would likely be no satisfactory end to the search without retracing back to birth or thereabouts. Yet for an adult's mind to accomplish a review back to infancy would require an inordinate amount of time even though the brain works very rapidly.

To explain the way in which the latest level of the memory hierarchy is a complete meaning even though it does not seem to extend backward in time, the magician's "rabbit in the hat trick" can be helpful as an analogy. Just as the rabbit lies hidden in the hat before the audience observes the hat, the background for the meaning is in the memory hierarchy before the current observation of an environmental object.

For example, suppose we are asked the question, "What time does the plane arrive?" The term "plane" evokes for us a concept of a jet airplane. As a result of frequent current usage of the term and the concept, the concept requires little vertical support to provide a meaning. The vertical roots of the meaning may be little needed. But suppose we were not clear as to the meaning of "plane." Vertical support, involving various past experiences would then be utilized to make the meaning complete. It is important to keep in mind, too, that each hierarchy level is a meaning by virtue of the identity of the nerve cells with meaning. *The nerve cells comprising the latest hierarchical level are the latest identity, the latest meaning.* The present configurations of consciousness cores are the present complete meanings just as earlier configurations of cores were complete meanings, even those in infancy. The nerve cells are an independent identity, an independent meaning, with past hierarchical levels available if needed for sufficient embellishment. If the meanings within memory are present in the form of a DNA molecule (which may be more of an analogy than an actuality), the molecule need be no larger to indicate a current meaning than for an earlier meaning. All that would be required is that the consciousness cores be present. Whether they exist in the form of DNA, quantum phenomena or something else, the exact mechanism, while important in its own right, is only secondarily relevant to the concept of meaning.

The reiterations of a computer are similar in a way to the development within memory. It will be illustrative to describe the way a computer manages to count from one to ten as an analogy to the latest meaning's being a complete meaning. The computer can be programmed so that it does not necessarily have to go back to the beginning of a content in order to produce an end result. We type into the computer the "command" that X equals X plus one. (The command in at least one "basic language" is actually "Let X = X + 1") This does not make sense in ordinary algebra but it does make sense in "computerese." The computer "reads" the directive from left to right, the same way we do, and uses the latest character that it reads. At the beginning, X has no numerical value. Therefore, upon reading the first X, its value equals zero. As the computer continues to "read" from left to right, X becomes equal to X plus one, that is, zero plus one. This adjustment now gives X the value of one. The computer then obeys our second directive, which would be typed on line 2, to return to the first directive and reread it. ("Go to line 1"). Upon the second reading of the command, since X already equals one, X equals one plus one, which is two. The process then continues, that is, the reiterations continue as long as you wish to permit them. If you desire them to stop at ten, you merely direct the computer in advance to stop the iterations when X equals ten. ("If X = 10 then stop").

Each X is analogous to a new meaning. To get the meaning of X, the computer does not have to recreate the meaning from the beginning. If, for example, X has become 5, the computer merely takes that figure and proceeds from there. In our scheme of hierarchical memory, the mind does the same. The latest meaning is floating free of the past, so to speak. The new meaning becomes the memory base which is built into any related new meaning. If we alter our understanding of something, that is if we alter its meaning, the altered memory hierarchy is the new meaning. And let us add, the involved nerve cells or their activity become the new meaning by virtue of identity. They simply *are* the new meaning.

In an earlier chapter, I have stated that consciousness may reside in neuronal molecules, or cellular activity, etc. Such a concept causes one to easily fall back into the thinking that consciousness requires a "central observer" or a homunculus-like entity. ("What is it that becomes aware of the molecules?") However, identity, that is, the concept that consciousness simply *is* sensory cells or sensory activity (which has been processed as memory hierarchies, etc.,) renders it unnecessary to postulate an observer of sensory inputs.

Computer Intelligence.

Progress in the area of artificial intelligence offers much in connection with explaining the processing of meanings. But with computers the meanings would have to be artificial in the sense that they would require some way of simulating emotions and other qualitative cores. This could easily be accomplished in the case of emotion, for example, by assigning different letters of the alphabet to represent the different emotions and by assigning numerical values from one to ten in proportion to the intensity of the emotion. But such a system would only represent emotion. The emotion would not be genuine. It would not be felt. It would not be the "inside" perspective of neurons.

We regard the sensory inputs as the only genuine contacts with the external world.

Computers can have contact with the "external world" by means of cameras and microphones but these do not furnish the qualitative sensations which the nervous system provides. They do not contribute impulses which *are* light, touch, or pain and the like. As we have explained, it appears to us that these are the raw materials of consciousness and without them the computer can do no more than manipulate symbols which simulate consciousness. Granted, if computers become sufficiently sophisticated they may even be able to perform adequately for most purposes which now require a human being. They may even be able to pass a Turing test, that is, they may sound human to many people. This would still not mean that they are conscious. However, our consciousness cores are, in the final analysis, physical entities which are conscious by virtue of the identity principle. As we elaborate in the next chapter, our nervous systems cause us to perceive what we know as reality. We believe one can expect that eventually artificial consciousness cores, including emotions, will be produced and computers and robots will then possess consciousness.

Context

Recognition of the relationship between consciousness and memory hierarchies as well as the idea that consciousness and meaning are the same enables us to understand the mechanism of context. We can readily fit contexts into our plan: As has been explained, memory hierarchy levels give sensory inputs their meanings. Context is simply the set of meanings from the memory hierarchy which are brought to bear in the matching of sensory inputs against the hierarchy.

A feature of meanings is that their composition changes according to the contexts surrounding them and, in addition, they can be present in any number of contexts. At one time juiciness may be what "tomato" connotes. At another time, in the context of art, a certain red color is what "tomato" means—the color is called "tomato red" or just "tomato." The neurophysiological mechanism for the two contexts would be as follows: The situational meanings surrounding "tomato" in the first example involves the random access search for an association of red fruit or food, while in the second example the search follows the associations of color or art. A switch in context is very often the basis for humor. The "punch line" conveys an unexpected meaning to a term, a context different from the one according to which the "build up" from previous inputs had been associated and matched in the memory hierarchy.

Summary

Meaning develops in the same manner that consciousness is built. This is in accord with the concept that *consciousness is meaning.* Levels of memory hierarchy are preconscious meanings (premeanings) and can become conscious meanings (consciousness). The latest hierarchy level is the latest meaning. The hierarchical connections of a new meaning are mostly horizontal (relatively current) rather than extending back in time indefinitely. Contexts are the hierarchical connections surrounding current inputs. The "mind" of a computer and computer intelligence lacks actual consciousness cores including emotion which are basic components of human mentality.

Chapter Twenty-six

Elaboration and Completion

In this chapter the reader may notice that we adopt a more discursive and repetitious style than we ordinarily do. We do so for purposes of emphasis and exposition and trust that the reader will be indulgent.

Identity and Reality

It will be well to elaborate once more upon the concept of identity. *It is not easy to imagine that nerve cells really comprise consciousness contents.* It is totally foreign to our experience. One has to understand it strictly intellectually. This is similar to the manner in which we understand that the earth is billions of years old. We believe the reason for the difficulty is basically the same as the one we combated in chapter five. In chapter five we attempted to inculcate the concept that *the brain invents light and sound and the myriad of other sensations in reaction to environmental stimulation.* This concept is deeply counterintuitive. Throughout all of their lives people generally accept, with no sense of doubt, that light and sound are in the environment. There is ordinarily no need to become aware of the fact that one's brain creates these sensations.

The more we approach the concept of identity within different contexts, the more we become accustomed to the idea and the more reasonable and correct it seems. In order to further heighten the meaning of the identity theory let us turn to the stories of "Alice's Adventures in Wonderland" and "Through the Looking Glass" as analogous to our own lives. When we observe nerve cells through a microscope, we see them in a third person perspective; but to understand identity, like Alice, who stepped into the looking glass, we must step inside nerve cells. *Our conscious experiences are within nerve cells and their activities.* Our nerve cells create our world within the cells from sensory stimulations similar to the way in which Alice in her mind created Wonderland.

Yet our experiences have an important difference from those of Alice. To us the external world appears normal but to Alice the external world seemed very "peculiar." Wonderland seemed strange to Alice due to the fact that she carried her background with her into the mirror. She viewed the characters in Wonderland from her outside perspective, not from the inside perspectives of the characters themselves.

We suggest that we are in a Wonderland of sorts but we are natives there. *Instead of being inside the mirror, it is as if we, insofar as our experiences are concerned, are inside nerve cells.* Let us call our location Nerve Cell Land or simply Cell Land for the sake of brevity. Unlike Alice, but similar to the Queen of Hearts, we were born in Cell Land and have lived there all of our lives. We have never had any knowledge of anything different and assume that our experiences reveal reality. From birth onward we have constructed our entire Cell Land hierarchically out of such experiences. Yet that which we take to be external reality is largely created internally.

Recall that our perception of reality rests on two feet, one foot standing in the outer world and the other planted in our brains; our brains create the sensory perceptions, having received stimuli from the outside world. Nevertheless, we do not normally assume that our experiences are "interpretations" of external reality or even that they "represent" reality but that they *are* reality. In making that assumption we seldom even entertain any doubt about its correctness. We do not consider our experiences of external reality to be strange. Like the Queen of Hearts or the Mad Hatter, we look upon our world as entirely normal. We perceive light energy as light, and not as energy; we feel molecular jiggling motions as heat, not as motions; to us certain molecules are smells, not molecules, and so on.

Our central point is that our conscious experiences are "inside" our nerve cells but we look upon ourselves as if we are "outside" the cells. The nerve cells which are appreciated from the "outside" perspective as cells or impulses are appreciated from the "inside" perspective as consciousness. Our view of the identity theory states that consciousness is neuronal activity, the inside aspect of nerve cell functioning. In terms of the first and third person perspectives, we normally think of ourselves as living in a third person world, a world that we see as outside of ourselves. But we actually live in a first person world, a world in which our nerve cells create all of the qualities. Just as the brain creates light, having been stimulated from the outside, since consciousness results from sensory inputs, the brain also creates all of consciousness. Again, we live inside a Cell Land in which our world is initiated from reality and reflects it, but its qualities are of our own making.

In this writing we have asserted that experience or consciousness is constructed upon earlier experience; that our entire memory system is such a construction. Even the concept of one's self or "I" results from the experiences one has had. We have also indicated that what we regard as abstractions, such as motherhood or patriotism, are hierarchical constructions built of our Cell Land experiences. (Incidentally, that is another oddity, not unlike the oddities that Alice came upon: As we have explained previously, abstractions arise out of concrete experiences, yet abstractions according to the usual definitions are not concrete.)

Pilots, in their training, wear equipment over their faces and practice flying in what is called a "virtual world." In actuality their "virtual world" is a copy of the "virtual world" in which we all live. As Kant said, reality is "unknowable." We do not know the world as it is in itself. In our understanding, Kant's expression implies that reality as we are aware of it is limited to our sensory inputs and is to a considerable extent a construction of our minds.

Be assured that our concept is different from pure idealism or solipsism. We are not proposing that objects and events which we consider to be reality are entirely a product of our brains or imaginations. Our "virtual world" results from objects in the real world. (In regard to objects, we do not know what they are in an ultimate sense; perhaps a relatively lasting accumulation of energy of some sort, etc. Yet, let us add that we also do not know in an ultimate sense what energy or several other basic concepts are. We do not even know if there is such a thing as an "ultimate sense" in reality or whether such a concept results only from human experience which we attempt to apply to nature.) As odd as it may sound, it is only partly the case that external reality exists as we experience it. External reality is merely our view as human beings within the severe limitations of our senses and their extensions by means of instruments such as microscopes and telescopes.

We have stated before that the physiological basis of consciousness may already be well known in the form of quantum phenomena, or coordinated rhythm of nerve cell activity, etc., but, if so, we cannot causally connect it to consciousness since it is known only from the "outside" perspective. If nerve cells or some aspects of them are truly significant, which relatively few theorists would doubt, then it is their "inside" perspective which is important. From that perspective no physiological mechanism is needed to bridge the gap between physiology and psychology, between mind and body. The neurons or some components or combinations of them *are* consciousness. Once the proper cellular activity is produced, *no further creating or perceiving by a "higher center" is needed to result in a consciousness content.*

In a previous chapter we stated that consciousness cores are "simply what we call light or sound and consciousness contents in general. No matter how complex, the contents are composed of consciousness cores." Also, now that we have discussed the equivalence of consciousness and meaning, we wish to emphasize once more: *Light, sounds, emotions, memories, and all ideas and meanings are nerve cells or nerve cell activity.* One must regard this statement as true if one believes that the nervous system produces consciousness and meaning. Our bodies have nothing other than our nervous systems with which to accomplish the "miracle" of consciousness. We may add that nerve cells do not "cause" or "produce" consciousness; they *are* consciousness.

Rocks and Reality

In order to present our view of reality in another context and to do so more concretely let us describe it in terms of an object, a rock. *In so far as we can perceive or know directly,* rocks are no more than nerve cells and impulse patterns. How can we make such an assertion? Consider that we are aware of a rock *only as our senses make us aware.* We perceive its size, shape, color, hardness, weight, and temperature only through our senses. One might find this difficult to accept: "The rock is real. If we trip over a rock, is it no more to us than our senses reveal? What if we injure a toe?" If we injure our toe or fall, the pain in the toe or the hardness of the ground involves sensations *in addition* to the sensations we receive from the rock. To each of us, a rock is nothing other than our perceptions of it. And our perceptions are nothing other than nerve cells and impulse patterns. So, to repeat, a rock is no more than its shape and hardness, etc. One may still object, "But the rock is in the environment. It exists. I know more about a rock than my senses tell me. I know that it is of the sedimentary or igneous type, and much more." These statements are correct; but all that we know results ultimately from sensory inputs. Even if we receive information from someone verbally or if we acquire it through reading, the information is previously acquired through the senses of the person who informs us and it is relayed to us through our senses. Furthermore, indirect observations such as chemical analyses, X-rays, etc., are known through recordings which we perceive by means of vision. In one manner or another every aspect of a rock which is known to us is known by means of our senses. That which applies to a rock also applies to our perceptions of people and to reality in general.

Notice that we do not say that a rock, or something that we call a rock, does not exist. Things exist but we know them only by means of our sensory impulses. The rock as it exists apart from our sensory impulses is "unknowable." We have explained that the brain creates the sensory qualities. They are "projected", that is, interpreted as being in the environment. The "projected" qualities constitute the objects in the environment in so far as we can know them.

The common understanding is that the act of perception transfers "reality" from the environment into our brains where reality becomes consciousness. Our version of the identity theory in large measure turns the transfer around and explains how *our brains project our perception of "reality" into the environment after* first receiving *stimulation* from the environment. In that sense, our brains literally create much of our "reality" for us.

Hierarchical Development of Objects and the "Binding Problem"

In the previous chapter we discussed the concept of the latest hierarchy level as being a single meaning. There is a more fundamental explanation of the means by which we become aware of objects as being the objects that they are. We can now offer an explanation of how the inputs of a sensory modality, as well as inputs of different sensory modalities, all of which are separate nerve cell impulses (separate volleys), become for us a single object. If we look at an object, we do not see it as individual "light rays", or individual spots of color with touch sensations available over its surface. We perceive it as a single object such as a rock or a cup or a chair.

In the theory we have presented we began with consciousness cores or sensory inputs and ended with sensations becoming consciousness on the basis of identity. This statement leaves a large explanatory gap between the sensory inputs and consciousness. At the level of sensory impulses, Crick and Koch have called the need for an explanation of this phenomenon the "binding problem." How do colors, shapes, sizes, touch sensations, and so on, become "bound" together into a single perception?

The "binding" relates to sensory inputs which are "bound together" *at the time of the perception*. In distinction from this concept, we offer that *the inputs are "bound" mostly in the past*. They are bound (associated) step by step, sensory input by sensory input, hierarchy level by hierarchy level, over the course of one's lifetime. When an adult sees an external object, the sensory inputs originating with the object are matched with memory hierarchy levels relating to the object. Most of the perception of the object has been developed hierarchically. Further, as we discussed in the previous section, *each new level of the memory hierarchy simply is the object* in so far as the perceiver is concerned. The brain creates the perceptual object. The creation is the only object known to us. If we acquire new sensory inputs from or about the object, then these, together with the previous perception, constitute the new object. An object is, for each person, nothing more than the perception of it.

The balance or net effect between inhibitions and facilitations of the relevant nerve cell impulses determines which preconscious memory levels become consciousness. In our view the nerve cells of the memory levels which are preconscious contain the elements of consciousness. When the controlling influences favor facilitation, the cells become consciousness itself.

Journey Into the Realm of Consciousness

Objects as Concepts

In keeping with our theory of memory hierarchies we regard perceptions of objects to be comprised mainly of memory organizations. We have previously called such organizations "memory levels" or "items" of memory. We include under "objects" any sensory inputs which we perceive, such as ordinary objects as well as sensations from within our bodies, that is, anything which becomes consciousness. We also include words under the category of "objects." Words not only represent objects but in themselves are objects of perception.

One readily recognizes that words and their meanings are acquired over the course of an individual's development from birth onward. The point we now wish to offer is that the meanings (consciousness) of ordinary objects are acquired in the same manner that the knowledge of words is acquired; their meanings are developed and reinforced through repeated experiences. Children, for example, learn the meaning of "horse" by means of a number of experiences. Further, in our discussion of objects it would be well to remember that we actually mean the synecdoches of physical objects; we do not register as sensory inputs all of the features of an object.

Our view of the mechanism of perception, allows for two ways of considering their sources: 1) As resulting from energies emanating from objects. 2) As resulting entirely from our memory hierarchies.

Since we regard objects, in so far as we are able to perceive them, as being largely memory hierarchies there is a further point which becomes available: In the form in which they are perceived, all objects, to the extent of our knowledge, are actually concepts. If we stumble over a rock, as described above, our perception of the rock is a concept and not the same as it exists in "unknowable" nature. Let us not be misinterpreted. Indeed, something we know as a rock exists in nature. Nevertheless, *after we have been stimulated from the environment, objects as we know them, are concepts.* The brain creates the consciousness and the concepts of objects based upon current and past stimulations.

Objects and Emotions

Yet another point which we feel is important in relation to objects, and which we have clearly implied a number of times in earlier chapters, is that the perceptions of objects have some emotion associated with them. In chapter fifteen we stated, "Incoming stimuli are immediately tied to the interests and anxieties from which the stimuli receive appropriate emotional tone." Under the section heading of "Higher Centers and Memory" (chapter 24) we asserted that "The memories all carry emotional associations and it is the emotions which provide weight and direction." Subject matter and emotion are both aspects of any experience (Brooks, 1994).

215

We feel that the association of emotion with objects is sufficiently important to warrant our express attention particularly in considering objects as concepts or meanings. For example, I perceive a magnifying glass lying before me on my desk. There is little or no conscious emotion connected with it. Yet I recall that as a child, like many children, I was intrigued by magnifying glasses. I marveled at how they made objects appear much larger. I also marveled at the way one could set paper afire by focusing the sun's rays upon it. At the present time a magnifying glass is kept on my desk in order to assist me in discerning some punctuation marks on a printed page as well as on my computer monitor. It is fairly frustrating when I am attempting to proofread something, to be unable to distinguish between a comma and a period, for instance. I believe the magnifying glass is perceived by me with an unconscious residue of the fascination from my childhood as well as a sense of comfort in feeling that it enables me to see more clearly.

In our judgment the same principle applies to all objects. If we give them any attention at all, it seems reasonable to think that they have some interest to us; and interest implies emotion. On the other side of the coin, we could have a measure of disdain for an object which comes before our notice. We could shift our glance elsewhere with little or no conscious thought of doing so. But even the occurrence of a lack of interest implies at least a minimum of emotion. We are inclined to believe that any object of which we are aware carries with it some emotion. We can therefore state that, as we perceive them, there are two aspects to objects, an objective or descriptive aspect as well as an emotional aspect.

Time and Space

Attempts to understand or explain time and space are traditional concerns of philosophy. Our theory of consciousness lends itself not only to objects and abstractions in general but also specifically to time and space. Our perceptions of both depend entirely upon our sensory inputs. We are aware of time as the separation between events, the events having been perceived by means of the senses. Similarly, space is the separation between objects which, again, are perceived through the senses. Time and space are therefore inferences or concepts which, like all perceptions, are based on sensory inputs. Of course, we are not stating that time and space are not real in nature. Our comments are merely about our consciousness of them. Once more, we may call upon our principle that "reality rests on two feet", one in environment and the other in the mind.

Synecdoche as Reality

In a previous section our discussion of the perception of reality was cast at the level of neurons. In the next to last section we moved to a high level of organization, the level of the "top of the hierarchy." Now let us round out our discussion of reality by including the role of synecdoche. Recall that a synecdoche is a part which represents the whole.

We will use the term 'reality' in the generally accepted, 'folk psychology', sense. The first two chapters of this book described different theories about how consciousness occurs, the three main traditional theories being realism, representationalism, and idealism. The problem was considered to be how the mind manages to represent reality for us—how the environment is brought into the mind. In order to be more complete and more comprehensible, we must bring synecdoche into our discussion. We believe that the mind perceives external reality mainly in terms of synecdoches. The mind manages to become aware of reality by reducing it to small parts, to individual features of objects.

Now, we are in a position to make the same point which we made earlier in relation to the level of neurons: The synecdoche does not *represent* reality; *it is reality* in so far as the individual is concerned. As we have stated we do not know the actual reality of objects. Such reality is unknowable. The reality we know, and that which we take to be real, usually consists, in our minds, of synecdoches. There are usually a number of synecdoches of any one item of reality. One synecdoche is conscious at any single instant. It, possibly together with backup synecdoches at later instants, constitute the entire item for our minds.

For an example let us use a dog. In a previous section we used a rock for our example, but we believe a dog will now serve better. Also let us say that the dog has only four features. Actually the features are innumerable but we will treat the dog as if it has only four. These are color, size, shape, and fuzziness. In order to consciously think of the dog we use any of the four features as a synecdoche. A split second later we may (or may not) think of a second feature or even a third or fourth. But in either case, to our minds the feature(s) *is* the dog at any instant under consideration. Remember the dog has only four features. But even if we allow innumerable features, the number of features, of which we become aware, are limited. We ordinarily do not need to become aware of more than one or two to know or think of the dog. And, as we mentioned, to our minds, that feature, at that instant, constitutes the dog. The synecdoche *is* the dog and by the same principle, to each of us it *is* all of reality. No two of us perceives the world in exactly the same way. As psychoanalyst (and philosopher) John Dorsey, M.D. used to say (in teaching the medical residents in psychiatry at Receiving Hospital in Detroit), "My you is different from your you."

Nerve Cells are Consciousness

It would probably be advisable to elaborate once more upon the concept of the identity of nerve cells with consciousness. Even if one acknowledges that light energy is transduced into nerve cell activity which in turn becomes light, a very reasonable question is, by means of what possible mechanism does nerve cell activity become light? Or more correctly, how can we assert that nerve cell activity *is* light? After all, light or objects as we know them, seem to have no resemblance to nerve cells. How does the one become transformed into the other? The answer which we offer is that the questions are based on an incorrect assumption; *nerve cell activity does not have to be transformed into light but is what we know as light. Light is nothing other than the inside perspective of neurons.* As we discussed in the first section of chapter twenty-four, to state it plainly, that is what light is and always has been. The propensity for the identity is inborn and is actualized when we experience light vibrations. Again, we are like the fish to which the universe consists of water or like the Queen of Hearts in Wonderland whose reality was normal to her but was most "peculiar" to Alice. The nerve cell activity is our reality. We normally do not realize this because we "project" the nerve cell activity to outside objects and consider them to constitute reality.

In support of our thinking that an explanation of how nerve cell impulses become light, we should understand that light as we perceive it is a psychological and not a physical phenomenon. Light energy is transduced into nerve cell energy but nerve cell energy is not *transduced* into psychological light. We believe the particular nerve cell activity simply *is* psychological light. Also, according to the same principal, the nerve cell activities involved in the other senses simply *are* those senses as we perceive them. We apply the same principal in all of the cases which we have included under the description of "sensory." This application is clear and customary except for those sensory inputs which are generally regarded as being entirely cerebral. By "entirely cerebral" we refer to the emotions, to items of memory, and to any other inputs which we will include under the general category of "thoughts." In regard to emotions, we have previously explained that we regard these to be similar to the other senses in that they are inborn sensory qualities. As to memory items and to thoughts in general, we regard these as being compounded of all of the other sensory qualities.

Difficulties with Accepting Theoretical Statements

The concept that nerve cell activity simply *is* consciousness, is, of course, the heart of our view of the identity theory. We have used light as an example of sensations in general. When we expand our description to include not only simple sensations but also to encompass all of consciousness, the expansion probably still reawakens a feeling of incredulity. Even if one can accept the bare premise that consciousness is nerve cell activity, which we think has become acceptable in the abstract to a majority of theorists, it still seems almost impossible for most theorists to have a sense of conviction about it. The ingredient which is lacking is the support of a developmental theory. One needs the further understanding of other concepts which fill in the explanatory gaps.

Of course, one problem which adds to the unacceptability of the identity theory is the manner in which one becomes genuinely convinced of something scientific. What is genuinely convincing is experience, not argument alone. But it is impossible to know from direct experience that the identity theory is correct, that nerve cells simply *are* consciousness and meaning. The phenomenon cannot be demonstrated in the laboratory. *Because sensory inputs are the bedrock experiences for our acquisition of knowledge, there are no more basic psychological observations to explain them.* Further explanation may eventually fall into place in the form of intra- or intercellular activity. However, convincingly demonstrating that these activities actually are consciousness promises to be quite difficult and will probably require more than a small leap of faith. Consider the fact that a fair number of people, including some philosophers, doubt that animals possess consciousness, that is, even the definition of consciousness is in debate.

A further difficulty with acceptance of the identity theory as an explanation of consciousness is that there is a marked difference between accepting a simple statement that brain activity *is* consciousness and accepting a statement which addresses the *complexity* of consciousness. There are a number of factors in the causal chain leading to consciousness. Several of them are counterintuitive yet most of them must be understood and accepted for the theory to hold together. The theory involves considerable complexity but complexity is not a problem for innumerable combinations of sensory impulses. The seeming difference between the appearance of simple colors and the appearance of a sunset is a matter of complexity. That which applies to solitary colors or other sensations also applies to complexes of them. Our theory of impulses and their combination has offered an explanation of the intricacy.

In approaching the concept of the identity theory intellectually, it can seem to be correct. The reasoning can be convincing—just as we recognize that light and sound, etc., are the inside perspective of nerve cells, we can recognize the contents of consciousness as the further derivatives of the cells and that consciousness includes the perception of objects, meanings, and reality in general. Yet, even if one accepts the logic, as once mentioned by Crick (1995), it is very difficult to avoid falling back into one's habitual mode of thinking—that consciousness needs an entity (a "higher center", or a homunculus) which becomes aware of the contents.

Another difficult problem is presented by the fact that all of our experiences of the world external to our own consciousness are observed in the third person perspective. All objects, including our own bodies, are "its." We assume that objects as we know them are outside of ourselves, outside of our minds, yet the perceptions are within our minds. In order to understand consciousness or to experience it in the manner that sentient beings normally experience the world, we do so from the third person perspective. But it is *impossible* for us to experience our own consciousness in that manner. As we explained in the section on introspection (chapter twenty-one), we have memory of consciousness in the third person but we *experience* consciousness only in the first person. Searle (1992, b) seems to miss this point in his argument against the identity theory: He states that in attempting to identify anything mental (such as a pain) with anything physical (nerve cell activity, etc.,) there is a "dilemma" which forces one to abandon the mental side and in having done so "we have left out the mind." This appears to be viewing both sides from the third person perspective. Our resolution of the "dilemma" is that the two sides of the identity should be considered from two different perspectives. The mental side must be considered from the first person perspective but the physical side must be viewed from the third person perspective. *Our own consciousness is known to us only in the first person perspective.* It is experience. It is not an "it" except in retrospect (in memory),

We have discussed the notion that it is difficult to accept the concept of our sensations residing not in the environment but in our minds. Three other concepts in particular, which we have previously discussed and which are central to our theory, are also difficult to accept. We wish to suggest reasons as to why this is so. The popular views of all three are conscious or semiconscious in almost everyone's thinking. The concepts have in common that they cannot be proved or disproved, at least not at the present time. Further, they are strongly contrary to popular opinion even among theorists of consciousness. We feel that our thinking in regarding the concepts as we do, as discussed in the previous chapters, considerably outweighs the reasons for the common views.

1) The first of our concepts is that consciousness is not a single entity, instead it is a rapid sequence of separate contents. We refer to our concept

(in chapter seven) as the "multiplicity" of consciousness. A person has no experience of consciousness as being multiple and has much difficulty believing it.   If told there is more than one consciousness, people feel confused or incredulous.   We believe the difficulty with accepting the multiplicity concept is simply that the concept is heavily based on neurophysiology while the usual notion is based on introspection. Multiplicity does not subtract is any way from the subjective impression of being conscious.

We suspect there is a deeper and much more interesting reason why the second and third concepts so completely "go against the grain" for most people. The reason is the same in both cases.

2) The second idea we wish to single out is that the self is merely a concept based on memory of experiences (as explained in chapter seventeen). Again, many theorists regard the self as being the same as consciousness.   Contrary to this view we believe the "mental self" is an illusion.   We hold that it is memory which informs us that we are single entities.   We recall having had particular sensations and particular experiences.

3) The third concept is that there is no free will, that there is a prior cause for every thought or action both within human beings and in nature in general.   People feel they are entirely free to raise an arm or to utter a particular word if they choose to do so.

What then might be beneath the popular intuitions? In the cases of both of the latter concepts we feel that there is a single theme which makes them difficult for most people to accept. *It lies in the implication that our minds function automatically. We might even say that we do not control our minds* and, that despite our illusions, we are the mind's subjects rather than its rulers. This statement is radical and unacceptable to most people and its opposite normally impresses one as being incontrovertible.   Very few individuals would agree that there is no free will even though logic dictates that this is the case. When logic is confronted by emotion it seems that it is almost always logic which succumbs. If told there is no self and no free will, an individual is made to feel that one is an automaton. We believe we have completely explained that these impressions are not correct; but allow us to expound further: As we explained in chapter twenty-three, *it is the automaticity of the memory hierarchies* which causes us to "will" as we do. We react automatically based on our past experience and are therefore similar to automatons in a most important yet limited sense.   Actual automatons react according to their prior programming. Indeed, people are also programmed; they are programmed by past experience. But the huge difference between people and automatons is that the past experience of people includes emotion. The net effect of emotions automatically steers us

221

toward or away from situations. Automatons or computers, even if they are self-programming based on "experience", are extremely limited relative to human beings.

In order to further explain the relation of automaticity to the concept of the self and to the illusion of free will, let us review the role of the memory hierarchies, a role which is central. In the process of perception, when the sensory inputs are matched against the levels of the memory hierarchy, *the categorization and matching (association) take place automatically and at an unconscious level* based on similarities. This is the inherent manner in which the memory system operates. Reactions to stimulations occur based on experiences which have occurred in the past, including those which occur immediately prior to the moment of the reaction. Note that we do not voluntarily choose the memory of a former experience to which a new experience is associated. Also, when an experience causes us to have a particular recollection, we do not choose the recollection. Neither our consciousness, nor our "selves", nor our "wills" determine to which former experience a new experience will be related. If something prompts us, our minds access the memories and there is a sense of free will in the accomplishment. Yet we overlook the emotion, the thought, or the motivation which performs the prompting. Therefore, in a very important sense, we (our selves) are not the controlling entities. We do exist, of course, in a physical sense and it is our memories which provide us with the knowledge that we exist in a mental sense.

We believe it is the automaticity which fundamentally runs counter to our belief that "we" perform the various activities. We maintain that "we" do not perform these activities. They are performed automatically by our brains. That there is no self as a separate agent and that the supposed will is not free, seems totally unacceptable, even incomprehensible, if one is not mindful of the extensiveness of automaticity. We normally feel that there is an "I", a self, which controls our minds. It is the automaticity, with the resulting implication that there is no "I" which is in control, which is counterintuitive and is so profoundly unacceptable.

Revisiting the Initial Premise

We are now in position to recognize that there is a problem in the attempt to explain consciousness which is even more fundamental than the difficulties with accepting the identity theory or the other problems which we have described in the preceding two sections. A major problem in explaining consciousness has been the general belief that one must clarify how perceptions bring objects from the environment *into the mind.* We stated in chapter one that "For a mind to become conscious of objects which are perceived as being external to itself, requires either that objects have to be brought into the mind in order for perception to occur, or that objects do not exist external to the brain but are present only in the mind (some form of idealism)." With the possible exception of solipsism, which denies external reality in the first place, the conveying of objects into the mind, has throughout history been either an expressed understanding or a definite implication. Realism wished to rely on empiricism but had no explanations of consciousness except that it occurred "directly" without representations. Representationalism, which struggled futilely with the nature of possible representations, required that objects had to somehow be shifted from the environment into the mind. Idealism, at least in the Kantian version, was a step in the right direction. However, even the Kantian version of reality, as we interpret it, still considered objects to be "out there" despite their being "unknowable" as they existed "in themselves."

In our view, the traditional manner of construing the problem constituted a major explanatory hurdle. It was based on a fallacious initial premise. It is impossible to explain *how* something happens which does not happen and cannot happen in the first place. Objects, *in the only form in which we are conscious of them, are projected from the mind into the environment.* This is a clear extrapolation of Locke's and Muller's statements which we explained in chapter three. Just as the brain creates colors and other qualities after being stimulated by energies from the environment, objects. *in so far as we are able to perceive them*, consist of qualities. We are conscious of objects only in terms of sensory inputs. We literally do not perceive what is "out there." Everything which we perceive is "in here", in our brains. What is "out there" *instigates* our perception of what is "in here" but our perceptions are only the effects of the instigations, that is, we perceive the light and sound energy, molecular jigglings (heat), and so on. As we explained in the earlier section entitled "Objects as Concepts", we know objects only as we construe them. What objects *seem* to be is in consciousness not in the environment. We believe that a major obstacle to the explanation of consciousness has been that the attempts at explanation have historically begun with a fallacious assumption.

Eugene M. Brooks, M.D.

General Summary

The most established historical approaches to an explanation of consciousness have been realism, representationalism, and idealism. Epiphenomenalism and panpsychism have also often been promulgated. The identity theory, with little or no elaboration, is another theory which has been on the shelf for many years. More recent important theories attempting to explain consciousness include among others, neural networks, the coordinated rhythm of brain cells, and quantum mechanics.

In our own explanation of consciousness, we adopt and expand upon the identity theory. The central concept of our version of the identity theory is that some brain cells or their activities are identical with consciousness. They constitute consciousness as it is known to us. We begin our explanation with the understanding that light, sound, and the other sensations are within the mind and not in the environment. Extending this physiological fact, we believe the explanation of consciousness does not require that objects be brought from the environment into the mind but that emanations from objects stimulate sense receptors and perceptions are then "projected" into the environment.

We find it desirable to adjust the uses of some of the common terms which are closely related to consciousness. The terms "consciousness", "awareness", "perception", and "sensation" are equated to the extent that they all involve perception. We define "sensory" as meaning any inputs which become consciousness, including the emotions, memories, and "thoughts" in general.

We postulate that consciousness is reducible to "consciousness cores." The cores are a heuristically very useful concept as was the case with atoms in the centuries prior to modern atomic theory. The cores are considered to be the primary elements or building blocks of which consciousness is composed. They are defined as consisting of all of the sensory qualities. They may be identical with particular nerve cells in the cerebral cortex but could possibly arise in neurons which extend to all areas of the body.

The qualitative diversity among the various sensations inherent in the consciousness cores results from anatomical and physiological differences. There are variations in the peripheral sense receptors and in the neuronal destinations in the brain. There are also diversities in cellular arrangements, the internal chemical composition of disparate nerve cells as well as variations in intercellular transmitters and in the timing of impulses.

Due mainly to the rapidity of the nerve cell "firing" rate as well as the speed of impulse transmission, particularly between cerebral neurons, the functioning of the brain is extremely fast. In addition, the brain regularly uses mechanisms of "shorthand." One such mechanism is synecdoche, by which a part represents the whole.

We believe that all sensory nerve cell stimulations move toward becoming consciousness but due to the results of mutual inhibitions and facilitations, occurring at both lower and upper levels in the nervous system, probably only one item becomes conscious in any single instant. We do not regard consciousness as a single entity. Instead we consider it to be multiple in the sense of a series of separate contents, each lasting only milliseconds, with imperceptible temporal separations between events. The process is similar in this respect to a motion picture film which is composed of individual frames but which appear as unbroken motion. The self is viewed neither as being the same as consciousness nor as a perceiving entity but as a concept based on the memory of experiences.

It is important in understanding the identity theory to differentiate between the inside and the outside perspectives of nerve cells. The usual description of nerve cells is in terms of appearance under a microscope or traces on an oscilloscope. Such descriptions are from the outside perspective. We consider the inside perspective in an entirely different manner. In accordance with the identity theory, the inside perspective is subjective and consists of the contents of consciousness. The inside and outside perspectives correspond to the first person and third person perspectives. Many attempts to explain consciousness have failed because the attempt is made from an "outside" perspective. An explanation of consciousness must necessarily be made by utilizing an understanding of an "inside" point of view. No characterization from the "outside" position can adequately describe subjective qualities.

Memory is considered to be hierarchical with its related items thoroughly interconnected. The memory hierarchy provides context and meaning for sensory inputs. In addition it directs the monitoring and selecting of material, which is to become consciousness, and exercises control over motor activity. Psychologically the control is accomplished not by virtue of being a mind within the mind but, by the automatic influence of the emotional associations of hierarchy levels. Neurologically the hierarchy levels exert control by means of facilitations and inhibitions of nerve cell impulses.

Consciousness and meaning are considered to be the same function in that all consciousness contents are meanings. There are unconscious meanings which we designate as "premeaning" corresponding to the term "preconscious." Introspection is not viewed as necessary for consciousness but, instead, is deemed to be consciousness of an earlier consciousness content.

In the mechanism of perception, attention is regarded as an inborn tendency under the control of the memory hierarchies. It may result evolutionally from the advantages of perceiving information from the environment. Perceptual inputs have random access to the levels of the memory hierarchy, the inputs being recursively matched against and combined with hierarchy elements of sufficient similarity. The associated units become new elements of the hierarchy and the new elements which are the least inhibited or most facilitated move "upward." The memory levels have the same neurological structure as consciousness and those which outdistance all other elements become consciousness. They do so by virtue of the identity of consciousness with the "inside" perspective of the involved nerve cells. The identity implies that the physical and the mental are two sides of one coin, two ways of considering the "inside" and "outside" perspectives of neurons. The identity of the physical and the mental closes the "mind-body gap."

The reactions of the mind are automatically determined by the influence of past experiences but one feels as if one determines the actions and has freedom of will because actions result from one's unique memory hierarchy components and their emotional qualities.

Ultimate reality is "unknowable" but the brain, having received relatively limited stimulations from the environment, completes our perception of "reality" largely from previous experience. Perception thus rests on two feet, one planted in the environment and the other in the mind.

Bibliography

Acton, Harry Burrows. (1965). *Idealism*. Encyclopaedia Britannica, Vol. 11, p. 1062.

Ayer, A. J. (1940). *The Foundations of Empirical Knowledge*. London: Macmillan, p. 24.

Armstrong, D. M. (1993). *A Materialist Theory of the Mind*. London: Routledge.

Armstrong, D. M. (1968). *A Materialist Theory of the Mind*. London: Routledge & Kegan Paul.

Berkeley, George. (1952). *A Treatise Concerning The Principles of Human Knowledge*. In Great Books of the Western World. Robert Maynard Hutchins, Ed. in Chief, 413 ff.

Blakemore, Colin. (1979). *Representation of Reality in the Perceptual World*. In Ciba Foundation Symposium, 69, 139-152.

Bleuler, Eugen. (1924). *Textbook of Psychiatry*. New York. Macmillan, p. 40. In Rapaport, David (1951). *Organization and Pathology of Thought*. Columbia University Press, p. 638, f.n. 140.

Boring, E. G. (1933). *The Physical Dimensions of Consciousness*. New York: Century.

Brain, W. Russell. (1951). *Mind, Perception, and Science*. Oxford. Blackwell Scientific Publications, p. 66.

Brill, A. A. (1938). *The Basic Writings of Sigmund Freud*. The Modern Library. p. 209.

Britannica, Encyclopaedia. (1965). "Descartes, Rene". Vol. 7, p. 281.

Broad, C. D. (1923). *Scientific Thought*. New York. Harcourt Brace: p. 23 ff.

Brook, A. (1998). Unified Consciousness and the Self. *Journal of Consciousness Studies*. Vol. 5. No. 5-6, p. 584.

Brooks, Eugene M. (1994). Toward an Understanding of Perception, Consciousness, and Meaning. Copyrighted and submitted for publication Feb. 28.

Brooks, Eugene M. (1995a). Consciousness and Mind, the Answer to the Hard Problem. Copyrighted and submitted for publication.

Brooks, Eugene M. (1995b). An Explanation of Consciousness. *Society for Neuroscience Abstracts*, November 11-16, Part 3, p. 1764.

Bruner, Jerome S. (1973) *Beyond the Information Given*. Edited by Jeremy M. Anglin. New York: W. W. Norton & Company, Inc.

Chalmers, David. (1995). Facing Up to the Problem of Consciousness. *Journal of Consciousness Studies*, (a) Vol. 2, No. 3, p. 210; (b) p. 212.

Chrisholm, Roderick. (1957). *Perceiving*. Ithaca. Cornell University Press.

Clark, J.C.S. (1995). The Nonlocality of Mind. *Journal of Consciousness Studies.* Vol. 2, No. 3, pp. 231-240.

Clark, Thomas. (1995). Functions and Phenomenology: Closing the Explanatory Gap. *Journal of Consciousness Studies.* Vol. 2, No. 3, (a) p. 246; (b) p. 241.

Crick, Francis, H.C., Koch, Christof. (1990). Towards a Neurobiological Theory of Consciousness. *Seminars in the Neurosciences,* Vol. 2, pp. 263-275.

Crick, Francis, H.C. Thinking about the Brain. *Scientific American,* Copyright 1991, "The Laureates' Anthology", Vol. II, p. 85.

Crick, Francis, H.C. (1994). *The Astonishing Hypothesis.* New York: Charles Scribner's Sons (Maxwell Macmillan International).

Dalton, J. W. (1997). The Unfinished Theater. *Journal of Consciousness Studies.* Vol. 4, No. 4, p. 316.

Dennett, Daniel C. (1991). *Consciousness Explained.* Boston: Little Brown and Co.

Dennett, Daniel C. (1981) *Where Am I?* See under Hofstadter.

Ducasse, C. J. (1942). Moore's "The Refutation of Idealism" in P. A. Schlipp (ed), *The Philosophy of G. E. Moore.* Chicago: Northwestern University. p. 223-251.

Earle, William. (1955). *Objectivity.* New York: The Noonday Press, p. 63.

Efron, Robert. (1966-68). What is Perception? *Boston Studies in the Philosophy of Science.* IV, pp. 137-173.

Fantino, Edmund and Reynolds, George S. (1975). *Contemporary Psychology.* San Francisco: W. H. Freeman and Company.

Farrell, B. (1995). Review of Bermudez et al. *Journal of Consciousness Studies.* Volume 3, No. 5-6. pp. 157-19.

Feigl, Herbert. (1958). *The "Mental" and the "Physical".* Minneapolis: University of Minnesota Press. Also 1967, *The "Mental" and the "Physical."* Minneapolis: University of Minnesota Press. p. 3-131.

Fischback, Gerald D. *Scientific American,* Sept '92, p. 55.

Forman, Robert K. C. What Does Mysticism Have to Teach Us About Consciousness? *Journal of Consciousness Studies.* Vol. 5., No. 2, p. 189.

Freud, Sigmund. (1913). *The Interpretation of Dreams.* New York. Macmillan.

Freud, Sigmund. (1936). *The Problem of Anxiety.* New York, Norton.

Freud, Sigmund. (1938). *The Basic Writings of Sigmund Freud.* Edited by A. A. Brill. New York. Modern Library.

Freud, Sigmund. (1948). *Collected Papers.* London. Hogarth Press. Vol IV, p. 15.

Freud, Sigmund. (1950). *Collected Papers.* London. Hogarth Press. Vol V, (a) p. 177, (b) p. 167

Freud, Sigmund. (1953). *The Complete Psychological Works of Sigmund Freud.* London. Hogarth Press Limited. Vols V and VI.

Gallager, Shaun. (1997). Editors' Introduction. *Journal of Consciousness Studies.* Vol. 4, No. 5-6, p. 399.

Gleitman, Henry. (1981). *Psychology.* New York, London. W. W. Norton & Company. (a) p. 288. (b) p. 272. (c) p. 275.

Hameroff, S. R., and Penrose, R. (1996). Orchestrated Reduction of Quantum Coherence in Brain Microtubules: A Model of Consciousness. In S. R. Hameroff, A. Kaszniak, and A. C. Scott, eds., *Toward a Science of Consciousness—The First Tucson Discussions and Debates,* Cambridge. MIT Press.

Hebb, Donald O. (1949). *The Organization of Behavior.* New York: Wiley and Sons, Inc., p. xiii.

Hebb, Donald O. (1980). *Essay on Mind.* Hillsdale, NJ: Erlbaum.

Hirst, Rodney J. (1959). *The Problems of Perception.* New York: Macmillan.

Hodgson, D. (1994). Why Searle Has Not Rediscovered the Mind. *Journal of Consciousness Studies,* Vol. 1, No. 2, p. 274.

Hofstadter, Douglas R. and Dennett, Daniel C., composers (1981). *The Mind's I.* New York: Bantam Books/Basic Books, Ch.13, p. 217.

Holt, E. B. (1922, copyright 1912). *The New Realism.* New York: The Macmillan Company. p. 32.

Horgan, John. (1994). Can Science Explain Consciousness? *Scientific American.* Vol. 271, July, pp. 88-94.

Hubel, D. H., Wisel, T. N. (1962). Receptive Fields, Binocular Interactive and Functional Architecture in the Cat's Visual Cortex. *London Jour Physiology,* 160, pp. 106-154.

Hume, David. (1974). *Dialogues Concerning Natural Religion.* In The Empiricists, Anchor Books, Anchor Press/Doubleday. Garden City, New York, 431 ff.

Hume, David (1978). *A Treatise of Human Nature.* Oxford at the Clarendon Press, 2nd Edition. p. 252.

Hut, P., van Frassen, B. (1997). Elements of Reality: A Dialogue. *Journal of Consciousness Studies,* Vol. 4, No. 2, p. 169.

Kolers, P. A. and von Grunau, M. (1976). Shape and Color in Apparent Motion, *Vision Research.* Vol. 16, pp. 329-335.

James, William. (1950). *The Principles of Psychology.* Vol I, New York. Dover. Publications. (First published 1890 by Henry Hold and Company). (a) p. 278. (b) p. 687.

Joad, C. E. M. (1957). *Guide to Philosophy.* New York. Dover Publications, p. 41-42.

Kant, Immanuel. (1965). *Critique of Pure Reason.* Trans. Smith, Norman K. Reprinted New York: St. Martin Press.

Kelly, David. (1986). *The Evidence of the Senses.* Baton Rouge and London: Louisiana State Press.

Kenny, A. (1998). *The Self.* (Marquette: Marquette University Press).

Kirk, Robert. (1994). *Raw Feeling: A Philosophical Account of the Essence of Consciousness.* Oxford: Clarendon Press.

Land, Edwin H. (1960). Experiments in Color Vision. *Scientific American,* pp. 80-96.

Land, Edwin H. (1983). Recent Advances in Retinex Theory and Some Implications for Cortical Computation: Color Vision and Natural Image. *Proceedings of the National Academy of Sciences of the USA,* 80, pp. 5163-5169.

Lewis, Clarence Irving. (1956). *Mind and the World Order* (1st edn 1929). New York: Dover Publications. pp. 61-5.

Libet, B. (1985). Unconscious Cerebral Initiative and the Role of Conscious Will in Voluntary Action. *The Behavioral and Brain Sciences,* Vol. *8,* pp. 529-66.

Libet, B. (1994). A testable field theory of mind-brain interaction. *Journal of Consciousness Studies.* Vol. 1. No. 1, pp. 119-26.

Libet, B. (1996). Solutions to the Hard Problem of Consciousness. *Journal of Consciousness Studies.* Vol. 3, No. 1, p. 34.

Livingston, M. S., Hubel, D. H. (1988). Segregation of Form, Color, Movement and Depth: Anatomy, Physiology, and Perception. *Science,* May 6, 240, pp. 740-9.

Locke, John. (1974). *An Essay Concerning Human Understanding.* In The Empiricists, Anchor Books, Anchor Press/Doubleday, Garden City, New York, Chs. 1-3.

Locke, John. (1975). *An Essay Concerning Human Understanding.* Peter H. Nidditch (Ed.), Oxford: Clarendon Press, ch. VII, sec. 10, p. 135.

Lockwood, Michael. (1989). *Mind, Brain, and the Quantum.* Cambridge, Massachusetts. Basil Blackwell, Inc.

McCullough, Warren S. (1947) Lecture at Fort Sam Houston, San Antonio, Texas.

Macdonald, Cynthia. (1992). (Published in hard cover 1989.) *Mind-Body Identity Theories.* London. Routledge. (A division of Routledge, Chapman, and Hall, Inc., New York.) p. ix.

McGinn, Colin. (1995). Consciousness and Space. *Journal of Consciousness Studies.* Vol. 2, No. 3, p. 228.

Merikle, Philip M. (1998). Psychological Investigations of Unconscious Perception. *Journal of Consciousness Studies.* Vol. 5, No. 1, p. 5-18.

Michaels, Claire F. and Carello, Claudia, *Direct Perception,* Prentice Hall, 1981, p. 105.

Moore, G. E. (1942). A reply to my critics. In Paul Arthur Schlipp (ed), *The Philosophy of G. E. Moore,* Library of Living Philosophers, La Salle, IL: Open Court, 629-31.

Moore, G. E. (1953). *Some Main Problems of Philosophy.* London: George Allen & Unwin. ch. II.

Nagel, Thomas (1974). "'What is it like to be a bat?'." *The Philosophical Review,* LXXXIII, No. 4, p. 43-50.

Nagel, Thomas (1986). *The View from Nowhere.* Oxford: Oxford University Press, p. 49.

Ornstein, Robert. (1991). *The Evolution of Consciousness.* New York. Prentice Hall Press, p. 129.

Panksepp, J. (19``98). A Naturalistic Proposal of How Feelings Emerge from the Neurodynamics of the Self. *Journal of Consciousness Studies.* Vol. 5,. No. 5/6, p. 580.

Pavlov, Ivan. 1927. *Conditioned Reflexes.* Oxford, England: Oxford University Press.

Penfield, Wilder. (1975). *The Mystery of the Mind.* Princeton, New Jersey. Princeton University Press.

Penrose, Roger. (1989). *The Emperor's New Mind.* Oxford, NY: Oxford University Press, p. 437.

Penrose, Roger. (1994). *Shadows of the Mind.* Oxford University Press, p. 263.

Piaget, Jean (1963). *The Origins of Intelligence in Children.* New York: W. W. Norton Company, Inc.

Pillsbury, W. B. (1913). Fluctuations in Attention and the Refractory Period. *Journal of Philosophy, Psychology, and Scientific Methods.* Vol. 10, pp. 181-185.

Popper, Karl R., Eccles, John C. (1977). *The Self and Its Brain.* New York: Springer International.

Pribram, K. H. (1999). "Brain and the Composition of Conscious Experience." *Journal of Consciousness Studies,* Vol. 6, No. 5, May.p. 28.

Price, H. H. (1973). *Perception.* Westport, Conn.: Greenwood Press, p. 66.

Pylkkanen, Paavo, (1994). On Baking a Conscious Cake with Quantum Yeast and Flour. *Consciousness at the Crossroads of philosophy and Cognitive Science,* Selected Proceedings of the Tempus Project, Imprint Academic, August, pp. 68-78.

Ranson, Stephen Walter. (1943). *The Anatomy of the Nervous System.* Philadelphia: W. B. Saunders Company, p. 309.

Rapaport, David. (1951). *Organization and Pathology of Thought.* New York. Columbia University Press.

Restak, Richard. (1991). *Your Mind Has a Brain of Its Own.* New York: Harmony Books.

Russell, Bertrand (1914). *Our Knowledge of the External World.* London: George Allen & Unwin Ltd., p. 109.

Russell, Bertrand. (1927). *The Analysis of Matter.* London: Kegan Paul.

Russell, Bertrand. (1929). *Mysticism and Logic.* New York: Norton Publishers, pp. 145-147.

Russell, Bertrand. (1949). *The Analysis of Mind.* (1st edn. 1921). London: George Allen & Unwin.

Ryle, Gilbert. (1949). *The Concept of Mind.* New York: Barnes & Noble Books.

Searle, John R. (1992a). Newsweek Magazine. April 20, p. 72.

Searle, John R. (1992b) *The Rediscovery of the Mind,* A Bradford Book, MIT Press, Cambridge, Massachusetts, p. 37.

Searle, John R. (1997a). *The Mystery of Consciousness.* New York: The New York Review of Books, xiii. (b) p. 30.

Sellars, Wilfred. (1963). Empiricism and the Philosophy of Mind. In *Science, Perception, and Reality.* London. p. 169, and p. 192.

Smart, J.J.C. (1959). Sensations and brain processes. *Philosophical Review,* Vol. 68, pp. 141-56.

Smart, J.J.C. (1963). *Philosophy and Scientific Realism.* London: Routledge & Kegan Paul.

Strawson, Galen. (1997). "'The Self'." *Journal of Consciousness Studies.* Vol. 4, No.5/6, p. 408.

Tye, Michael. (1995). *Ten Problems of Consciousness.* A Bradford Book, The MIT Press, Cambridge, Massachusetts, p. 104.

Underwood G., Paterson, K., Chapman, P. (1997). "Attention and Consciousness in the Processing of Novelty." *Journal of Consciousness Studies.* Vol. 4, No. 4, p. 340.

Vallentine, E. R. (1994). "Dissociation and the Delimitation of Consciousness." *Consciousness at the Crossroads of Philosophy and Cognitive Science, Selected Proceedings of the Tempus Project,* Imprint Academic, August p. 29.

Velmans, Max. (1991). "Consciousness from a First Person Perspective." *Behavioral and Brain Sciences,* Vol. 14, No. 4, pp. 792-26.

Velmans, Max. (1993). "Consciousness, Causality and Complementarity." *Behavioral and Brain Sciences,* Vol. 16, No. 2, pp. 404-16.

Velmans, Max. (1995). "The Relation of Consciousness to the Material World." *Journal of Consciousness Studies,* Vol. 2, No. 3, (a) p. 256; (b) p. 262; (c) p. 258.

Wittgenstein, Ludwig. (1969). *On Certainty.* Sections 95-105, 151-2, and 162.

Weiskrantz, L., Warrington, E. K., Sanders, M. D., and Marshal, J. (1974). Visual Capacity in the Hemianopic Field Following a Restricted Occipital Ablation. *Brain,* 97, pp. 709-729.

Zeki, S. (1992). The Visual Image in Mind and Brain. *Scientific American,* Sept, 69 ff.

Zeki, S. (1974). The Mosaic Organization of the Visual Cortex in the Monkey. In *Essays on the Nervous System.* Edited by Bellairs, R. and Gray, E. G. Oxford: Clarendon Press. pp. 327-343.

Zohar, Danah. (1990). *The Quantum Self.* New York: Wm. Morrow & Co.

Index

A priori, 80, 160
Abstract concepts, 134
Abstractions, 132, 133, 134, 204
Access, random, 113, 145, 151,
  155, 204, 208, 226
Activity, 79, 81, 126
Acton, 9, 227
Adverbial theory, 204
All-at-once, 95
Anaxagoras, 8
Anglin, 164, 227
Animism, 10
Anticipations, 35
Anxieties, 69, 118
Aristotle, 8, 86, 112
Armstrong, 127, 190, 227
Artificial intelligence, 13, 19,
  124, 158, 199, 207
Associated, consistently, 102,
  103, 104, 105, 159
Association, 112, 159
Atom, 21, 22, 23, 25
Attention, 173, 176, 185, 203,
  231, 232
Augustine, 8, 80
Automatic, 19, 50, 81, 154, 173,
  175, 176, 177, 178, 180, 182,
  193, 225
Axon, 126
Ayer, 7, 227
Berkeley, 10, 26, 46, 79, 93, 112,
  227
Birds, 104, 112, 122
Blakemore, 111, 227
Bleuler, 173, 227
Blindsight, 36, 152
Body, 16, 29, 48, 49, 87, 90, 230
Boolean, 151

Boring, 64, 227
Boyle, 45
Brain, creations of, 40
Brain, W. R., 149
Brill, 121, 227, 228
Britannica, 227
Broad, 7, 227
Brook, 76, 227
Brooks (1994), 20, 30, 68, 142,
  215
Brooks (1995a), 20
Brooks (1995b), 20
Bruner, 7, 46, 69, 150, 164, 227
Carbon monoxide, 114
Cartesian theater, 7, 61, 135, 156,
  169, 193
Cell, nerve, xii, 1, 2, 16, 20, 23,
  29, 30, 31, 32, 35, 36, 40, 41,
  43, 44, 56, 58, 59, 62, 64, 65,
  67, 69, 70, 73, 81, 87, 88, 90,
  106, 107, 108, 110, 114, 115,
  116, 118, 119, 123, 124, 125,
  127, 128, 129, 130, 131, 132,
  135, 140, 141, 144, 147, 149,
  150, 151, 156, 157, 160, 164,
  166, 167, 168, 170, 171, 172,
  179, 181, 182, 183, 184, 185,
  187, 197, 199, 204, 205, 206,
  207, 210, 211, 212, 213, 214,
  218, 219, 220, 224, 225, 226
Centers, higher, 69, 89, 120, 121,
  153, 156, 157, 160, 192
Central observer, 7, 8, 12, 63, 75,
  98, 118, 135, 138, 140, 164,
  166, 177, 182, 183, 195, 205,
  207

Cerebral cortex, 22, 29, 30, 31, 36, 40, 56, 59, 61, 74, 81, 93, 110, 115, 153, 170, 172, 190, 193, 224

Chalmers, 15, 34, 227

Chapman, 18, 139, 230, 232

Children, 215, 231

Chrisholm, 204, 227

Clark, JCS, 14, 228

Clark, Thomas, 228

Cochlea, 25, 40, 107

Cognition, 79

Color, 41, 55, 229, 230

Competition for consciousness, 69

Computers, 1, 12, 102, 124, 207

Conceptions, 35

Consciousness, 7, 9, 16, 18, 20, 27, 30, 33, 35, 36, 58, 61, 62, 64, 67, 68, 72, 77, 86, 87, 89, 91, 92, 114, 124, 125, 126, 130, 132, 135, 136, 138, 143, 146, 157, 165, 166, 169, 172, 181, 184, 185, 187, 188, 189, 193, 195, 197, 199, 200, 201, 218, 225, 227, 228, 229, 230, 231, 232, 233

Consciousness and meaning, 225

Consciousness and memory, 188, 189, 192, 208

Consciousness neurons, 188

Consciousness, becoming, 126, 150, 169, 170, 175, 186, 189, 214, 225

Consciousness, content, 59, 62, 64, 65, 66, 67, 125, 135, 138, 139, 140, 141, 143, 159, 166, 167, 181, 182, 183, 184, 185, 186, 188, 189, 190, 191, 192, 194, 195, 196, 200, 202, 205, 210, 212, 225

Consciousness, definition, 219

Consciousness, examination, 74

Consciousness, location of, 61, 86

Consciousness, multiplicity, 55, 69, 87, 140, 193

Consciousness, origins, 4, 31

Consciousness, outside, inside, 71

Consciousness, physiology of, 23

Constancy, size, shape, 56, 57

Core, consciousness, xi, 20, 21, 22, 23, 24, 25, 26, 27, 28, 29, 30, 31, 32, 34, 43, 45, 46, 56, 58, 59, 60, 62, 63, 70, 92, 106, 107, 108, 109, 114, 115, 124, 125, 130, 131, 145, 159, 160, 166, 169, 183, 184, 185, 194, 195, 199, 202, 203, 204, 206, 208, 209, 212, 214, 224

Core, qualitative, 20, 26, 30, 41, 57, 92, 108, 124, 130, 132, 143, 157, 158, 159, 168, 181, 182, 203, 207

Cores, connecting of, 87

Counterintuitive, xii, 19, 42, 66, 73, 129, 152, 205, 210, 219, 222

Create, 26, 42, 133, 184, 210, 211, 214

Crick (1990), 13, 106

Crick (1994), 61, 69, 168, 193

Curiosity, 179, 180

Cycles, 40 per second, 106, 167

Dalton, 16, 228

Darkness, 42, 83

Day dreams, 35

Democritus, 11, 21

Dendrite, 106, 115

Dendritic spines, 111

Dennett, 2, 16, 17, 26, 27, 69, 76, 136, 138, 169, 183, 193, 194, 228, 229

Determined, 25, 52, 53, 54, 59, 120, 153, 179, 180, 185, 203, 226
Direct vs indirect, 84
Directionality, 45, 50
Distance, 50, 51
DNA, 8, 147, 159, 206
Dreams, 69, 120, 178, 228
Dualism, 12
Ducasse, 204, 228
Duck, 112
Dynamic, 3, 68, 69, 86, 117, 120
Dynamicity, 61, 68, 169
Earle, 79, 228
Earthworm, 24
Eccles, xi, 9, 77, 231
Efron, 114, 228
Ego, 69, 118, 157
Electromagnetic, 44, 130
Emotions, 30, 34, 82, 145, 170, 215
Empirical, 227
Encyclopaedia, 227
Energy, 26, 36, 40, 43, 44, 47, 68, 81, 82, 103, 110, 125, 126, 130, 150, 161, 173, 199, 202, 211, 212, 218, 223
Entity, 21, 24, 59, 61, 62, 63, 64, 66, 69, 70, 76, 77, 88, 91, 92, 118, 126, 131, 137, 138, 139, 140, 141, 164, 181, 183, 184, 185, 190, 199, 207, 220, 225
Epiphenomenalism, 11, 12, 224
Epistemology, 197
Erotic, 34, 42
Evolution, 66, 231
Experience, 103, 142, 159, 231
Experiments, light, 114
External, 212, 232
Extracting, 100, 102, 103, 104, 105
Extracting and memory, 105

Extracting and motor skill, 103
Eye, 7, 10, 23, 24, 26, 30, 51, 60, 71, 83, 87, 88, 89, 107, 114, 122
Facilitate, 69, 70, 119
Faction, 55
Fantino, 228
Farrell, 136, 228
Feet, on two, 38, 44, 201, 211, 216, 226
Feigl, 126, 228
Fibers, sensory, 30
Fischback, 228
Flatworm, 24
Forman, 195, 228
Frassen, 16, 229
Freud (1913), 69
Freud (1936), 68
Freud (1938), 122, 147, 173
Freud (1948), 162, 173
Freud (1950), 229
Freud (1953), 121
Galileo, 9, 79
Gallager, 75, 229
Gap, bridging, 29, 37, 74, 129, 212
Gleitman, 40, 82, 112, 113, 147, 148, 229
God, 9, 93
Greeks, ancient, 4, 21, 46, 61, 91
Hallucinations, 38, 122, 147
Hameroff, 11, 14, 167, 229
Hearing, 24, 25, 33, 34, 40, 43, 50, 55, 63, 65, 84, 86, 102, 104, 112, 131, 146, 190, 191
Hebb (1949), 5
Hebb (1980), 69, 157
Hierarchy, 158

Hierarchy, memory, 111, 142, 143, 150, 152, 156, 162, 163, 164, 165, 173, 174, 175, 176, 180, 181, 182, 184, 185, 186, 188, 189, 191, 193, 195, 200, 201, 205, 206, 207, 208, 214, 222, 225, 226

Higher level, 35, 69, 111, 113, 117, 118

Hirst, 4, 7, 229

Hodgson, 95, 229

Hofstadter, 228, 229

Holt, 2, 4, 5, 6, 229

Homunculus, 7, 8, 63, 75, 78, 91, 98, 103, 118, 135, 138, 140, 141, 156, 161, 164, 166, 169, 177, 183, 192, 193, 207, 220

Horgan, 2, 10, 15, 229

Horizontal, 38, 110, 111, 112, 115, 143, 144, 145, 205, 209

Hubel, 110, 229, 230

Humanoid, xi

Hume (1974), 93, 229

Hunger, 34, 41, 130, 133

Hut, 16, 229

I, 1, 3, 6, 16, 47, 48, 49, 59, 65, 71, 75, 76, 85, 95, 100, 101, 128, 137, 139, 141, 142, 149, 152, 153, 166, 173, 177, 178, 183, 185, 186, 187, 190, 191, 193, 207, 211, 213, 216, 222, 228, 229

Idea, 47

Idealism, 5, 9, 10, 83, 223, 227, 228

Identity theory, 7, 15, 16, 17, 19, 28, 29, 41, 61, 69, 70, 109, 125, 126, 127, 129, 130, 132, 135, 138, 140, 149, 150, 166, 169, 171, 184, 210, 211, 213, 219, 220, 222, 224, 225

Illusion, 1, 8, 62, 64, 75, 82, 125, 141, 169, 194, 221, 222

Illustrations, 134

Image, 230, 233

In itself, 201, 212

Inborn, 24, 27, 55, 56, 80, 145, 156, 160, 175, 176, 180, 218, 226

Infants, 43, 103

Inhibit, 69, 70, 119

Inhibitory, 69

Inputs, 202

Inside, 72

Integration, 35, 81, 89, 144, 194

Intercellular, 107

Interests, 69, 118

Internal, 4, 5, 9, 18, 19, 20, 30, 42, 67, 108, 120, 121, 126, 130, 132, 142, 161, 162, 184, 198, 224

Introspection, 73, 190, 192, 225

Jackson, 46

James, xi, 3, 61, 148, 162, 173, 186, 229

Joad, 2, 46, 93, 230

Judgment, 6, 51, 52, 53, 56, 60, 79, 92, 104, 138, 216

Kant, 10, 42, 79, 83, 84, 160, 163, 212, 230

Kelly, 2, 4, 5, 6, 8, 35, 46, 84, 85, 98, 230

Kenny, 75, 230

Kirk, 25, 230

Kittens, 112

Knowledge, 142, 160, 227, 232

Koch, 167, 214, 228

Kolers, 36, 229

Land (1960), 114, 230

Land (1983), 114, 230

Learning, rote, 102

Leibniz, 11, 17

Level, memory, 163, 182, 189, 190, 191, 214, 215, 226
Lewis, 152, 230
Libet (1985), 36, 230
Libet (1994), 16, 230
Libet (1996), 15
Light, 40, 41, 43, 49, 55, 81, 114, 130, 199, 212, 218
Light energy, 81, 130, 218
Linguistics, 13
Livingston, 114, 230
Locke (1975), 45, 46
Lockwood, 126, 128, 152, 230
Logic, 159, 160, 232
Macdonald, 16, 230
Matching inputs with memory, 181
Materialist, 227
McCullough, 1, 89, 165, 230
McGinn, xi, 15, 230
Meaning, 197, 201, 205, 208, 227
Meaning, unconscious, 116
Meditation, 194, 196
Memory, 23, 100, 105, 139, 145, 146, 149, 150, 151, 153, 155, 177, 186, 187, 188, 189, 192, 215, 225
Memory and higher center, 192, 215
Memory and perception, 13
Memory, and consciousness, 31, 147, 149, 187, 188
Memory, motor, 19, 153
Memory, reinforcement, 148
Memory, searching, 154
Merikle, 152, 231
Michaels, 90, 231
Microtubule, 14, 63, 131, 147, 167, 168, 170, 183
Millisecond, 225
Mind-body gap, 31, 226

Mind-body problem, 2, 9, 11, 29, 90, 92, 128, 132, 179
Modules, 109, 111, 114, 115
Molecule, 8, 21, 22, 30, 206
Monad, 11, 17
Monism, 12
Monitor, 113, 216
Mood, 13, 187
Moore, 5, 152, 228, 231
Mother, 104, 111, 112, 120, 133, 161, 199
Motion, 49, 52, 53, 229
Muller, 40, 41, 42, 47, 48, 223
Multiple drafts, 138, 169, 194
Multiplicity, 61, 66, 67, 70, 199, 221
Mysticism, 124, 228, 232
Nagel (1974), xi
Nagel (1986), 14
Nerve cell impulses, 2, 29, 30, 31, 36, 40, 41, 43, 44, 58, 59, 62, 64, 69, 73, 81, 88, 107, 116, 118, 119, 123, 124, 127, 130, 131, 132, 135, 144, 151, 160, 166, 167, 168, 170, 172, 183, 184, 199, 214, 218, 225
Nervous system, 1, 7, 10, 23, 25, 30, 31, 36, 37, 41, 50, 58, 67, 69, 87, 89, 90, 92, 94, 100, 108, 119, 126, 130, 131, 135, 168, 170, 175, 181, 207, 212, 225
Network, 13, 29, 63, 124, 144, 158, 167, 170, 183, 185, 224
Neuroanatomy, 106
Neurons, consciousness, 168, 170, 193
Neurophysiological, 63, 80, 99, 100, 111, 116, 118, 123, 148, 149, 153, 177, 192, 197, 200, 208
Neurophysiology, 111

Object, 55
Objective, 50, 55, 56, 60, 194, 216
Objectivist, 6
Observer, central, 7, 8, 12, 63, 75, 98, 118, 135, 138, 140, 164, 166, 177, 182, 183, 195, 205, 207
Ornstein, 112, 231
Outside, 2, 4, 6, 10, 11, 15, 26, 30, 33, 37, 38, 41, 43, 57, 72, 73, 74, 79, 80, 83, 85, 120, 127, 130, 131, 132, 154, 156, 166, 167, 168, 171, 180, 181, 182, 198, 199, 202, 210, 211, 212, 218, 220, 225, 226
Pain, 130
Panksepp, 9, 231
Panpsychism, 11, 12
Passivity, 79
Patterns, 149, 150
Pavlov, 102, 104, 159, 231
Penfield, 74, 231
Penrose (1989), 14
Penrose (1994), 106
Perceive, 6, 33, 34, 41, 42, 43, 49, 57, 63, 84, 85, 93, 97, 98, 99, 119, 135, 148, 162, 163, 194, 198, 202, 208, 211, 213, 214, 215, 216, 218, 223
Perception, 4, 37, 38, 44, 47, 55, 79, 80, 84, 98, 119, 149, 154, 161, 164, 169, 173, 204, 205, 226, 227, 228, 229, 230, 231, 232
Perception and meaning, 98
Perception, activity vs passivity, 79, 81
Periphery, 30, 87, 89, 106, 108, 115, 116, 171, 172
Person, first and third, 74, 127, 211

Personify, 91
Perspective, first, third person, 71, 74, 77, 109, 127, 128, 131, 132, 167, 168, 181, 183, 210, 220, 225
PET scan, 86
Peterson, 18
Phenomenal quality, 8
Physical/mental, 16, 29, 226
Physiology, 106, 229, 230
Piaget, 43, 231
Pillsbury, 64, 231
Plasticity, 111
Plato, 8, 11, 80, 160
Popper, xi, 9, 11, 77, 91, 231
Power, 47
Preconscious, 116, 117
Premeaning, 200, 225
Preperceptual, 36, 69, 179
Pribram, 126, 231
Price, 7, 231
Processing, parallel, 23, 68, 150
Protoconscious, 14
Pylkkanen, 14, 231
Qualia, 27, 28, 163
Qualitative, 20
Qualities, primary, secondary, 45, 46, 49, 50, 52, 53, 55, 56, 57, 58, 60, 83, 194
Quality, 47
Quantum, 14, 95, 147, 229, 230, 231, 233
Ranson, 193, 232
Rapaport, 227, 232
Real, 187
Realism, 4, 5, 12, 223, 229, 232
Realism, Common Sense, 6
Realism, Modern, 5, 229
Reality, 42, 134, 210, 213, 217, 227, 229, 232
Reality, external, 12, 13, 120, 125, 133, 211, 212, 217, 223

Recall, 27, 58, 93, 120, 127, 132, 139, 174, 176, 181, 182, 183, 211, 217
Recognition, 161, 169, 173, 205, 208
Recursive comparison, 164
Reduction to the absurd, 7, 9, 12, 63, 75, 78, 138, 183
Reductionism, 21, 32, 35, 62
Reflection, 20
REM, 122
Representationalism, 6, 7, 12, 37, 223
Representationalism, perception in, 37, 43
Representations, 161, 163
Repression, 200
Restak, 111, 232
Retina, 55
Reynolds, 55, 228
Rhythm, 13
Robot, 62, 92, 208
Rorschach, 85
Russell (1914), 28
Russell (1927), 126, 232
Russell (1929), 7
Russell (1949), 126, 232
Ryle, 7, 8, 9, 90, 232
Schopenhauer, 27
Searching, 150, 151, 154
Searle (1992a), 68, 169, 232
Searle (1992b), 232
Searle (1997a), 232
Selection, 69
Self, 75, 136, 138, 139, 186, 187, 227, 230, 231, 232, 233
Self-consciousness, 17, 77
Sellars, 13, 232
Semantics, 197, 203
Sensation, 35, 49
Sensation, sexual, 35, 204
Sense data, 80, 164

Senses, 230
Senses, five, 24, 31, 33, 35, 39, 50, 52, 58, 88, 170
Senses, physics and physiology, 40
Sensory, 35, 151, 152, 165, 170, 172, 182, 202
Shape, 52, 56, 57, 229
Shorthand, 100, 159
Size, 51, 52, 56, 57
Smart (1959), 127, 232
Smart (1963), 127, 232
Smell, 24, 25, 26, 40, 41, 50, 55, 57, 60, 85, 109, 119, 130, 183
Socrates, 11, 75
Solidity, 48, 49, 53, 55
Solipsism, 10, 83, 212, 223
Soul, 5, 9, 10, 11, 72, 77, 90, 124, 136
Sound, 40, 54
Sound, perception of, 43
Spinoza, 11, 15
Strawson, 75, 136, 137, 232
Subconscious, 17, 117
Subjective, 13, 24, 28, 42, 46, 50, 51, 52, 55, 56, 60, 71, 74, 130, 131, 221, 225
Summation, 158
Symbols, 96, 101, 208
Synaptic knobs, 111
Synecdoche, 93, 95, 96, 97, 98, 99, 100, 104, 163, 201, 204, 217
Synecdoche and representationalism, 98
Taste, 24, 25, 40, 41, 46, 50, 55, 57, 59, 60, 109, 119, 130, 139, 146, 180
Tennis, 94, 95, 96, 120, 153
Thoughts, 34
Touch, 58
Transduce, 131

Tye, 146, 232

Unconscious, 17, 18, 152, 200, 230, 231

Understand, 1, 14, 16, 29, 33, 42, 58, 64, 79, 93, 100, 101, 128, 130, 139, 140, 147, 158, 167, 168, 172, 179, 183, 198, 201, 202, 208, 210, 216, 218, 220

Underwood, 18, 139, 232

Unitary, 24, 61, 62, 63, 64, 66, 70, 178, 184, 199

Unknowable, 42

Vallentine, 232

Velmans (1991), 232

Velmans (1993), 15

Velmans (1995), xi, 15, 32, 233

Vibrations, electromagnetic, 40, 41, 47

Vibrations, molecular, 40

Vision, neurophysiology, 193

Volition, 178

Weiskrantz, 36, 233

Whole object, 47, 93, 94, 95, 97, 98, 111, 150, 152, 161, 163, 201

Will, 178, 230

Wish, 1, 3, 19, 31, 57, 59, 85, 87, 99, 105, 109, 120, 121, 126, 127, 144, 146, 149, 154, 161, 168, 175, 177, 181, 189, 201, 207, 212, 215, 220, 221

Wittgenstein, 13, 233

Zeki (1974), 114, 233

Zeki (1992), 36, 233

Zohar, 11, 14, 106, 233

Printed in the United States
809700003B

9 781403 328878